ation
d the
unity
itain

esearch
aken for
Equality

the

# Dr Mary Hickman
## and
## Dr Bronwen Walter

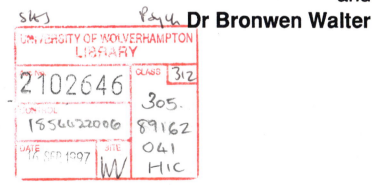
Commission for Racial Equality, 1997

## Acknowledgements

We would like to thank the following people and organisations, all of whom have provided us with assistance, advice or some other contribution without which it would have been immeasurably more difficult to complete this research. The responsibility for the final product remains our own.

CMU at the University of Manchester which provided the Samples of Anonymised Records, SARS, with the support of ESRC/JISC. All tables containing the SARS are reproduced with the permission of the Stationery Office and are Crown Copyright.

Jackie Taylor, David Bolsdon, Janet Heyden and Melanie Legg who drew the maps and diagrams.

The research team which included: Sarah Morgan, Mairead Dunne, Jackie Harnett and Jim McCool.

All the staff of the community groups and agencies who answered our postal questionnaire and those who subsequently agreed to be interviewed for the survey in Part Two.

All the Irish people in Birmingham and London who consented to be interviewed for the survey which forms Part Three of the report.

All the academics, staff of race equality and community relations units and members of Irish organisations in Glasgow and Edinburgh who assisted our study of Scotland.

In addition the following individuals were immensely helpful: Mary Connolly; Sean Hutton; Gail Lewis; Tony Murray; Pat Murphy; Robert Miles; Chris Myant; Greville Percival; Paddy O'Sullivan; Alistair Ross; Ruth Silverstone; Robin Skinner; Seamus Taylor.

Bronwen Walter wishes to acknowledge the support of ESRC Research Grant R000234790.

Finally, we would both like to acknowledge the support in completing this research provided by our respective academic institutions: the University of North London and Anglia Polytechnic University.

**Mary J. Hickman**

**Bronwen Walter**

**Dr Mary Hickman** is the Director of the Irish Studies Centre at the University of North London

**Dr Bronwen Walter** is a Senior Lecturer in the Geography Department at Anglia Polytechnic University

Published by the Commission for Racial Equality
Elliot House
10/12 Allington Street
London SW1E 5EH

First published June 1997
ISBN 1 85442 200 6
Printed by Biddles, Kings Lynn

# Contents

# Foreword

The Commission for Racial Equality is publishing this research report as an important contribution to a necessary debate about the problems and opportunities facing the Irish community in Britain. The CRE was urged to undertake the work by Irish community organisations, which had been convinced by the experience of the cases brought to them over several years, that Irish people in Britain faced discrimination. The work was commissioned in 1994 and we are pleased to offer this report to the public and to those in positions of responsibility in institutions across British society.

Using materials from the 1991 and earlier Censuses, discussing with the many agencies now at work assisting Irish people, and, finally, conducting a pilot survey of Irish members of the British public, the authors of this report have highlighted evidence of inequality and a of deep sense of hurt among people of Irish origin at the way they have been treated.

Before the research project was completed, the Commission for Racial Equality decided to include an Irish category in those that it recommends for use in ethnic origin monitoring systems. An Irish category had been long recommended by Irish organisations and several bodies had taken that up, particularly in housing, health, education and local government employment. Clear evidence of inequality experienced by Irish people across a range of indices convinced us that this was a necessary step.

It is to be hoped that the findings contained in this research report will persuade all involved in monitoring - and all who should be - to include an Irish category. But, of course, monitoring, the collection of data, is only a first step toward tackling discrimination and inequality. There is a wealth of fact, argument and analysis in these pages that will help anyone who seriously intends to deal with the problems revealed.

The findings and analysis are the responsibility of the authors, but their recommendations have been accepted by, and have the support of, the CRE. There has been a failure, at an official level and at the level of general discussion of race relations, to recognise the nature of the experience faced by many Irish people in Britain. In addition to recommending that further research is undertaken, the authors point to the need for institutions across British society to examine their practices to ensure they are offering equality of opportunity to all and not just those from some groups.

As the authors say, 'the substantial body of evidence presented here strongly suggests that discrimination does play a significant role in generating these experiences, although in individual cases it might be hard to establish the exact causal circumstances'.

That is a matter of serious concern for the CRE, as it should be for all agencies responsible for public policy decisions and implementation. A steady stream of Irish people have brought complaints of alleged unlawful discrimination to the CRE over the past few years. They have come from all parts of the country and the problems they have highlighted are not limited to one area of experience. In a number of cases, their allegations of discrimination have been supported by the relevant tribunal or court. In a larger number of cases, involving both employers and those providing services to the public, we have been able to secure favourable settlements under which institutions have agreed to change their practices. The findings in this report reinforce the view that the number of cases which are brought to the CRE is just a small part of the total number of acts of unlawful discrimination directed against people of Irish origin in Britain today.

As with all discrimination, this represents a terrible and unnecessary waste of talent, resources and time.

In the last few years, long standing dismissive attitudes toward the Irish in Britain have been challenged, not only by the activities of community organisations, but also by the growing popularity of Irish culture in Britain. Against the background of this changing mood, there is a opportunity for real progress on the issues raised in this report.


**Sir Herman Ouseley,**

Chairman, Commission for Racial Equality

# Introduction

## 1. The Invisibility of the Irish in Britain

The Irish are the largest ethnic minority element in Britain's workforce and have been the most important source of migrant labour for the British economy for 200 years. Within the Irish population in Britain, women form a majority and represent, for example, the largest ethnic minority element in London's work force. Both these phenomena are usually ignored in studies of migration, ethnicity, racism and discrimination in Britain.

Unlike the other large-scale labour migrations to Britain, principally from the Indian sub-continent and the Caribbean, Irish migration, if considered at all, is treated as if it was some sort of 'natural occurrence'. There is little acknowledgement that Irish people might have experiences or be subject to practices which are based on ethnic differentiation or racist discrimination. The Irish are excluded from consideration in these terms because they are white and the dominant paradigm for understanding racism in Britain is constructed on the basis of a black-white dichotomy.

This exclusion of the Irish whenever issues of differential ethnic access to scarce resources is discussed is a dominant theme in the reports of every Irish welfare and advice agency in the country. Every agency records, either in its annual reports or in special research reports, the monumental task it faces in trying to persuade funding authorities of specific Irish needs in service provision and of the necessity of earmarking resources accordingly.

As a result of these difficulties over 20 Irish organisations systematically lobbied the Commission for Racial Equality from the late 1980s onwards about Irish issues. The case these groups made to the CRE is that the Irish should be included in ethnic monitoring, there should be an Irish category in the ethnic question in the Census and that there was a need for research about the ways in which the processes and practices of racism and discrimination impact on Irish people in Britain.

The 1976 Race Relations Act and the equal opportunities policies of local authorities and other bodies do not restrict their definitions of which groups may experience racism or 'racial' discrimination to those who are visibly different. The 1976 Act defines discrimination on racial grounds as being on grounds of colour, race, nationality or ethnic or national origins.

The definition of a racial group to include ethnic or national origins obviously includes the Irish and this has been readily acknowledged by the Commission for Racial Equality, which over the years has taken up a number of cases of alleged discrimination brought to the Commission by Irish people.

The Irish groups were, therefore, lobbying the CRE in the full knowledge that the

1976 Act covered the areas of concern Irish people were raising and knowing that the CRE had already responded to individual Irish cases.

One consequence of this lobbying was the commissioning of this research report. In announcing its research initiative on the Irish community, the Commission for Racial Equality indicated that the main purpose of the research was to establish the extent to which Irish people in Britain experience various forms of racial discrimination. The CRE commented that, apart from a small number of formal complaints which had been made to it under the Race Relations Act, there was only anecdotal evidence of discrimination against the Irish.

The major objective of the research project, therefore, was to evaluate existing and new evidence in this area. The CRE was inviting a close examination of both the reports of Irish welfare agencies and an examination of the implications of the consistent patterns of social disadvantage which the census statistics and other surveys revealed the Irish population in Britain to experience.

A wealth of empirical data indicates that the location, circumstances and experiences of many Irish people in Britain are consistent with structured patterns of disadvantage and possible discrimination. This should be unsurprising because one role of Ireland within the British economy for the past 200 years has been that of a frequently resorted to source of surplus labour. During the period in which we conducted this research (1994-95), for example, hospitals in north London were recruiting in Ireland for nursing staff.

In West European societies research has shown that it is frequently labour migrant groups who are the object of discrimination (Castles et al, 1984; Miles, 1993). Migrants are frequently differentiated, racialised and subject to exclusionary practices on the basis of ascribing them certain (real or imagined) characteristics. These characteristics are utilised to justify the assignment of specific economic, social and political roles to these groups and consequent exclusionary practices towards them.

It is important to emphasise this relationship of Ireland as a source of migrant labour for the British economy because many academic and policy-oriented accounts assume that Britain ceased to be a country of large-scale immigration with the passage of various immigration control laws in the 1960s-70s. The movement of thousands of Irish people to Britain in the 1980s, for example, is completely ignored.

In Britain, there is a reluctance or resistance, on the part of officialdom and those involved with 'race relations', to include Irish migrants within the definition of a ethnic minority group in British society. The frequently used term 'black and ethnic minorities' refers in most people's usage to those from the Caribbean and the Indian sub-continent and their descendants.

There is, therefore, confusion about whether the Irish are an ethnic minority group or not. This confusion also exists amongst the Irish themselves because of the interchangeability of the term ethnic minority with 'black'. Does the absence of the Irish from the discourse of ethnic minorities in Britain reflect a material reality of easy assimilation or does the denial of the specificity of being Irish in Britain mask processes and practices of differentiation, racialisation and discrimination which should be addressed? These are some of the questions we set out to address.

## 2. The status of Irish migrants in Britain

Migrants coming from the Republic of Ireland are travelling from a foreign country. However, they are migrating from a country which stands in a unique legal relationship to the United Kingdom. This was enshrined in the 1948 British Nationality Act. That Act created a distinction between citizens of the United Kingdom and colonies, and citizens of Commonwealth countries, but stipulated that both categories of citizen had the status of British subject. All such persons were thereafter to be known as either British subjects or Commonwealth citizens, but were identical in terms of their rights (Miles 1993).

Thus citizenship in a particular Commonwealth country was the qualification for being a British subject. The government of Ireland was not willing that all Irish citizens should automatically be British subjects and the 1948 Act therefore made special provision for Irish citizens. The 1948 Act:

> ensured that any law in force on 1st January 1949 shall apply to Eire citizens as to British subjects. In other words, an Eire citizen in the United Kingdom gets automatically the same treatment under our existing laws as if he were a British subject; if he is resident here he can vote and he is liable for military service (if resident for two years or more).

(Attlee speaking in the second reading of the Ireland Bill, Hansard 1949, Vol. 464, Col. 1859)

On independence in 1922, the Irish Free State was accorded the status of a dominion in the Commonwealth. Citizens of the Irish Free State remained free to enter, and to take up residence in Britain. And British subjects were accorded the same right with respect to the territory of the Irish Free State.

Irish people in Britain, along with people from other Commonwealth countries, had the right to vote as British citizens. No change to this situation was made by the British Nationality Act of 1948.

In 1948 the Irish Government formally withdrew from the Commonwealth and in 1949 the Irish Republic was inaugurated. Once Ireland had been declared a Republic and had left the Commonwealth, Irish citizens were not formally British subjects, neither were they aliens. The immediate response of the British government to Ireland leaving the Commonwealth was to consider taking retaliatory measures in the areas of citizenship and trade. The government was dissuaded from this by the Prime Ministers of New Zealand, Australia and Canada. Attlee, speaking in the House of Commons during the debate on what would become the Republic of Ireland Act 1949, spoke about why the status of Irish citizens would remain unchanged, that is as outlined in the 1948 Nationality Act.

Attlee made it clear that the difficulties caused by the land frontier between Northern Ireland, which is part of the United Kingdom and the Commonwealth, and the Republic of Ireland were particularly pertinent. It was decided, therefore, that 'the people of Eire and the people of Britain should not be foreign to one another' (Hansard 1948-49, Vol. 464, Cols 1854-5). Later in the same speech, Attlee confirmed that the Bill included a proviso that Northern Ireland would never be detached from the United Kingdom without the consent of the Northern Ireland legislature. In the new Republic, this was viewed as the retaliatory action because of the Irish decision to leave the Commonwealth.

The motives which informed this decision by the Labour government to maintain the position whereby the citizens of two foreign countries, the United Kingdom and the Republic of Ireland, would not be aliens to each other were varied: the need to address a severe shortage of labour for its massive reconstruction programme after the Second World War, the significance of Ireland for security issues in the post-war world, and Britain's economic, military and political connections in Ireland and its continuing rule of one part of that island.

These factors meant that it was more in Britain's interests not to treat the Irish as 'aliens' and political co-operation between Britain and Ireland was viewed as essential. Also, as was made clear by Herbert Morrison's speech in the debate, another consideration was the need for Irish votes in Britain (Hansard 1948-49, Vol. 464, Cols 1854-5).

Despite this settlement in 1949 the Commonwealth Immigration Bill in 1962 in its original form made the Irish subject to immigration control, but, by the second reading, the government had dropped this provision on the ground that it was impossible to police the border between Northern Ireland and the Republic (Dummett & Nicol, 1990). In the debate on the Bill it was broadly accepted that it would be impossible to enforce immigration controls between Britain and Ireland because of the border with Northern Ireland and the proximity of the two countries. It was also broadly accepted that Irish labour was needed, especially for the unskilled labour slot. This did not prevent some MPs expressing their views that the Southern Irish were a social liability.

The problematisation of the Irish in the debates on the Bill echoed many debates of the 1930s when there had been an upturn in Irish immigration (Glynn, 1981). In the 1962 parliamentary debate reference was made to the fact that the Irish, in bringing over tuberculosis, were more likely to create health problems than West Indian immigrants and created worse housing problems (Hansard 1961-62, Vol. 649, Cols 753-762). It was also argued that stopping Commonwealth immigration would not have any effect on the demands placed on social services because, in view of the demands placed on maternity services and the evidence of overcrowding and delinquency, these problems were 'just as great, if not greater, in the case of the Irish as they are in the case of any Commonwealth immigrants' (Hansard 1961-62, Vol. 654 Col 1251).

These parliamentary debates reflected both an acquiescence on pragmatic grounds that the Irish could not be designated as 'immigrants' in the same way as people from the New Commonwealth and a continuing problematisation of the Irish as a source of social contamination and a drain on the public purse.

The 'race relations' paradigm has rather unquestioningly accepted the myth of British homogeneity prior to the 1950s. There has been little querying of the discourses and practices of the British state which have masked the internal ethnic, regional and national differences which characterise the 'United Kingdom'. Constructions of whiteness are one means by which these differences have been masked. Consequently, 'colour' has become a marker of national belonging and being of the same 'colour' can be equated with 'same nation' implying 'no problem' of discrimination.

Those active in the 'race relations' field have quite rightly protested that exclusion from the nation on grounds of colour is discriminatory. However, it has led to a too-ready equation of 'whiteness' with an homogenous way of life. Examining the experiences of Irish people in Britain highlights the extent to which it is necessary to deconstruct 'whiteness' (see Hickman, forthcoming 1998, for further development of the points in this section).

The above discussion has focused on the status of migrants from the Republic of Ireland because there is sometimes confusion about this. Migrants from Northern Ireland are citizens of the United Kingdom and, therefore, there should be no confusion about their status. However, this does not prevent British citizens from Northern Ireland being perceived as 'Irish' rather than as 'British' (Kells 1995). This was demonstrated in the recent cases of anti-Irish discrimination, involving Trevor McAuley and Alan Bryans, both of whom are from Northern Ireland, which the CRE brought successfully to Industrial Tribunal.

### 3. The organisation of the Research Report

We have divided the report into three parts, each of which deals with a different stage of the research. The CRE in its initial brief for the research outlined a three-stage research process. Our submission had followed their guideline for the first two stages but had suggested a different third stage. This proposal was accepted by the CRE.

Part One comprises a statistical analysis of the present day demographic and socio-economic characteristics of the Irish population in Britain, with a particular emphasis on the migrant generation. It also includes the results of a survey to assess the extent to which the Irish are included as a specific category in ethnic monitoring by local authorities and housing associations in England, Wales and Scotland.

Part Two gives the findings of a survey of Irish community groups and advice centres. The aim of this stage of the research was to establish and document the evidence of discrimination as presented by Irish clients to these agencies. The final stage of the research was designed to extend the investigation of experiences of discrimination to a representative sample of the total Irish-born population in Britain. It comprised  in-depth interviews with a sample matching the range of demographic and socio-economic characteristics of the Irish-born population identified in the first stage of the research. The findings of this survey are presented in Part Three of the report.

## REFERENCES

Castles, S. with Booth, H. & Wallace, T. (1984), *Here for Good. Western Europe's New Ethnic Minorities*, Pluto Press, London.

Glynn, S. (1981), Irish immigration to Britain 1911-1951: patterns and policy, *Irish Economic and Social History*, Vol VIII.

Hickman, M.J. (1998 forthcoming), Reconstructing deconstructing 'race': British political discourses about the Irish in Britain, *Ethnic and Racial Studies*, Vol. 21, No.2.

Kells, M (1995), Ethnic Identity amongst Young Irish Middle Class Migrants in London, *Irish Studies Centre Occasional Papers Series, No. 6*, University of North London Press, London.

Miles, R (1993) *Racism after 'race relations'*, Routledge, London.

# Part One
# The Irish population in Britain in 1991:
## demographic, geographic and socio-economic circumstances

# 1. Introduction

The first stage of the research comprises a statistical analysis of the present day characteristics of the Irish population in Britain, with a particular emphasis on the migrant generation. This was specified by the Commission for Racial Equality in order to establish the demographic, geographic and socio-economic circumstances of the Irish community through the collation of the available evidence from secondary sources, including large published datasets and ethnic monitoring records.

The aims of this section are therefore:

1. to bring together existing statistical data, and create relevant new datasets, in order to provide a clear public profile of an under-researched ethnic minority group in Britain;

2. to identify areas of disadvantage in the labour market and in access to resources which might be indicative of discrimination;

3. to provide a background for the evidence presented in the subsequent parts of the report, particularly highlighting the distinctive features of the Irish population, in order to

   - contextualise the characteristics of the subset of the Irish population presenting cases to the community groups and advice agencies;

   - facilitate the selection of a representative cross-section of individuals for interview about their individual experiences.

# 2. Sources

## 2.1 1991 Census: availability and deficiencies of data

The 1991 Census was published by the Office of Population Surveys and Censuses (OPCS) and is by far the most accurate and complete dataset available for the study of the Irish population in Britain. It was held on 21 April 1991, when every household in Britain was required by law to complete a census form.

Final coverage was estimated to be 97.8% of the resident population. Census data at 100% and 10% levels is available in published tables, the prime source being the two volumes of the Ethnic Group and Country of Birth tables (HMSO, 1993). Unpublished Local Base Statistics provide a larger number of pre-selected cross tabulations.

However, analyses of the Irish-born population face two serious problems in the use of Census data. One is the issue of under-enumeration, involving approximately 1.2 million people overall, which is likely to have a disproportionate effect on Irish numbers. Although no specific correction factors have been calculated for the Irish, young white men (20-29) are estimated to be under-enumerated by 10% and the proportion is even higher for Black Caribbeans (14% for the age group 20-24, 16% for 25-29). The proportion is boosted yet again for those in inner cities. For young men aged 25-29 in Inner London, for example, 22% are estimated to be missing (OPCS User Guide 58).

Taking all these factors into account, a conservative increase of 15% for young Irish men (20-29) would raise the total Irish-born population by 7,593. Since London has been the prime destination of young Irish male migrants during the 1980s, this serious under-enumeration must be borne in mind. Although the correction factor calculated by the OPCS for young women is much smaller (for example, white women 25-29 3%, Black Caribbean 5%), it cannot be assumed that Irish women have equally low rates. Their migrant status places them in a different category from both these groups and makes it likely that under-enumeration is much closer to the estimates for young Irish men.

A second problem is the ambiguous position of the Irish in the Ethnic Group tables. Despite representations from a number of Irish community groups, the category 'Irish' was not included in the new ethnic origin question in 1991. However, the OPCS went some way to meeting expressed needs for such a category by including an additional column headed 'Born in Ireland' in a number of the subsequently published tables.

Although these are useful additional statistics to those provided on birthplace alone, two important issues are raised by the form of this column. One is that its inclusion of only one generation makes numerical comparisons with other groups misleading. A correction factor to allow for at least one more generation is needed here. The second issue is that the amalgamation of data relating to people born in the Irish Republic and Northern Ireland disguises significant differences in the two population groups.

These will be examined in more detail later in this section, but it should be noted that the socio-economic characteristics of the Northern Irish-born population are often intermediate between those of Great Britain and the Irish Republic. The effect of adding them together is to reduce the gap between the Irish Republic-born and British-born populations.

The last issue can be resolved by use of two valuable extensions to the published Census volumes, the Samples of Anonymised Records of the 1991 Census of Great Britain (SARS) and the OPCS Longitudinal Study (LS), although each has weaknesses for the study of the Irish population. Moreover, these sources are unpublished and not easily available to those outside the academic community.

The SARS provide full Census details on a 2% sample of individuals and a 1% sample of households in Britain, making possible the selection and cross-tabulation of all variables. They are thus a much more flexible data source than published tables or unpublished Local Base Statistics. They do allow those born in the Irish Republic and Northern Ireland to be distinguished. However the small total numbers in the Irish-born samples limits the scope for detailed breakdown for use in more specific investigations.

The sample of individuals contains 11,880 people born in the Irish Republic and 5,094 born in Northern Ireland, which is large enough for most cross tabulations on two or three dimensions. However in a table showing numbers of Republic- and Northern Irish-born people by gender, age, housing tenure and region, for example, the numbers in each category would be too small to be meaningful (Walter, 1996).

The LS allows a different anonymous sample of 1% of the population in England and Wales, initially drawn from the 1971 Census and continuously updated, to be traced in successive censuses. Changes occurring over the lifecycles of clusters of individuals can be analysed. This is especially valuable for study of the Irish community since parents' birthplace was recorded for the only time in 1971, allowing second-generation Irish people to be traced subsequently. However small numbers again limit subdivision of the data, for example by age, gender or social class, and an important drawback is that Scotland has not been included in this sample.

## 2.2 Other large datasets

Irish birthplace is also recorded in the Labour Force Survey (LFS) and General Household Survey (GHS). However these rely on small total sample sizes (LFS approximately 60,000 households in total; GHS approximately 10,000) which are then weighted, and also have lower response rates (approximately 80%). Although detailed questions are asked, results must be treated with caution unless very large differences are observed, especially when groups are further subdivided. The GHS, for example, yields only about 400 Irish-born individuals in total (Pearson, Madden and Greenslade, 1991).

A particular problem is the use of areal sampling frames, which rapidly reduce the accuracy of statistics on spatially clustered populations such as the Irish. Effects include an under-representation both of the total size of the Irish population and of the particular characteristics of those in larger centres of settlement such as London. Census data, where available, is thus much more accurate.

## 2.3 Ethnic monitoring

Statistics produced by ethnic monitoring may also be more focused and include data not covered by the Census. As yet, however, the Irish are included in only a very small proportion of ethnic monitoring.

A nationwide survey of 514 local authorities in Great Britain was carried out for this project in May/June 1994 (63% response rate), showed that only 26 authorities (14 in Greater London) included the Irish as a category. This represents 8% of responses (5% of local authorities). Ethnic monitoring by housing associations is much more extensive, many now including the Irish as a separate group. A further survey carried out for this project showed that 51 of the largest 88 associations (70% response rate) collect this information systematically (see Part One, Section 7).

# 3. Statistical profile

## 3.1 Population characteristics

### 3.1.1 The size of the Irish community in Britain

#### 3.1.1.1 Present day Irish population

In 1991 the Census of Great Britain recorded 837,464 people born in Ireland, 1.5% of the total population. Of this number 72.7% (592,550) were born in the Irish Republic and 27.3% (244,914) in Northern Ireland. Women outnumbered men, comprising 53% of the Irish-born total.

The 1991 total represented a small decrease (-1.5%) over the 1981 total (849,820) despite the sharp rise in immigration from Ireland during the 1980s which has been described as a 'third wave' following those which peaked in the 1850s and 1960s respectively (Figure 1.1). The number of Irish-born people in England and Wales alone remained almost unchanged (1981: 789,426; 1991: 788,280) decreasing by 0.1%. If correction is made for under-enumeration, however, by including the 7,593 missing young men estimated above, the total in Britain would be raised to 845,057, much closer to the 1981 figure. It seems likely, therefore, that there has been no net change over the decade, the renewed immigration in the 1980s being matched by higher mortality amongst the ageing 1950s generation.

Most of the total decline took place in Scotland, which had a single peak of Irish immigration in the mid-nineteenth century (Figure 1.1). Numbers there have fallen sharply since 1881, so that the Irish-born population in 1991 (49,184) was only 32.8% of the 1881 figure, whereas the combined England and Wales total had grown by 131.0%. Immigration to Scotland has continued throughout the twentieth century, but at a substantially lower rate then to England and Wales.

### 3.1.2 Origins in Ireland: Irish Republic and Northern Ireland

After 1921, population totals are recorded separately for birthplace in the Irish Republic and Northern Ireland. Over the period 1921-1991 the proportion originating in Northern Ireland has increased from 18.0% to 27.3% (Figure 1.2).

Throughout the period the rate of emigration from the Republic has been higher, but since 1971 the Northern Ireland share, relative to population size at home, has increased sharply. Whereas in 1971 Northern Ireland represented 34.0% of the island's population and contributed 24.2% of migrants to Britain, in 1991 it had only 30.9% of the island total but contributed 27.3% of all Irish migrants. Changes in emigration patterns are strongly related to economic factors in Britain, especially demand for labour, rather than unemployment levels or political instability in Northern Ireland (Compton, 1991).

Growth in the Northern Irish component contributed significantly to the stability in numbers of the Irish-born population in England and Wales. It rose from

209,042 in 1981 to 218,521 in 1991 (+4.5%) in contrast to the fall in numbers of the Republic Irish-born from 580,384 to 569,759 (-1.8%) over the period. In Scotland, however, where the Northern Irish-born population outnumbers the Republic-born population, their numbers declined much more steeply. The Northern Irish-born total fell from 33,927 to 26,393 (-22.2%) compared with a drop from 27,042 to 22,791 (-15.7%) for the Republic Irish-born. Thus, England is increasingly the focus of migration from Northern Ireland as well as that from the Republic.

It is not possible to disaggregate the Northern Irish-born population in Britain into its constituent Catholic and Protestant parts, so that the statistics presented in this report represent the average of two divergent populations. For example, in some instances there may be greater similarities in demographic and socio-economic characteristics of Northern Irish Catholics and Republic Irish-born people than between Catholics and Protestants from the North. In others, common institutional provision, such as shared education and social welfare systems, may place all Northern Irish-born people closer to other United Kingdom-born groups.

### 3.1.3 Second generation

The Irish community in Britain includes children of Irish parents, often called the 'second generation'. This group is omitted from most statistical coverage, but its inclusion becomes more important as self-identified multi-generation ethnic identities are recognised in monitoring procedures. In comparisons such as those made possible by certain ethnic group tables in the 1991 Census, the size of the Irish community, drawn from birthplace data alone, is greatly understated.

Only one British Census (1971) has included a question on parents' birthplace, allowing for a full enumeration of those with one or two Irish parents. Fortunately the choice of 1971 as the starting point of the OPCS Longitudinal Study means that an initial 1% of the second generation can still be traced over time. Other datasets with much smaller samples identify Irish parentage to some extent, including the General Household Survey (since 1971) and the Labour Force Survey in a single year (1983).

In 1971, 1,303,450 people in the United Kingdom had at least one parent born in the Irish Republic (two parents 361,800; one parent 941,650) (Table 1.1). Since the number of Republic Irish-born people in Britain was 615,820 this gives a ratio of just over 2:1 and a total community size of almost two million. However, it must be remembered that the analysis omits people born in Northern Ireland, who were included in the United Kingdom total, so that at least another half million should be added. At the same time, people born in Northern Ireland to Republic-born parents are included, inflating the ratio applied to Britain alone. The ratio will of course vary to some extent over time, depending on the size and age structure of the migration flow. But, clearly, the Irish are by far the largest ethnic minority by immigration in Britain.

The size of the joint first and second generations is confirmed in the 1991 Census. The SARS show that 1.95 million people in Britain lived in households where either the household head or his/her partner had been born in Ireland (Owen, 1995). This would give a ratio of 1 Irish-born person to 1.3 second-generation Irish people for Britain as a whole where the two generations still live in the same household. However, this is a considerable underestimate of the total numbers in the second generation.

Many second-generation Irish people will have left the parental home and established new households, especially the children of the 1950s bulge of immigrants who are now in their thirties. The importance of this group is brought out clearly in Figure 1.3 showing the age structure of the population with one or two Irish-born parents, living in London in 1983 (LFS, 1983). It is also confirmed by GHS data in 1984 where the 15-34 age group accounted for nearly half of the second generation with Republic-born parents (43.8%) and a third of those with parents born in Northern Ireland (31.8%) (Pearson, Madden and Greenslade, 1991). A conservative estimate of the ratio of second to first generation would therefore be 1.5:1 and the true figure may be closer to 2:1.

The apparent rate of mixed-origin partnerships is high, though 'UK-born' partners may include Northern Irish-born or second generation Irish people (Table 1.2). In 1971 Irish men were more likely to live with United Kingdom-born marriage partners (56.6%) than were Irish women (50.4%). Irish women were three times more likely to marry men born in the New Commonwealth and twice as likely to marry men born elsewhere in Europe. By 1991 the rate of mixed-origin partnerships had increased sharply. Of all households containing an Irish-born partner, in only 20.2% were both partners born in Ireland (Owen, 1995). This, in turn, contributes to the growth of numbers in the second generation, since more of the group will have one rather than two Irish-born parents.

Further research is needed in order to make an accurate assessment of the size of the second-generation Irish population. A conservative correction factor of the Irish-born population to include this group is 2.5 and the true figure is probably closer to 3. This means that the number of Irish-born people given in the Census should be multipled by 3 to give the size of the Irish community. For the Britain as a whole the total would be 2.5 millions, or 4.6% of the total population. In particular localities, however, the proportion would be much higher. In Greater London, for example, the conservative estimate (2.5) gives a proportion of 9.6%, whilst the more realistic one (3) makes a total of 11.5% of the population Irish (Table 1.3).

In order to make the Irish Census totals strictly comparable with those of Census-defined ethnic groups, it would also be necessary to include a third generation. However, only very broad estimates of this total could be made. Some light on the wider diffusion of the Irish population within England and Wales can be drawn from the Longitudinal Study, which recorded the number of Irish-born grandparents to children aged under 16 and living at home. That is, parents' parents' birthplace can be linked back to these children. The results show that

9,190 (6.9%) of this 1% sample had at least one Irish-born grandparent, of who 3,590 were British-born of UK-born parents, that is third generation. They comprised 2.8% of all those with two UK-born parents. Multiplied through to the total population, this would give an additional 1,456,000 people in the third generation. However, this is likely to be a considerable underestimate.

### 3.1.5 Travellers

Statistics on Travellers are patchy and inaccurate. Mobile Travellers are largely missing from Census returns and the settled group are not identified separately. Estimates of numbers are based on families in some cases and on individuals in others. In 1987 the Minority Rights Action Group gave the figure of 11,500 Traveller families in Britain, of whom 13,000 individuals were Irish, suggesting that they comprised a quarter to a third of the total. However a table of figures produced in 1990 showing an ethnic breakdown of the Gypsy population of England, gave an estimate of 8,000 Irish Travellers out of a total population of 63,000, only 13%. The other Traveller groups were estimated at Romanies (53,000), Roma (2,000), Scots (200) and Kale (50). Although this survey estimated that the Irish comprised a much smaller proportion of the total, it also showed that far more Irish Travellers were living in vans (75% compared with 52% overall), and therefore both more visible and in need of parking sites (Kenrick and Bakewell ,1995).

Monitoring of Traveller numbers is collated by the Department of the Environment on a bi-annual basis. But it is simply a count of the numbers of caravans and pitches on council, private and unauthorised sites based on returns from individual Local Authorities. These returns are not mandatory and are, therefore, incomplete. No information is collected on numbers, ages, sex and ethnic origins of the people living on the sites.

A large proportion of the Travelling population lives in London. Estimates place the number of families at 3,200, one third of whom have no official status. A survey of London boroughs by the London Irish Women's Centre in 1994 identified a wide variation in monitoring procedures (LIWC, 1995). Department of Environment statistics show that 24 London boroughs are Designated Authorities, having made official provision for at least some of the Travellers in their area (DOE, 1994). A total of 22 London boroughs responded to the survey. Of these 17 claimed to keep records on the number of Travellers, whilst only 14 supplied figures, which were admitted to be broad estimates in most cases. Only four Local Authorities included Travellers living in houses in their estimates though many reported large numbers settled in their borough.

The most detailed figures were produced by the London Borough of Harrow, which had carried out a snapshot survey on a particular day (16/06/94) recording numbers, gender and school age of children. The results showed 124 Travellers in houses and 85 on the authorised site. They included 58 adult women, 30 adult men and 121 children (30 pre-school, 64 primary and 27 secondary school age).

However, the Council believed these totals to be a considerable underestimate since they did not reflect cumulative numbers who had passed through the Borough over the year, nor those Travellers who stayed on unauthorised sites for approximately 3 weeks. The latter were estimated to have been 25 adults and 50 children.

Only two London boroughs, Bromley and Lewisham, carried out ethnic monitoring of Travellers. Individual officers in other boroughs claimed to know the ethnicity of Travellers in their boroughs, stating that they were either all Irish, or a mixture of Irish, Welsh, English and Scottish. Clearly Irish Travellers were perceived as numerous, even though precise evidence was lacking.

### 3.1.6 Comparison with other ethnic groups in England

Britain is a plural society, including several different ethnic groups based in its constituent nations/regions as well as those originating principally in former colonies. Comparisons between the groups are made difficult by the difference drawn in the 1991 Census between birthplace and ethnic groups, the latter being based first on skin colour and second on self-identification. Although an 'Other' category was provided it was clearly not intended for use by 'white' groups. All white people were invited to tick this first category, which then overrode any subsequent choice.

In fact two thirds of the 31,000 people writing in 'Irish' were disqualified in this way (OPCS/GRO(S), 1993). Of the remaining 11,050, 9,860 (89%) lived in Greater London, over half (54%) in 7 boroughs - Brent (1,170), Haringey (1,030), Islington (7,40), Camden (690), Barnet (660), Hackney (560) and Ealing (520). The distribution probably reflects areas where the option was publicised, as well as the large size of the local Irish-born population. The highest proportion of 'write-ins' in relation to the size of the Irish-born population was in Haringey, only 6.2%. However a substantial proportion (40%) of the qualifying 'write-ins' were from non-Irish-born people (3,960 of 9,860 in Greater London), suggesting that a boxed Irish category would be the first preference of many second, and possibly subsequent, generation Irish people as well as the Irish-born. Census-defined ethnic groups thus include at least two generations, and often three, greatly augmenting their size when tabulated beside those defined by birthplace alone.

Table 1.4 examines the ethnic composition of England alone, placing the Irish population in relation to the other internal national groups of the United Kingdom, the Scots and the Welsh. It is necessary to limit the consideration to England in order to place Irish migrants on a similar footing to those originating in Scotland and Wales. Table 1.3 compares the totals of groups defined firstly by birthplace, that is the constituent parts of the United Kingdom, together with the Irish Republic, and then by Census-defined ethnic group. The geographic logic of the British Isles is applied to the birthplace question in the Census, for no stated reason, illustrating the special status of the Irish Republic. In total, the Irish (767,439) slightly outnumber the Scots living in England (743,856) and exceed numbers the Welsh (545,381).

The size of the first, that is migrant, generation of the Irish population (767,439) alone exceeds all Census-defined ethnic groups, with the exception of the Indian population (823,821). However when two generations of the Irish community are included, applying the multiplication factor of 2.5, the total Irish population in England alone reaches 2.7 millions (3 millions in Britain as a whole). It can thus clearly be seen to be substantially the largest ethnic group by migration.

Geographical clustering of the Irish population within Britain underlines the importance of including the second generation Irish population in comparative Census tables. This is brought out by the example of Greater London. Table 1.4 shows that inclusion of the second generation places the Irish population well above the numbers in other recognised ethnic minority groups, nearly three times the size of the two largest, those labeled Indian and Black Caribbean.

### 3.1.7 SUMMARY

- The size of the Irish-born population in Britain has remained stable overall since 1981 at about 845,000. However, the proportion in Scotland, where immigration has continued at a lower rate, has declined continuously since 1881.

- In 1991, 73% of the total Irish-born population in Britain originated in the Irish Republic and 27% in Northern Ireland. Published Census figures often combine the two groups under the heading 'Born in Ireland', but they have different characteristics in important respects.

- Estimates of the size of the 'second generation' population (born in Britain, but with one or two Irish-born parents) are necessary to count the Irish ethnic group on the same basis as others. A conservative correction factor of 2.5 is suggested on the basis of available evidence, though this may be a considerable underestimate, and 3 may be more accurate.

- Irish Travellers are monitored in a patchy way. Estimates from different sources include 13,000 individuals in Britain and 8,000 in England alone. Although the Irish appear to comprise perhaps a quarter of the total Traveller population, they are more visible since a higher proportion are live in caravans. A high proportion are located in London, one estimate being 3,200 families.

- Compared with other ethnic groups the Irish form a very large minority in Britain. When two generations are considered, numbers greatly exceed those of non-White Census-defined groups. There are also more Irish-born than Scots or Welsh in the population of England.

## 3.2 Patterns of settlement

### 3.2.1 Significance of geographical distribution

The Irish population in Britain has never been evenly spread. Overall statistics for Britain are thus extremely misleading. Although the Irish-born comprised 1.5% of the total British population in 1991, for example, they made up 3.8% of the Greater London total, augmented as was shown earlier to 13.4% when the second generation is included. Irish-born people have also been concentrated into the larger urban areas, where they have had specific needs such as access to housing and employment.

Certain parts of Britain, therefore, have much higher than average proportions of their populations born in Ireland. Thus when large statistical samples such as the Labour Force Survey are drawn on the basis of an even geographical spread of population throughout Britain, they underestimate the true size of the Irish-born population and distort its characteristics, over-emphasising those of more scattered Irish-born populations.

Distribution at a regional scale has also changed sharply over time, with important consequences for later arrivals. In the nineteenth century the major centres of Irish settlement were in the heavy-industrial areas in the north and west, notably Lancashire and Clydeside. As a result there are long-established traditions of Catholic adherence and school provision in these areas. Newly arrived migrants are not seen as a challenge to resource allocation as they have been in parts of southeast England without previous experience of Irish settlement, for example Luton (Walter, 1984). In northwest England the spread of Irish ancestry through outmarriage now includes a much wider section of the population than in other parts of England where settlement has been on a much smaller scale. People of Irish descent in Merseyside readily accept the identity of 'Liverpudlian' whereas in London many remain firmly 'Irish' (Hickman, 1990).

The age distribution of the present day Irish-born population differs sharply by geographical location, as result of changing cycles of migration. The largest group is the older generation who arrived in Britain during the 1950s and early '60s boom years of the British economy. Many were directly recruited to work in manufacturing industry, transport and the health service. The strongest demand for labour was in the West Midlands, especially in Birmingham. Since the 1970s employment prospects in these areas has declined sharply, leaving an ageing Irish-born population and a large second and third generation community. In the 1980s, an upturn in demand for labour in the service sector was concentrated in London, where the largest number of young Irish-born people is now located.

### 3.2.1 Change over time

The late twentieth century distribution of Irish-born people in Britain is sharply different from that of the nineteenth century. Traditional areas of Irish settlement were in Scotland and North West England, but in the post-War period these regions have received only small numbers of new immigrants and their share of the total Irish-born population has fallen steeply (Figure 2.1).

Greatest growth has taken place in the South East where almost half of the British total of Irish-born people was recorded in 1991 (49.3%) (Table 2.1). Six of the other nine regions registered a fall in their Irish-born populations between 1981 and 1991. The other regional increases were in East Anglia (+12.5%), which had only a very small proportion of the total (2.2%), and South West England (+7.6%).

The Irish-born population is thus increasingly clustered in South East England, to a much greater extent than the population as a whole (Figure 2.2). Whereas slightly less than a third (31.4%) of the total population of Britain lives in South East England, half of the Irish-born population does so (Figure 2.3). There is still a slight, though declining, over-representation of Irish-born people in the West Midlands (10.9%, compared with 9.4% of the total population) and for the first time since 1841 the proportion in North West England almost exactly equals that of the total population (11.7%, compared with 11.4%). This pattern is similar to that of other ethnic minorities by migration, with the exception of the higher percentage of Irish people in North West England, and lower percentage in Yorkshire/Humberside.

In all other regions the Irish-born are under-represented and regional shares declined 1981-91. The North region of England, for example, contains 5.5% of the total population, but only 1.9% of the Irish-born. This proportion has steadily decreased since 1881.

### 3.2.2 Settlement by origin: Irish Republic and Northern Ireland

The settlement patterns of those originating in the Irish Republic and Northern Ireland differ in important ways. There is a substantially higher degree of clustering amongst the Republic-born, of whom over three-quarters (76.9%) live in only three regions - the South East, North West and West Midlands (Figure 2.2).

Those born in Northern Ireland, on the other hand, have a distribution much closer to that of the total population and are more evenly spread over the ten regions (Figure 2.2). In this case three quarters (76.7%) live in five regions - including Scotland and Yorkshire/Humberside as well as the three where the Republic-born cluster. A particularly distinctive feature is the high proportion of Northern Irish people in Scotland (10.8%). Overall a much lower percentage live in the South East (36.6%).

Mapping at the finer scale of districts (Figures 2.6 and 2.8) confirms the distinctive clustering of the Irish Republic-born population in Greater London and the urban areas of Manchester, Birmingham and Luton. By contrast, the Northern Irish-born pattern (Figures 2.7 and 2.9) shows a much more even spread, with slightly more noticeable clustering in southwest Scotland.

Because of the clustering of Irish-born people within urban areas and within particular urban localities, local importance may be brought out more clearly by listing areas where they are most prominent. Table 2.2 shows percentages at local authority district and parliamentary constituency levels. All but three of the local authority districts with over 4% Irish-born population were in London. Outside London, Luton (5.4%), Coventry (4.6%) and Manchester (4.6%) all had relatively high proportions, showing that areas of previous high immigration continue to have substantial Irish populations. This is underlined even more clearly when parliamentary constituencies are considered. Although London still features most prominently, parts of Manchester and Birmingham also have large numbers of Irish voters. The Manchester Gorton constituency, for example, has Irish-born population of 6.3%, including the highest proportion of Northern Irish voters (1.2%). Two Birmingham constituencies also have high proportions, Erdington (5.8%), also with a larger than average Northern Irish-born component (1.1%) and Sparkbrook (5.7%).

### 3.2.4 Recent migrants 1990-91

The destination of recent migrants is a very important influence on the changing pattern of settlement in Britain and its character. New migrants, following changing demand for labour, attract friends and relatives, who learn about job opportunities from them and look for help in obtaining accommodation. New arrivals need to find employment and low-cost, rented housing as well as advice about the institutions with whom they need to deal. If they set up households in the area and raise children, they may need appropriate schools and health facilities. Reception of migrants in areas with little previous experience of Irish people is likely to be different from that in established settlement clusters.

The 1991 Census records by birthplace migrants living outside the United Kingdom one year previously. In fact the number of new arrivals from the Irish Republic in 1990-91 was substantially lower than a few years previously, so that the total is not representative of the 1980s as a whole. In 1985 alone, for example, the net outflow from the Irish Republic was 28,000 people leading to an absolute decrease in the total population of the state for the first time since the 1950s. Emigration increased rapidly to reach a net loss of 43,900 in 1989 (outflow 70,600; inflow 43,900), according to official figures (CSO, 1994). Totals declined sharply thereafter so that in 1990-1, 12,429 entered Britain according to the Census (HMSO, 1993). In 1992 there was a slight net inflow to Ireland, but by 1994 there was again a net outflow of 10,000, mainly due to falling in-migration to Ireland. However, the true figures for net migration are likely to be considerably higher than official estimates, which are widely believed to be conservative. Not all emigrants settled in Britain, of course, official estimates showing that 59% of outmigrants from the Irish Republic moved to the United Kingdom (CSO, 1994).

The majority of new migrants from Ireland settling in Britain were young, 71.4% aged under 30. The regional distribution of these new arrivals can be compared with that of the Irish-born population as a whole (Table 2.3). A striking feature of this pattern is its focus on South East England. In 1991 66.1% of all new arrivals were located there. Women were even more strongly attracted to this region than men, 73.0% of Republic Irish-born and 45.1% of Northern Irish-born women settling in the South East region, compared with 68.5% and 41.7% of men respectively (Table 2.4). The South West is the only other region to have a higher proportion of new arrivals than its share of the total Irish-born population, and this is due to its attraction for relatively large numbers from Northern Ireland.

Very few recent arrivals chose the traditional areas of Irish settlement of the North West (6.2%) and the West Midlands (4.5%). Despite strong networks of contacts in these regions, they no longer appear to attract many young people. However the effects of under-enumeration of young migrants must be borne in mind, and the true numbers are likely to be higher.

A changing pattern over time can also be traced. Figure 2.11 shows a sharp increase in popularity of the South East, from 49.0% of new arrivals 1970-71 to 66.0% in 1990-91. This is especially clear in the case of recent migrants from the Irish Republic who shifted sharply towards the South East during the 1980s, away from the North West and West Midlands which were still favoured in the 1970s.

### 3.2.5 Migration within Britain

The main form of redistribution taking place after arrival appears to be an outward movement from Inner London to Outer London and to a lesser extent the Outer South East (Table 2.5). However, there is also a smaller counter-current of migrants moving back into Inner London from outer areas of the region, perhaps to independent rented accommodation after a period staying with longer-established relatives.

A net outward movement from the South East as a whole can also be identified, the most favoured destination being the South West, probably for retirement. But by far the greatest number of moves are within the same region, suggesting that migrants tend to remain in the area of initial settlement, though they often relocate within it.

### 3.2.6 Settlement in conurbations

The Irish in Britain have always clustered in large cities to a greater extent than the population as a whole. Seven major conurbations in England are identified by the Census: Greater London and the six metropolitan counties of Tyne and Wear, South Yorkshire, West Yorkshire, West Midlands, Greater Manchester and Merseyside (Table 2.6). In 1991 61% of the Irish Republic-born population in England lived in these conurbations, and 41% of the Northern Irish-born but only 37% of the total population. Scottish conurbations are not identified in the Census, but the Strathclyde district contained 58% of the total Republic Irish-born population in Scotland, and 47% of the Northern Irish-born. Again therefore a clear distinction can be drawn between those originating in the Republic and Northern Ireland, people born in the Republic being distinctly more urbanised.

By far the largest concentration of Irish-born people was in Greater London, 30.6% of the total living in Britain compared with 27.7% in 1981. By contrast the proportion of the total population living in Greater London had remained almost static (1982,12.3%; 1991,12.2%).

Within the South East region migrants in 1990-91 chose Greater London to a greater extent than in 1980-81. This was particularly true of Northern Irish-born migrants. In 1981 33.5% of women and 31.4% of men first located in the South East, but in 1991 the proportions were 41.9% and 45.7% respectively. Many more Republic-born migrants moved directly to Greater London, rising from 68.8% in 1981 to 72.2% for women though appearing to fall slightly for men from 72.4% to 71.4%.

There is a small difference in gender patterns with a slightly higher proportion of Irish-born men living in the conurbations (Republic-born: men 61.2%, women 59.9%; Northern Irish-born: men 43.0%, women 39.4%: Table 2.7). The difference would be reinforced if more Irish men were omitted from the 1991 Census. This pattern was not found amongst the population as a whole, women having a very slightly higher propensity to live in large urban areas (37.0%, men 37.4%). Moreover, in Greater London the position is reversed and Irish Republic-born women greatly outnumber men (115,865 women to 98,362 men).

Within conurbations, further clustering takes place. In Greater London, for example, Figure 2.4 shows clear zoning in the northwest sector, represented by strong concentrations in the boroughs of Brent (9.0%) and Islington (7.1%), as well as Hammersmith and Fulham (6.8%), Camden (6.5%) and Ealing (6.0%). An outer arc adjacent to this core includes the boroughs of Harrow and Barnet which have high numbers of young Irish-born people aged 16-24, 13.5% and 11.6% respectively compared with an average for London of 6.5%. Total numbers of Irish-born people are relatively smaller in more easterly inner boroughs such as Newham (2.1%), Tower Hamlets (2.5%) and Lewisham (3.4%).

In Birmingham a pattern of greater clustering in inner wards can also be seen (Figure 2.5). However, the two wards with the highest proportions of Irish-born population, Erdington (6.9%) in the north and Fox Hollies (6.5%) in the southeast, are located towards the periphery of the city, suggesting an outward movement to the suburbs over time (Figure 2.5).

### 3.2.7 SUMMARY

- The Irish-born population has always been strongly clustered at regional, urban and local scales. Percentages relating to Britain as a whole are thus misleading, as are large official datasets based on areal sampling frames.

- The pattern of settlement has changed sharply over time. In the nineteenth century clustering was greatest in northwest England and Clydeside in Scotland. More people in these areas thus have Irish ancestry. The large-scale immigration of the 1950s focused particularly on cities in the English Midlands, especially Birmingham, as well as Coventry. Recent migrants have settled most strongly in London.

- The Republic Irish-born population is particularly concentrated. Over three-quarters live in three regions of England - the South East, North West and West Midlands. Northern Irish-born people are more widely spread, and more strongly represented in southern Scotland.

- In the past Irish-born women were strongly clustered in South East and North West England, but the gender balance is now almost equal between the regions.

- Recent Irish migrants (1990-91) were strongly attracted to South East England: 66% of the total. Most were young, more than 70% under 30.

- Migration within Britain by the Irish-born population was mainly within each region, including a shift from Inner to Outer London and to a lesser extent to the Outer South East and South West England.

- The Irish-born population has clustered in large urban centres to a much greater extent than the population as a whole. Within Britain 57% of the Republic Irish-born (36% Northern Irish-born) live in the seven major English conurbations, compared with 32% of the total.

- London accounted for 36% of the Irish Republic total (17% of the Northern Irish-born). The second largest concentration was in the West Midlands (9% and 5% respectively). In Scotland over half the Irish-born population lived in Strathclyde alone (58% of the Republic-born and 47% of the Northern Irish-born).

- Within conurbations there are strong clusters of Irish settlement. For example, in London there is a clear northwesterly clustering, especially of the Republic-born. Highest proportions are in Brent (9% of the total population), Islington (7.1) and Hammersmith and Fulham (6.9%). In Birmingham the suburban wards of Erdington (6.9%) and Fox Hollies (6.5%) had the highest proportions of Irish settlement in 1991.

### 3.3 Demographic characteristics

### 3.3.1 Age

### 3.3.1.1 Significance of age

The age distribution of the Irish community in Britain provides important evidence about its character. Lifecycle stages are intricately related to family formation, participation in education and training, employment patterns, housing requirements, health and welfare needs.

Age structure itself reflects cycles of migration. Past peaks of immigration now appear as bulges in the population pyramid and are similarly associated with the changing pattern of second generation numbers and age distributions. For example the 'second wave' of emigration from Ireland in the 1950s is now associated with very large numbers of people in their early retirement years. In turn, the children of migrants from these 'bulge' years form an unusually large second generation, who passed through the British education system at a time of expanding opportunities particularly in higher education in the 1970s (Figure 1.3). This group is now approaching middle age and raising a third generation.

### 3.3.1.2 Age structure in 1991

Age distributions of the total and Irish-born populations in Britain are distinctly different (Figure 3.1). The two Irish-born populations show a typical labour migrant pattern with very small numbers of children. This is particularly marked in the case of the Republic-born where there is a sharp bulge in the age group 20-24. Children form a relatively higher proportion of the Northern Irish-born population, reflecting greater family migration in the last twenty years. Those aged 0-19 comprise 8.8% of the Northern Irish population, but only 4.4% of the Republic-born. By contrast they make up 25.3% of the total population. In all comparisons between the Irish-born and total populations, therefore, only adults aged 16+ should be included, or the results will be distorted.

A distinctive feature of the Republic-born age pyramid is the bulge of older middle-aged people aged 40-69 who comprise 58.0% of the total. The bulge is less marked for the Northern Irish-born where it accounts for only 46.6%. This reflects the much greater importance of the outflow from the Republic in the peak years of the 'second wave' during the 1940s and 50s. The small dip in numbers of Republic-born people in their thirties reflects the downturn in net immigration during the 1970s, reversed strongly again in the 1980s as the rise of numbers in the 25-29 age group indicates.

The Northern Irish pattern differs in significant ways. It has less extreme fluctuations and there is a slight bulge amongst the younger middle-aged (25-49), who comprise 45.2% of the total, compared with 37.0% for the Republic-born. Emigration was exceptionally high during the early years of the current phase of the Northern Ireland conflict, the net figure totalling 39,484 between 1972-75, compared with 24,600 in the following three-year period. People now in their forties would have left at this time, often with young families. The larger proportion of new migrants from the North is also clear, forming 38.4% of the 25-29 Irish-born age group compared with 21.8% of those aged 55-59. A smaller proportion of the elderly Irish-born is from the North, 24.8% of those aged over 70.

Gender differences are highlighted by Figure 3.1. Women outnumber men in all adult age groups of the Republic-born. Differences are greatest in the oldest age groups where women comprise 63.7% of those aged over 75. However the gender gap amongst the Irish-born population is slightly smaller than in the total population of Britain where women make up 65.8% of the age group. This is rather surprising given the greater propensity for men to return to Ireland and the number of widows leaving Ireland to joining their families in Britain, or seeking work when jobs as housekeepers or carers in Ireland come to an end (Kelly and Nic Giolla Choille, 1995). It may reflect an historically smaller difference in life expectancy between men and women in Ireland than in most other Western industrial countries, though this has now disappeared (Kennedy, 1973; Walter, 1989).

Young women 20-24 also substantially outnumber men in their age group, though it is not known how much of this difference arises from uneven Census under-enumeration. Numbers of women and men are more closely balanced in the Northern Irish-born population, and in several age groups men are more numerous than women (25-34, 45-49, 55-64).

### 3.3.1.3 Age profiles by region

The balance of young, middle aged and old Irish people varies considerably by region, mainly reflecting period of arrival of the majority of migrants (Figures 3.2 and 3.3). The South East of England is the only region to have above the average proportion of young people aged 16-29, while the strongest representation of middle-aged people (30-59) is in the West Midlands followed by Yorkshire/Humberside, North West England and the East Midlands.

The older age group (60+) of the Irish-born population is strongly over-represented in Scotland and South West England. In the case of Scotland, this constitutes a residual population from larger immigration flows earlier in the century. High mortality rates because of old age help to account for the very steep fall in the Irish-born population between 1981 and 1991 (-19.3%). Although immigration continues to take place, net new migration at present into Scotland is low, making it likely that the total will have fallen substantially again by the time of the next Census. Between 1981 and 1991 the number of Irish-born people of pensionable age in Scotland actually fell by 11.1% whilst it rose sharply in other regions with large elderly populations, including the North, North West, Yorkshire/Humberside, East Midlands and Wales, where this is a relatively new phenomenon.

The large proportion of older Irish-born people in the South West, on the other hand, reflects immigration to the region rather than ageing-in-place. Numbers of Irish-born people of pensionable age rose by 31.8% between 1981 and 1991, exceeding growth in the total population (+13.6%). These older Irish people are sharing in the migration patterns of other sections of the British population and choosing the milder climate and seaside attraction of this region.

### 3.3.2 Gender

Despite the common British stereotype of Irish 'Paddies' and 'Micks', Irish women have outnumbered men in Britain for most of the twentieth century. In 1991 there were 45,774 more Irish-born women in England and Wales (women 417,027; men 371,253) and 4,622 more in Scotland (women 26,903; men 22,281). This pattern was first recorded in 1921 in England and Wales and has become more marked since 1961. There are now 112 Irish-born women to every 100 men. In Scotland, the trend is much more recent, becoming apparent for the first time in 1961 and now reaching 121 women per 100 men. Although more women have left Ireland in most census years since 1851, they chose to emigrate to the United States in greater numbers before the 1920s.

The gender imbalance is much greater amongst those born in the Irish Republic, where there are 115 women per 100 men in England and Wales and 129 in Scotland. In the Northern Irish-born population the respective ratios are 104 and 114. This difference between the two parts of Ireland may reflect a greater tendency for women from the North to return home. Compton (1991) suggests there may be a circular pattern of migration for young women from Northern Ireland, due to the segmentation of the labour market in which they are peripheral workers in the public sector and other service industries. Because Northern Ireland is part of the UK public services labour market, women can circulate within the same area of employment. Men on the other hand are core workers, who do not move interchangeably within one type of organisation, and become permanent settlers.

By contrast, Irish Republic-born women are more likely than men to settle permanently in Britain. They leave jobs in Ireland and move to a different type of work or join new organisations in Britain. Fewer women than men from the Irish Republic took the opportunity to return home in the 1970s when net immigration into Ireland was experienced, suggesting that they had found better jobs, were tied into networks of family and friends in Britain, or preferred aspects of the way of life in Britain (Garvey, 1985). There may be more opportunities for men from the Republic to establish themselves in business there, with capital accumulated in Britain. However, more research needs to be done on the patterns of labour migration between both parts of Ireland and Britain.

### 3.3.3 Household structures

### 3.3.3.1 Household heads

In order to examine the housing and income needs of the Irish population, household structures must be analysed and placed in context. However a serious weakness of the published Census tables is the classification of households by birthplace of 'head'.

Although designation of 'head' is now taken to be the first adult name appearing on the Census form, men are still greatly over-represented. (Data from the SARS 2% individual data show that men are 'heads' in 92.2% of households with female/male couples). Households where Irish-born women live with non-Irish-born men (over half of Irish-born mothers lived with non-Irish-born fathers in 1971, see Table 1.1) are thus omitted from tables based on head of household, which include those household composition and housing statistics.

### 3.3.3.2 Household composition

For this reduced sample (that is, missing a substantial number of households with Irish-born women) Tables 3.1 and 3.2 compare household and family structures for Irish-headed and total populations. The main points of contrast include the larger proportion of Irish-headed households with no families, that is single or groups of unrelated people. These constitute 34.9% of Irish-headed compared with only 29.6% of the total. This would be expected amongst a migrant population, but may point to problems of loneliness and social isolation for some people, especially if it is prolonged. Housing is also a particular problem for the single, since there is less provision and lower priority in access.

An analysis of single people by age and sex in the Irish-born and total populations throws more light on the extent of this situation (Table 3.3). In all age groups substantially higher proportions of Irish-born women and men are never-married and a larger number are likely to be living alone. The proportions are highest for men, following the trend in the total population. In the 50-54 age group, for example, where numbers of single Irish Republic-born women are closest to the population average (6.9%, compared with 5.1%), men diverge strongly (14.0%, compared with 8.2%). At younger ages, Republic-born men and women are also much more likely to be single. In the 30-34 cohort, 30.0% of women are single (18.1% total population) and 45.5% of men (28.2% total population). Reasons include cultural factors, a continuation of lower marriage rates in Ireland, and the migration process itself. For men an important factor has been the unsettled nature of construction work, necessitating frequent movement to new sites, for example in motorway construction.

There is a striking difference between the profiles of the Republic and Northern Irish-born populations. In the younger age groups, the Northern Irish-born occupy an intermediate position between the average and Republic-born totals. However, over the age of 45 the proportion of single men drops below average, whilst the rate amongst Northern Irish-born women was slightly higher.

Amongst households with one family, who form the majority, a higher proportion of Irish-headed households consists of a lone parent (10.8%, compared with 8.9% in the total population). However, more Irish lone-parent households have non-dependent children, suggesting an older age structure. This is also true of married couple and cohabiting families.

### 3.3.3.3. Household size

The higher proportion of single people is reflected in comparative household sizes (Table 3.4). Nearly a third of Irish-headed households (31.3%) have one person compared with the average of 26.0%. At the other end of the scale 9.0% of Irish-headed households are large, containing 5, 6 or 7+ people, while the average is 7.6%.

Single person households include a large number of lone adults of pensionable age, either never-married or widowed/divorced. In London, for example, the average is well above that of Census-based ethnic minority groups, though below that of the white non-Irish-born population. However, in certain Inner London boroughs, notably Westminster (25.5%), Kensington and Chelsea (22.0%) and Camden (20.2%) high proportions of the total Irish-born population fall into this category (Table 3. 5) (AGIY, 1995).

### 3.3.3.4. SUMMARY

- A distinctive feature of the Irish Republic-born age distribution is the bulge of older middle-aged people. These are the settled population from the large-scale immigration of the 1950s, who make up the largest section of the Irish-born population in Britain (58%).

- The Northern Irish-born population has a more equally distributed adult age profile, with a slightly greater younger middle-aged section (25-49), who comprise 45% of the total.

- Young migrants from Northern Ireland make up a larger proportion of the Irish-born age group than in the past (38%).

- There are marked differences in age profile by region. Young people are clustered in South East England, whereas the middle-aged are most evident in the West Midlands. Older Irish-born people form a larger proportion of the population in Scotland and South West England.

- Irish-born women outnumber men in Britain. In 1991 there were 115 Republic-born women per 100 men in England (129 in Scotland). The ratios for the Northern Irish-born population are lower, 104 and 114 respectively.

- Census statistics are biased towards households with Irish men and published data excludes more than a third of Irish households where Irish-born women have partners of another birthplace/ethnic origin.

- More Irish-headed households contain single people, reflecting lower marriage rates throughout the age range and many lone pensioners.

# 4. The Irish in the British labour market

## 4.1. Introduction

The position of the Irish in the British labour market is crucial in determining income and job security. It is also an indication of the extent to which the Irish

i.  are integrated on equal terms with the majority society;

ii. remain a migrant labour force filling specific gaps or;

iii. experience continuing disadvantage through exclusion.

Although a disadvantageous position is not clear evidence of discrimination, discrimination may be a contributory factor.

The Irish are a labour migrant group in Britain and rates of immigration are closely tied to demand for labour. Although the *push* factor of high unemployment has been experienced in Northern Ireland throughout the 1970s and 80s, and in the Irish Republic after a brief fall in the early 1970s, emigration takes place primarily in response to the *pull* factor of opportunities in Britain. Between 1975 and 1990, there was a strong positive correlation between outflows from Northern Ireland and vacancies in Britain (r = 0.60 for the gross outflow; r = 0.70 for the net outflow, that is 60% of the variation in the total flow could be explained by vacancies in Britain alone), becoming even stronger after 1980 (r = 0.87; r = 0.88 respectively). Correlation with unemployment levels in Northern Ireland was very weak (r =0.08 for the gross outflow; r = 0.27 for the net outflow, that is only 8% of total out-migration could be directly related to unemployment in Northern Ireland) (Compton, 1991).

Econometric models of emigration from the Irish Republic stress the importance of *relative* changes in labour market conditions in the two countries, and the strong impact of the buoyant demand for labour in Britain after 1984 which coincided with sharply increased unemployment levels in the Republic (NESC, 1991). In other words, although high rates of unemployment in both parts of Ireland make labour readily available, actual numbers emigrating respond very sensitively to the needs of the British labour market.

This section examines four aspects of Irish participation in the labour market:

(i) Occupation profiles of the Irish population, the types of work in which Irish women and men are employed, are examined. These indicate not only approximate income levels, but also degrees of segregation experienced and the extent to which these are associated with migrant labour.

(ii) Positions within the socio-economic hierarchy which these jobs, and the levels occupied within them, confer on the Irish relative to other sections of the population are identified. Social mobility over time is a particularly important indicator of integration within the mainstream structure.

(iii) Qualifications of the Irish population are compared with those of other sections of the population. These can be related to employment levels and any mismatches noted.

(iv) Experience of unemployment amongst the Irish is investigated and placed in a comparative perspective with that of other groups.

## 4.2 Work profiles

### 4.2.1 Types of occupation: 1991

The 1991 Census classifies the economically active population into nine broad occupation categories. Figure 4.1 shows the overall pattern of Irish-born women's and men's occupations.

### (i) Women

Irish women are far more strongly clustered than men into particular occupational groupings (Table 4.1). Much higher than average proportions of Irish women are recorded in associated professional occupations including nursing (Category 3), personal services (Category 6) where domestic and catering work is predominant and other elementary occupations (Category 9), mainly services.

At the same time, Irish women are noticeably under-represented in the major section of British women's work, clerical and secretarial work (Category 4) where only 20.1% of Irish-born women compared with 27.7% of the total are recorded. They are also missing to a certain extent from sales occupations (Category 7), which account for 6.3% of Irish-born women but 10.4% of the population as a whole.

Overall therefore, Irish women clearly fit the pattern of migrant workers, filling niches in the labour market unmet by the skills and preferences of the majority population. Two very different groups of Irish women are involved - highly qualified nurses and low-skilled personal service workers. Although Irish women are equally represented in professional occupations, their numbers are conspicuously low in middle-range 'white collar' clerical and sales work.

### (ii) Men

Irish-born men's occupations are more similar to those of the population as a whole. Like women they are under-represented in 'white collar' occupations (Categories 1, 3 and 4), but not professional work (Category 2), where there is a slightly greater proportion of Irish-born men (10.1%, compared with 9.3% in the total population).

Some clustering is apparent in Category 5, which includes skilled construction work, and industrial work, heavy machine operation and general labouring (Categories 8 and 9). These two categories account for 19.2% of Irish men's work compared with 13.8% of the male workforce.

### 4.2.2 Industries

(i) Women

The Industrial Classification places a very large proportion of women in the single undifferentiated category 'other services'. Irish women are over-represented in this amorphous area (50.7%, compared with 41.2% of the total population) and 71.9% fall into the two groups, 'other services' (Category 9) and 'distribution and catering' (Category 6) compared with 65.7% of all women.

(ii) Men

Clustering of Irish-born men's work in the construction industry is brought out more clearly when the Industrial Classification is used, that is categorisation by type of product rather then type of work (Figure 4.2). A quarter of all Irish-born men (25.3%) are engaged in construction, compared with only 12.0% of the total population. This is by far the greatest divergence from the general pattern.

### 4.2.3 Proportion of total labour force

The Irish-born constitute 1.5% of the total British population, but make up 1.8% and 1.6% of the female and male workforces respectively (Table 4.1). However within this average there are strong differences. For example, Irish-born people constitute over 3% of health professionals (2b) and health associated professionals (3b). In the case of women the proportions are 3.6% of health professionals, and 4.3% of health associate professionals. The figure for men is 3.0% in each category. Irish-born women also make up a higher than average proportion of the female workforce in other professional categories, including 2.5% of science and engineering associate professionals (3a).

Irish-born women and men both form a larger than average proportion of personal service workers (Category 6b, women 2.9% and men 2.2%; 9b, women 2.3%) and men make up 2.9% of the general labouring workforce. Overall therefore, Irish-born workers are over-represented in certain areas of work. For women these are the contrasting ends of the caring occupations, nursing and personal service. Irish men are still strongly clustered in construction work, but are also well represented in professional occupations.

Labour migration from Ireland thus has a dual pattern. It includes both highly educated and trained professionals for whom there is a skills shortage in Britain, the brain drain, and low paid manual workers filling secondary jobs which are rejected by the indigenous workforce. The migration of highly skilled workers from less-developed to highly-developed countries is part of a wider trend (Castles and Miller, 1993). In Britain in the late 1980s, 85% of work permits were issued to professional and managerial workers, and about two-thirds of all employed immigrants were in these categories (Salt, 1989).

### 4.2.4 Comparison of the Irish Republic and Northern Irish-born populations

Important differences are noted when the Irish-born population is disaggregated, pointing to the problem of uniting the category in the 1991 Census. These data are drawn from the 2% SARS (Table 4.2) so that smaller numbers are involved and the joint proportions are similar but not identical to those of the 10% published sample (Walter, 1996). However the contrasts observed between those born in the two parts of the island are clearly significant ones.

The main point to emerge is that most of the patterns identified in the previous section are much more strongly associated with the Republic-born population. Those born in the North are much closer in profile to the average population of Britain, although in some cases they show a pattern of clustering similar to, but less marked than, the Republic-born.

(i) Women

Women born in the Republic are more strongly represented in nursing (11.9%) than the Northern-Irish born (9.3%), though both groups are substantially above average (4.8%). Women originating in the Republic are much more likely to be in personal services (Category 6b, 15.2%; 9b, 19.4%) than the Northern Irish-born (Category 6b, 12.7%; 9b, 11.9%) who are closer to the female average (Category 6b, 12.8%; 9b, 10.8%). Generally, Northern-Irish born women are found in higher status occupations, 11.2% in Category 1, management and administration (Republic-born 9.6%) and 11.4% in Category 2, professional workers (Republic-born 5.8%). In the latter category the proportion is also considerably higher than average (7.1%).

(ii) Men

Occupation profiles of Irish men show a similar contrast, those of men from the North being much more similar to the British average. Whereas 9.0% of Republic-born men were in skilled construction trades (5a), only 5.1% of the Northern-Irish born are in this category, close to the average of 4.8%. The proportion in other elementary occupations (9b) is much higher amongst the Republic-born (16.2%) than amongst the Northern Irish-born (9.8%), again much closer to the average (8.5%).

Like women, Northern Irish-born men occupy higher status categories. Management and administration (Category 1), for example, includes 13.8% of the Republic-born but 17.3% of men from the North and 18.0% of all men. Northern Irish-born men are also particularly well represented in the professions (13.4%), almost twice the proportion of Republic-born men (6.4%) and considerably higher than average (8.9%).

It is important, therefore, to distinguish migrants by origin in Ireland when considering their place in the British workforce. Whereas both women and men from the Irish Republic show very clear labour migrant profiles, those from Northern Ireland have a more complex occupation pattern. Their greater similarity to the British average may be explained by a number of factors, including the shared education system and its resulting qualifications. Those with higher levels of education may emigrate within common employment structures, such as the civil service. Undoubtedly, therefore, the stereotyped manual occupations are more characteristic of migrants from the Irish Republic.

### 4.2.5 Occupations by age

Marked differences by migrant generation and lifecycle stage are brought out when further sub-division of occupational categories by age is made. It is essential to disaggregate the Irish population in Britain by age to avoid examining a misleading average. Figure 4.3 summarises the main differences between the young (18-29), middle-aged (30-44) and older (45-59) working age groups. It should be remembered that these comprise very different proportions of the Irish-born population as a whole (see Figure 3.1).

(i) Young working age group (18-29)

The young group, which comprises 11.8% of the total Irish-born population and represents 1980s migrants, has much stronger representation in occupations demanding higher qualification levels. Both women and men are strongly over-represented in managerial and professional occupations (Categories 1, 2 and 3) compared with the total population.

Nearly half of all Irish-born women aged 18-29 (45.4%) are in these three categories alone, compared with 26.5% of all women, the proportions for men being 39.0% and 26.5% respectively. Nurses account for an important part of this group and explain the higher representation of women in these occupations. If non-health occupations only are considered, 29.7% of Irish-born women (18.9% total population) and 36.3% of Irish-born men (24.2% total population) are included.

Even without an important niche occupation, therefore, there is still a significantly greater than average proportion of young Irish people in higher level managerial, administrative and professional work, evidence of a brain drain from Ireland during the 1980s.

Nevertheless, young Irish-born men also remain over-represented in areas of low-skilled, often casual work, notably personal services (Category 6: 10.3%, compared with 4.1% total population). Unusually, Irish-born women are not also over-represented in these categories, suggesting an important gender difference amongst recent migrants. Fewer young women appear to be entering low-paid, unskilled casual work than in the past, but young men continue to do so, taking on service jobs rather than the traditional general labouring ones. However, it is possible that young men missing from Census enumeration are mainly in the casual labourer category, so that the totals are misleadingly low.

(ii) Middle working age (30-44)

In the middle working age groups, which comprise 20.7% of the total Irish-born population, the occupational patterns of the Irish-born converge most closely with those of the population as a whole, though the broad differences noted earlier remain.

(iii) Older working age (45-59)

Sharp distinctions emerge, however, amongst older working age populations. This is by far the largest section of the Irish-born population, comprising 30.8% of the total and representing the 1950s bulge (see Figure 3.2). The experience of this group thus has a major effect on the socioeconomic structure of the Irish population as a whole.

Older working Irish-born women are strongly concentrated into the two personal service and catering categories, (Categories 6 and 9: 39.2%, total population 27.0%) and Irish-born men into the industrial and general labouring (Categories 8 and 9: 34.9%, total population 23.2%). The proportion of Irish-born men and women in the professional category is much lower than in the young working age group.

### 4.2.6 SUMMARY

- A new phenomenon in the occupational profile of the Irish-born population is the significantly high proportion of young people in the highest occupational categories. Whilst this is partly explained by traditional associations with skilled healthcare professions, especially for women, the spread of managerial and professional occupations is much wider than before. Both women and men are part of a brain drain from Ireland, helping to fill the skills shortage in Britain.

- However, by far the largest number of Irish-born people in the workforce are in the older age group 45-59, representing long-established migrants from the 'second wave' of the 1950s. These workers are still strongly clustered into occupations traditionally associated with the Irish population, particularly domestic work for women and general labouring for men (Jackson, 1963).

### 4.3 Social class patterns

This section takes a broader view of the socio-economic condition of the Irish-born in Britain and attempts to assess their class position. Class is a notoriously difficult concept to define and measure, but its hierarchical basis introduces a measure of relative advantage into the analysis of socio-economic structure and thus allows the discussion of occupational difference to be taken further. In addition to the issue of clustering by workplace, income levels, career prospects and status can be considered, as well as social mobility over time.

### 4.3.1 Registrar General's Social Class

Several methods of allocating individuals to social classes may be used. The simplest and most readily available is the Registrar General's index based on levels of skill in occupations. Although criticised for lack of systematic criteria (Prandy, 1990) and inadequate representation of women's work (Thomas, 1986), this has the advantage of summarising data on occupations.

Table 4.3 shows the distribution of women and men in England by Registrar General's Social Group for the main birthplace and Census-based ethnic groups. Though small numbers are inevitably involved (2% Individual SARS), broad patterns can be identified.

(i) Social Classes IV and V

The most striking finding is the clustering of Republic Irish-born women and men in the lowest social category, Social Class V. The proportions in this class are substantially higher than for any other group, 14.1% for women compared with 7.5% for white English-born, the closest being Black African women with 11.5%. For Republic Irish-born men the total is 12.0%, more than twice the proportion of the white English-born (5.4%) and closest to the Black Caribbean population (8.4%). There is a particularly marked contrast with Scottish and Welsh-born women and men in England, whose totals in this class are lower than for the English-born majority. If the lowest Social Classes (IV and V) are merged, an approximation to a 'working class' grouping, Irish Republic-born women are second only to Pakistani women in proportion, whilst men are very close to Black Caribbean and Pakistani men who have the highest proportions.

The greatest contrast is with the indigenous British ethnic groupings (English, Scottish, Welsh). Women and men from Northern Ireland are also much closer to these British ethnic groupings than to the Irish Republic-born.

(ii) Social Classes I and II

Conversely at the top end of the class scale, Republic-born Irish women and men have the lowest proportions of any of the birthplace/ethnic groups listed, with the exception of the Black Caribbean population. Irish Republic-born women have low proportions in Social Class I, similar to the English-born total and well below those of the Scottish, Welsh and Northern Irish-born groups. The difference is even more striking when the two highest Social Classes, that is the groups fitting most closely the description 'middle class', are taken together. Women originating in Wales (41%), Scotland (37.2%) and Northern Ireland (39.3%) are in much higher-ranking occupations than Republic-born women (32.9%), despite the number of well-qualified nurses. Amongst men, Irish Republic-born proportions in Social Classes I and II (25.1%) are well below those of men from Wales (49.0%), Scotland (40.9%), Northern Ireland (37.4%), aa well as England (33.6%).

Overall the patterns strongly reinforce the position of the Irish as a labour migrant group which cannot simply be categorised as part of the 'Celtic fringe' with Scotland and Wales. Although a substantial proportion of migrants from Northern Ireland do indeed share in the brain drain from these British nations, the overall profile of Republic-born migrants is much closer to that of the Black Caribbean population.

### 4.3.2 Socio-economic groups and social mobility

A number of studies of social mobility amongst the Irish in Britain, both over the lifecycle and intergenerational, have been made. Heath and Ridge (1983), for example, found a net downward mobility of Irish men in England and Wales in 1972 compared with English, Scots and foreign-born whites. This difference could not be explained on the basis of educational qualifications. The authors relate a similar pattern amongst non-white groups as the result of discriminatory practice. However, since they see this as a function of skin colour, they attribute the Irish experience to different causes. These include an inability to manipulate the necessary network of contacts and lack of 'know-how'. In other words, they provide a class-based explanation, with the added handicap of migration background. But their grounds for rejecting discrimination as a consideration rest on an unquestioned assumption that racism and discrimination can only be experienced by black people, and must therefore be scrutinised further.

Lower than average rates of mobility amongst Republic Irish-born men were also recorded in a study of mobility in both first and second generations by Hornsby-Smith and Dale (1988).

For the current project, change over time was examined at a more detailed level by use of the Longitudinal Study which permits comparison of mobility rates between 1971-81 and 1981-91. The analysis uses broad class divisions based on level of work, following Savage's (1988) classification based on clusters of socio-economic groupings. This identifies five categories, three of which can be broadly described as 'middle class', that is managers (MA), professionals (PR) and petty bourgeoisie (PB), and two as 'working class', that is white collar (WC) and blue collar (BC). These groupings are a better guide to income levels and relative social position than the Registrar General's Social Class categories which are simply based on occupation type.

Table 4.4 shows the change in socio-economic grouping for particular individuals between 1971 and 1981. The top left hand section of each table records upward mobility from working class to middle class categories, while the bottom right hand sections show downward mobility into white collar and blue collar working class groups.

Transition rates are calculated in Table 4.5 (for method, see Fielding and Halford, 1993). These give the proportions of the total in each category in 1971 who have entered each of the other categories in 1981. The total rate for each section is an overall measure of mobility. Thus in the total population, 14.40% were upwardly mobile and 26.50% downwardly mobile between these two Census years (Table 4.5A).

Although numbers of Irish-born people are small, differences are apparent and reflect the experiences of the 1% LS sample. Upward mobility was markedly lower for both Republic and Northern Irish-born groups than for the total population, with rates of 10.00% (Table 4.5B) and 10.45% (Table 4.5C) respectively compared with 14.40% in the population as a whole. Downward mobility was somewhat greater than average (26.50%: Table 4.5A) for the Republic-born (28.84%: Table 4.5B) but little different for the Northern Irish-born (25.69%: Table 4.5C).

Striking changes are recorded for all groups when new transition rates are calculated for the 1981-91 period and compared with those listed in Table 4.5. For the population of England and Wales as a whole, upward mobility increased sharply from 14.40% to 21.00% and downward mobility fell from 26.50% to 17.01%. The Irish-born population shared in these positive changes within the employed workforce, but the proportion who were upwardly mobile remained substantially below the average rate. The total for the Irish Republic-born increased from 10.00% to 17.51%, but remained well below the average of 21.0%. For the Northern Irish-born, the increase was from 10.45% to 16.89%, even further below that for the population as a whole.

These findings reinforce those of Heath and Ridge (1983) and Hornsby-Smith and Dale (1988) for the earlier period and highlight a continuation of the pattern of below-average upward mobility for the Irish-born, despite the arrival of well-qualified migrants in the 1980s.

Having settled in Britain, therefore, Irish migrants are less likely to move to better paid, higher status jobs over the course of their lifetime than the population as a whole. This finding is in accordance with Castles et al's (1984) analysis of labour migrants' experience in Europe. They are recruited to fill less desirable secondary sector jobs and are still needed in those areas when opportunities open up for movement into the tertiary sector. Ways in which this restriction may affect Irish people will be explored further in Part Three of the report.

### 4.3.3 Car ownership

Car ownership is closely related to income and a useful summary measure of standard of living overall. Substantially more residents in Irish-headed households live in non-car-owning households (35.7%) than average for white-headed households in Britain (24.6%) (OPCS, 1993).

In part, this may be explained by clustering in large urban centres (see Table 2.7). However, even within inner city areas, car ownership rates amongst the Irish-born are significantly lower than for white non-Irish-headed households. In London, where 53.9% of Irish-headed households have no car (white non-Irish-headed households 38.8%) (Table 4.6), the gap remains in every borough (Table 4.7). For example, in Camden 72.6% of Irish-headed household have no car, compared with 52.9% of white non-Irish-headed households. Throughout London, proportions are close to, but slightly below, those of the Black Caribbean community (average 57.1%).

## 4.4 Qualifications

### 4.4.1 Definitions

Educational qualifications are very important influences on the level of employment Irish people can obtain. The 1991 Census defines a group of qualified persons aged 18 and over possessing qualification levels above the United Kingdom GCE A-level and its equivalents. The published tables amalgamate the Republic and Northern Irish-born populations.

Within this category three levels of qualifications are distinguished:

a - higher university degrees

b - first degrees and same standard or higher, other than university higher degrees

c - qualifications generally satisfying three requirements, that is obtained at 18 or above, above GCE A-level and below first degree level, including non-degree teaching and nursing qualifications.

This is a very narrow definition of qualifications in the workforce, restricted to 13.4% of the total British population. It is of relevance principally to occupations in the first three occupational categories in the Census, administration/management (1), professions (2) and associate professions (3) (Table 4.1). Its main use is in assessing the position of the highly qualified Irish-born relative to other groups in the population and in comparing levels of qualifications with occupation and social class measures.

This data can be supplemented by the Labour Force Survey, which includes a much fuller range of educational qualifications but uses different ethnic categories. In order to reduce the problem of small sample sizes in subgroups of the population, three years (1989, 1990, 1991) have been averaged.

### 4.4.2. Higher level qualifications

(i) Comparisons by birthplace/ethnic group

Table 4.8 shows that Irish-born women, taken as a whole, have a markedly greater than average proportion of women with higher level qualifications (16.4%, total population 10.9%), exceeded only by Black African women (22.1%). The figure for Irish-born men is somewhat lower than average (13.2%, total population 15.5%), though the totals for Black Caribbean (6.0%) and Pakistani (9.8%) men are lower still.

When the three constituent levels are disaggregated, it can be seen that two thirds of Irish women's qualifications are in Level c, mainly reflecting nursing and teaching training. Irish men, on the other hand, are under-represented relative to the total male population in these vocational areas and over-represented in Level a, higher university degrees.

(ii) Differences by age

These overall trends mask distinctive differences by age group (Table 4.9). There is a general decline by age in the proportion of the total population with high qualification levels, reflecting the very marked increase in opportunities over three generations. Thus 19.5% of the total male population aged 25-29 had these qualifications, compared with 8.9% of men aged over 65. For women the change has been even greater over time, from 18.4% of 25-29 year olds, compared with only 4.7% of women aged over 65.

The pattern for the Irish-born population mirrors this decline with age, but with some important variations. Nearly one third (31.5%) of Irish-born men in their later twenties have these qualifications, mainly first and higher degrees, compared with 19.5% of all men. In their middle working years (30-45) the proportions are almost identical (20.7% Irish-born, 21.5% total), but for Irish-born men aged over 45 the proportions drop very sharply below those of the total population.

Irish-born women, on the other hand, demonstrate higher levels throughout the age range. As with men, the large gap between Irish-born and total population in the 18-24 range undoubtedly includes the effects of uncompleted courses by the home population set beside graduate emigration from Ireland. However in the 25-29 group, Irish-born women are also extremely well-qualified compared with the average for the age group in Britain. Over one third (34.2%) had higher-level qualifications, compared with 18.4% of the total population, with a higher proportion in categories a and b, higher and first degrees. Amongst the 45-64 age group the greater number of qualified nurses accounts for the somewhat higher levels amongst Irish-born women.

(iii) Change over time

The dramatic change by generation and period of migration is confirmed by the changes recorded in Table 4.10. A sharp rise in the proportion of Irish-born men with higher level qualifications from 5.1% in 1971 to 13.2% in 1991 mirrors and even exceeds the growth in the total qualified male population from 8.7% to 15.5% over the twenty year period.

Irish-born women have maintained higher proportions in Social Classes I and II between 1971 and 1991, though the rate of growth from 10.9% to 16.4% is slightly lower than in the population as a whole. Again, this parallels growth in the total female qualified population which has almost doubled from 6.2% to 11.6%.

(iv) Regional differences

There is an uneven distribution of highly qualified Irish-born people throughout Britain (Table 4.11). Overall, a slightly greater proportion have higher qualifications (14.9%) than the total population (13.5%). Only in two regions does the average of the Irish-born fall below that of the total population. In London, the Irish-born proportion is 14.5%, but the total population figure is exceptionally high at 17.7% reflecting its role as an 'escalator region' of high social mobility attracting in new graduates from the rest of Britain (Fielding and Halford, 1993).

In the remainder of South East England, however, the situation is reversed and the Irish-born population (17.8%) is relatively more qualified than average (15.3% total population). Only in the West Midlands is there a particularly low proportion of highly qualified Irish-born people (8.9%), reflecting its ageing population from the 1950s 'second wave' migration peak.

In the East Midlands (12.4%) and North West (12.8%) the proportions of Irish-born people with higher level qualifications are clearly below the Irish-born average, but higher than the total population figures, mirroring the generally low qualifications base of those regions. Proportions are particularly high in Scotland (20.4%), East Anglia (19.7%), the North (18.0%) and the South West (18.2%).

### 4.4.3 Lower level qualifications

Labour Force Survey data for four birthplace and ethnic groups are considered - White UK born (including the Northern Irish), White Irish (Republic-born), Asian and AfroCaribbean (Table 4.12). The Irish are the only group to have received their education outside the UK so there is a danger that the totals are distorted by non-recognition of equivalent qualifications, though an analysis in the Employment Gazette (1994) found only a small number of Irish qualifications classified as 'other' in the Labour Force Survey, that is unknown, and concluded that Irish qualifications were being successfully coded.

The results appear to show that the Irish had lower qualification levels at the A-level equivalent stage than either the White UK-born or the Afro-Caribbean populations, but higher rates than the Asian group. Proportions with no qualifications were also markedly higher amongst the Irish-born, especially men where a quarter were in this category compared with only 16.4% of the White

UK-born. For women the proportion was 29.9% (24.3% White UK-born population).

An attempt to measure the match between educational qualifications and level of work of the Irish-born in Britain was made in the NESC Report (1991). The findings suggested that the Irish-born were more likely to be found in the working class than would be predicted from their educational qualifications. From modelling the relationship between class and qualifications, it was concluded that the Irish with no qualifications were clearly more disadvantaged than either the British or second-generation Irish, while those with second-level qualifications were also less likely to achieve the intermediate non-manual positions (NESC, 1991: 207). The mechanisms producing this situation are examined further in Part Three of this report.

### 4.4.4 Overall position

These findings confirm the dual character of Irish migration to Britain. On the one hand are highly-qualified migrants who constitute a brain drain and comprise a more highly-educated proportion of their age group than average. At the other end of the scale, more Irish-born people have no qualifications.

### 4.5 Unemployment

(i) Comparisons by birthplace/ethnic group

A broader picture of unemployment amongst the Irish-born working population can be drawn, placing the experience of Irish women and men beside that of other groups within the total population. Unemployment levels are important measures of individual disadvantage and may also indicate discrimination against particular groups.

Table 4.13 shows that Irish-born men had a substantially higher than average rate of unemployment in April, 1991 (15.1%, compared with 11.3% amongst the total male population). However, this was still markedly lower than the rate for Pakistani (30.4%), Black African (25.2%) and Black Caribbean men (19.7%), suggesting the existence of a hierarchy of disadvantage. It also reflects the responsiveness of migrant labour to economic demand.

(ii) Rates by occupation

When the distribution of unemployment rates is examined by occupation (Table 4.13), rates for Irish-born men are quite close to the average in many occupations (Categories 2,3,6,7 and 8). However, they are noticeably higher in certain areas, particularly skilled trades, including construction (Category 5: 15.3%, total 10.7%), general labouring (Category 9: 21.4%, total 18.5%) and to a lesser extent, management and administration (Category 1: 6.4%, total 4.5%) and clerical and secretarial work (Category 4: 10.1%, total 8.2%).

Higher Irish unemployment is thus recorded in the major areas of Irish economic activity (Categories 1,5 and 9), which account for 48.7% of the Irish-born workforce. Irish men have been attracted to Britain by demand for labour in the skilled manual trades, but in times of recession these are disproportionately affected. However, rates in all occupation categories were much lower than for the non-White Census-based ethnic group workers.

The pattern of women's unemployment is quite different. In April 1991, Irish-born women had an almost identical rate to the total population (7.0%, total 6.8%). In the major areas of Irish women's employment (Categories 3, 6 and 9), unemployment rates amongst the Irish-born were lower than average for the female population. They were slightly higher in clerical and secretarial work (Category 4: 5.5%, total 4.3%) and skilled industrial trades (Category 5: 11.0%, total 9.0%) though these are areas where Irish women are under-represented. In all occupations, women in non-White Census-based ethnic groups had higher unemployment rates, often substantially so.

It appears, therefore, that there is a strong demand for Irish women's labour. Although marked similarities in the occupation profiles of Irish-born and Black Caribbean women have been noted, Black Caribbean women have much higher rates of unemployment in those areas, including personal service (Category 6: 7.2%, Irish-born 4.7%) and, associate professionals (Category 3: 3.1%, Irish-born 2.3%). By contrast, traditional occupations of Irish men have been particularly hard hit by the recession. It is noticeable that young Irish men have moved into personal service (Category 6) where they have close to average unemployment rates (8.7%, total 8.8%).

## 4.6 SUMMARY

- The Irish-born, both from the Irish Republic and Northern Ireland, are a migrant labour group, whose rates of immigration correlate closely with demand for labour in Britain.

- Irish-born people are clustered in particular occupation and industrial categories, reflecting gaps in the British labour market. Irish-born women are particularly strongly represented in the niches of nursing and personal service. Irish-born men have slightly higher than average representation in professional occupations, but also remain substantially clustered in the construction industry.

- Northern Irish-born people by contrast have profiles much closer to, or even slightly higher status, than the British average.

- Subdivision by age highlights marked differences within the Irish-born population by generation and lifecycle stage:
  - Young women and men (18-29) are more highly represented in professional and managerial categories than the British average, even when nursing is taken into account. However, young Irish-born men are also clustered in areas of low-skilled, casual work.
  - The older working age population (45-59), representing the 'bulge' of 1950s migrants, is strongly clustered in the areas of personal sevice for women and industrial and general labouring for men.

- Irish-born people are more strongly clustered in Social Class V, the lowest grouping, than any other major birthplace/ethnic group in Britain. The profiles of the Republic-born contrast with those of Welsh, Scottish and Northern Irish-born groups in England which are well above average.

- Measures of social mobility suggest that the Irish-born category do not share in upward mobility to the same extent as the population as a whole.

- Greater than average proportions of Irish-born women have high level (post-18) qualifications, while Irish-born men have lower than average rates. When age is taken into account, however, young Irish-born men had remarkably high rates, one third having post-A-level-equivalent qualifications. For men the rate fell very sharply with age, whilst women had higher rates at all ages.

- Percentages of Irish-born people with no recorded qualifications were well above the White British-born average. There is evidence that Irish-born people are more disadvantaged by lack of qualifications than the British population.

- Irish-born men's unemployment rate was substantially higher then average in 1991 (15%, compared with 11%), associated with traditional areas of Irish activity. That of Irish-born women was close to average (7%), reflecting strong demand for their labour.

- Car ownership, often used as an overall measure of standard of living, is much lower than average in Irish-headed households, and close to that of the Black Caribbean population.

# 5. Housing conditions of the Irish in Britain

## 5.1 Introduction

Housing is a central issue for the Irish-born in Britain. As migrants, they have to enter the housing market. The majority arrive as young people without any capital and are thus dependent on income from paid work. Unlike an increasing proportion of the British-born population, most cannot expect to inherit property in Britain during the course of their lifetime.

Published Census tables are an unsatisfactory source of data about Irish people's housing situation, because of categorization under birthplace of household head. This excludes about half of all Irish-born women who do not live in households with Irish-born men and includes many non-Irish people, although these live at least to some extent in an 'Irish' household (see Table 1.1).

In this analysis, therefore, data will also be drawn from the 2% Individual SARS where housing can be linked with birthplaces of both women and men (Walter, 1996). Figures relate to the housing situation of individual Irish-born people, some living in households with other Irish people and some not. Published Census data also fail to distinguish between people originating in the Irish Republic and Northern Ireland, who may have very different housing experiences.

Census indices of housing quality are increasingly marginal in application as most housing now has an inside WC and bath, while the provision of central heating is often a matter of council policy rather than a measure of better quality provision. Nevertheless, in the absence of more meaningful measures, they will be briefly examined here. Three measures of housing experience give more meaningful information about relative advantage and disadvantage - tenure, household space type and density. These are examined in more detail.

## 5.2 Tenure

Tenure provides some measure of comparison of the housing situation of the Irish-born compared with that of the total British population, though it no longer provides a clear-cut indicator of advantage or quality. This must be borne in mind when assessing change over time. The widespread effects of the Right-to-Buy policy have blurred the boundary between local authority housing and traditional private property ownership, although only the better quality former-rented sector has been included. Similarly the shift of local authority housing into housing association management has made technical rather than qualitative effects on tenure bands. Since Irish people have had a strong association with the local authority rented sector in the past, they have been disproportionately affected by recent changes.

### 5.2.1 Owner-occupation

Table 5.1 shows that Irish-born people are under-represented in owner-occupied housing in Britain. Although similar proportions of the Republic-born and total populations live in houses which have been bought outright (women 22.7%, total 20.3%; men 18.7%, total 18.2%), many fewer Republic-born people live in mortgaged property (women 37.6%, total 48.3%; men 39.7%, total 52.5%). Northern Irish-born people occupy an intermediate position between those of the Republic-born and the total population, slightly closer to the latter.

The average proportion of Irish-born people occupying outright-owned property is accounted for by the top-heavy age structure (see Figure 3.1A), so that many of the 1950s migrants have lived long enough in Britain to have paid off loans on small terraced or semi-detached houses. This is borne out by the lower than average proportions of Northern Irish-born women and men, whose age structure is younger (see Figure 3.1B) in this category. In fact, therefore, the proportion might have been expected to be even higher than average and, in reality, the Irish-born are under-represented in this category when age structure is taken into account.

When London is considered alone, a different picture emerges (Table 5.3). The proportion of owner occupiers owning their houses outright (13.5%) is substantially below that of the White non-Irish born population (20.0%). In part, this reflects the younger age structure of the London Irish-born population, but it also results from higher house prices in London which disproportionately affect the Irish-born population who are clustered there. This illustrates the importance of taking geographical clustering into account when examining statistics relating to the Irish population, so that national-level generalisations do not mask areas of disadvantage.

When mortgaged property is considered, a starker picture is drawn (Table 5.1). Much lower than average proportions of Republic Irish-born people were living as owner-occupiers in mortgaged property in 1991, providing even clearer evidence of disadvantage relative to the total population. In Britain as a whole, the averages for women and men are 48.3% and 52.5%, but for the Republic Irish-born, they are 37.6% and 39.7% respectively. In London, where owner-occupation is lower overall, a large gap is also present - 30.5% for Irish-headed households, compared with 39.2% for the white non-Irish-born. Republic Irish-born people do not have access to this form of tax-subsidised housing to the same extent as the population as a whole. In fact the proportions are substantially lower than in each of the three large, non-White Census-defined, ethnic groups, Black Caribbean, Indian and Pakistani. In London, the proportions of these groups with mortgaged housing is 37.4%, 66.9% and 56.9% respectively (Table 5.3).

Although owner-occupation is not necessarily an indicator of high quality housing, especially in London where much housing is structurally unsound and prices are high (Bennett, 1991), this tenure category is usually seen as offering a range of advantages, both direct and indirect. Tax-subsidies are greater than on rented properties, weekly outlays may be lower and a capital asset is often

54

acquired. Owner-occupiers may have a greater choice of locations, especially since the residualisation of the council rented sector has restricted its extent, especially to inner cities. Owner-occupation may thus be an important way in which households are able to leave the inner city, which has experienced rapid decay in its economic and social infrastructure during the 1980s. Higher rates of Irish male unemployment, for example, may be related to concentration of rented housing in inner city areas, whilst educational decline has been greatest in these marginalised areas.

Reasons for this reduced access to the owner-occupied sector must therefore be examined. Possible factors include:

(i) Discrimination by mortgage lenders, such as building societies and banks;

(ii) Low pay as result of clustering in the secondary sector of manual work (see Table 4.3), so that Irish-born people are less able to save the necessary deposit for a house purchase;

(iii) Feelings of impermanence amongst a labour migrant group.

These will be investigated further in Part Three of this report.


### 5.2.2 Private renting

Both Republic and Northern Irish-born groups are much more strongly clustered than average in the furnished private-rented sector, reflecting migrant status, low income and above-average proportions of single-person households (see Table 3.4). A further factor may be the employment of Irish-born men in the 'lump' system of the construction industry, which discourages them from applying for council housing where their irregular tax status may be exposed to official scrutiny (Bennett, 1991).

Rates of private renting amongst Irish-born women and men are well over twice the average. Thus, in Britain as a whole, 6.9% of Republic-born and 7.4% of Northern Irish-born women are found in this sector compared with only 2.9% of the total female population. Proportions are even higher for men - 8.8% of the Republic-born and 9.7% of the Northern Irish-born, compared with an average of 3.4%. The slightly higher figures for Northern Irish-born people are probably associated with the younger age structure.

In London, the proportion of Irish-headed households in privately rented accommodation is much higher (Table 5.3). In 1991, 16.8% of Irish-headed households were in this category, compared with 12.1% of white non-Irish households and much lower proportions of the main non-White Census-defined ethnic groups (Black Caribbean 5.4%, Indian 7.3% and Pakistani 11.2%). Only Black Africans had similar rates (16.5%).

Private rented accommodation has the worst record for unfitness and lack of amenities of any tenure category. Over a quarter of private tenants in furnished accommodation share a bath, shower or toilet (Connor, 1987). Irish-born people are therefore exposed to these conditions to a greater degree than other major ethnic minority groups (Table 5.1). In 1981, overcrowding (more than 1.5 persons per room) was much greater amongst Irish-headed households in both furnished (Irish 5.9%, total 1.3%) and unfurnished (Irish 12.9%, total 2.8%) rented accommodation (Connor, 1987).

However, as a labour migrant group, which includes young single new arrivals and a higher proportion of low-paid, never-married people in older age-groups (see Table 3.3), the Irish-born continue to need rented accommodation and have thus been disproportionately affected by the sharp decline in this sector. In London, for example, whereas in 1971 private rented accommodation comprised 33.9% of all housing, by 1981 this had fallen to 15.1% and in 1991 it was only 12.2% (Connor, 1987; AGIY, 1995). Yet the proportion of the Republic Irish-born population in this sector is 16.8%, higher than any of the six largest non-White Census-defined groups (see Table 5.3).

### 5.2.3 Local authority housing

People from the Irish Republic have been associated with local authority rented housing since its inception. The strong clustering has been continued throughout the post-War period. In 1991, 22.0% of women and 21.0% of men occupied this tenure group, compared with 17.4% and 15.7% respectively of the total population. Again, the Northern Irish-born are much closer to the average (women 17.5%, men 17.4%).

In London, the rates are considerably higher reflecting higher provision of this tenure type. Well over a quarter (28.9%) of Irish-headed households occupied local authority housing, compared with only 21.8% of the white non-Irish. Non-White Census-defined ethnic groups with higher rates included the Bangladeshi population (57.6%), Black African (46.1%), Black Other (40.0%) and Black Caribbean (39.0%).

Within the local authority housing sector, there is evidence that the Irish-born disproportionately occupy less desirable accommodation. The Docklands Housing Needs Survey (LRC, 1985) showed that a greater proportion of Irish-born households lived above the third floor in high rise blocks. The 1981 Census revealed that overcrowding (more than 1.5 persons per room) amongst Irish-born council tenants was three times the average rate (Connor, 1987).

### 5.2.4 Renting from housing associations

This pattern holds for housing association tenure which, although small overall, is relatively greater for those from the Republic (women 4.2%, men 4.0%), compared with the total population (2.7% and 2.4% respectively) and the Northern Irish-born (women 3.3%, men 2.2%).

Again, the proportions are higher in London, where 8.0% of Irish-headed households compared with 5.1% of white non-Irish-headed households rent from housing associations. However, the proportion is lower than for a number of other Census-defined groups, for example Black African (11.7%), Black Other (11.6%) and Black Caribbean (10.5%). This suggests that Irish people do not have the same access to housing association property as other non-White Census-defined ethnic groups, although their high demand for private rented accommodation, and its declining availability, indicates a need for rented housing.

## 5.3 Household space type

Household space refers to the character of the building occupied, specifically whether it is a house or a flat. Within the 'house' category a distinction is made between detached, semi-detached and terraced. Although the meanings of these descriptions varies from place to place, the general assumption is that there is a reduction in size and value from the first to the last. Flats are also divided into 'purpose-built residential' and 'commercial', that is attached to a business or workplace, and converted, usually from a house.

Table 5.2 shows that Irish-born people occupy generally smaller types of housing than average. Those from the Republic are strongly under-represented in detached housing which may be regarded as the most desirable, especially for families. Thus, only 13.7% of women and 12.1% of men are found in this type of housing, compared with 22.1% and 22.9% respectively of the total population. The Northern Irish-born are, again, much closer to this British average (19.4% and 18.7%).

Even in the semi-detached housing category, both Irish groups are under-represented, with approximately 25% of the Republic-born, compared with around 32% of the total. In this case, the Northern Irish-born have a closer proportion ,close to 27%. Slightly higher proportions of the Republic Irish-born population live in the generally smaller and cheaper terraced category.

The Republic Irish-born occupy an intermediate position between the total population, or average, and that of most non-White Census-based ethnic groups, for whom the gradient from large to small housing is even steeper.

As would be expected from the tenure patterns, Irish-born people are substantially over-represented in the smallest category of housing, flats. Again a gradient can be seen between the Republic-born and total populations. Whereas 26.6.0% of Republic-born women and 24.9% of men live in flats of all kinds, this is true of only 15.1% and 13.3% respectively of the total population. The Northern Irish-born figures are intermediate at 21.1% and 20.9%.

## 5.4 Density: measures of overcrowding

If overcrowding is represented by an index of 1.5+ persons per room, it can be seen that the Republic-born population is much more likely to live in these conditions than the population as a whole (Table 5.3). Although the figures are very small, they show that 1.7% of women and 1.6% of men originating in the Irish Republic live at these densities, compared with only 0.9% of the total population. The figures for the Northern Irish-born are closer to average at 0.9% and 1.1% respectively. However, the densities of households in non-White Census-defined ethnic groups, notably Pakistani and Black African, are much higher.

In London, a similar pattern is found, with Irish-headed households (1.6%) having twice the overcrowding rate of the White non-Irish (0.8%) (Table 4.6).

## 5.5 Other measures of housing quality: London

Table 4.6 shows that households in London with Irish-born heads have poorer facilities than average for the majority White population. Nearly twice the proportion (2.2% compared with 1.2%) lack, or share, a bath/shower and/or inside WC. The proportion is higher than for the other established large ethnic minority groups, Black Caribbean (1.4%) and Indian (1.0%), and similar to the Black Other category (2.4%).

Similarly higher proportions of Irish-headed households lack central heating, 21.9% compared with the White average of 18.9%. Again, this is higher than for the Black Caribbean (17.4%) and Indian-headed (10.9%) households and slightly above the Black Other category (20.2%).

## 5.6 Communal establishments

Irish-born people are over-represented in communal establishments relative to their proportions in the total population, though Census statistics are likely to be inaccurate with substantial under-enumeration. They are recorded both as employees in these areas of work, and as residents in various forms of establishment.

Communal establishments attract an Irish workforce both because of the demand for labour in what is often unattractive and low paid work and because the availability of accommodation is valued by newly arrived migrants. Irish-born women are particularly over-represented in hospital staff accommodation, forming 11.2% of the live-in population, but Irish-born men are also clustered here (7.9% of all men). Irish-born people form a disproportionately large section of staff in local authority homes (women 6.3%, men 3.4%), private residential homes (women 7.5%, men 2.7%), schools (women 5.3%, men 3.4%) and hostels/common lodging houses (women 7.4%, men 7.1%). In hotels, they form 3.5% and 3.1% respectively of the recorded live-in workforce.

Irish-born people are over-represented in accommodation for the homeless, especially men. In housing association homes and hostels, for example, Irish-born men comprise 6.8% of the total number of residents (women 2.5%), and in hostels/common lodging houses 8.6% of residents (women 4.1%). 'Other miscellaneous establishments' record high rates of occupancy, especially by Irish women (18.4%, men 6.3%).

## 5.7 Sleeping rough

Finally, part of the population 'sleeping rough' in Britain was captured by Census enumerators in April, 1991. Overall a far greater number of men than women fell into this category, 2,397 out of 2,827 (85%), including an even higher ratio amongst the Irish-born out of 422 (89%). The Irish-born were substantially over-represented, comprising 15.7% (377) of all men and 10.5% (45) of all women classified in this way in Britain, though the overall proportions of Irish-born people in the population are only 1.5% and 1.6% respectively.

The proportion of Irish people is likely to be greater in London, where estimates have placed it at about 28% (GLC, 1984). But there is a lack of accurate data about this issue which is compounded by failure to include an Irish category in research. A major study on homelessness in London published in 1989, for example, used the category 'white European', which included 88% of the sample (Canter et al., 1989). It is likely that a substantial proportion of this figure was Irish, but this was not recorded, although categories described as Afro-Caribbean, Asian and Oriental, with extremely small numbers, were.

## 5.8 Conclusion

The Irish-born occupy poorer than average housing in Britain. As labour migrants, predominantly working in low paid manual jobs, they need low cost housing which does not demand capital investment. However, rented accommodation is declining as a proportion of the housing stock and the Irish have not shared in the sharp shift to owner occupation of the White population as a whole.

Within the rented sector, Irish people have traditionally relied strongly on private renting. However, this has the greatest problems of structural defects, lack of privacy and overcrowding. Housing association accommodation, where greater control over quality and prices may be expected, appears to be less available to the Irish-born than to other ethnic groups, suggesting less recognition of their need for this type of accommodation.

The Irish-born are over-represented in all forms of communal establishment, again reflecting the specific needs of a migrant group for work-related housing and for temporary, or permanent, cheap shelter for single people who are low paid or unemployed.

This housing pattern reflects inadequate provision for the needs of a migrant labour force recruited formally and informally to fill low-paid secondary sector jobs in the British labour market. Moreover, demand for such labour is strongest in South East England where housing costs are highest. Migrants are expected to adapt to changes in the housing market which run counter to their need for flexibility and affordability.

It is possible that the Irish are further disadvantaged by discrimination, either direct in the form of exclusion from, or delay in, access to mortgage or local authority waiting lists, or indirect in the form of non-recognition in ethnic group housing allocations. These will be examined further in Part Three when individual Irish people are questioned about their housing experiences.

## 5.9 SUMMARY

- The Census categorises housing tenure and amenities by birthplace/ethnic group of 'Head of household', 92% of whom are male in households with couples. About half of all Irish women and their families are thus excluded from published totals. These tables also do not distinguish between Irish people from the Republic and Northern Ireland.

- Irish-born people are under-represented in owner-occupied housing, particularly among those with mortgages. In Britain as a whole, about 50% of the total population are buying their own homes, but the figure is only 38% for the Republic Irish-born (45% Northern Irish-born). In London the proportion is 30%, much lower than for Black Caribbean (37%), Indian (67%) and Pakistani (57%) populations.

- Rates of private renting by the Irish in Britain are well over twice the average (7% compared with 3%). In London the proportion is 17% compared with 12% for the white non-Irish-born. This is also much higher than for the large non-White Census-defined ethnic groups and similar to the rate for another largely-migrant group, Black Africans.

- The Irish-born have a continuing need for rented accommodation - as new arrivals, low-paid workers and single-person households - but the sector is shrinking. The private-rented sector declined from 15% to 12% of the housing stock between 1981 and 1991.

- Above-average proportions of the Irish-born population rent local authority housing (21% Republic-born, 17% Northern Irish-born: total population 16%). In London, the proportion is 29% compared with 22% of the White non-Irish born. Within the sector, the Irish disproportionately occupy less desirable accommodation.

- Although above-average proportions of Irish people have housing association tenancies, these are well below those of non-White Census-defined ethnic groups.

- The Irish-born are disproportionately located in smaller-sized houses, especially terraced housing and flats. However, the household sizes of those with two or more people are slightly higher than average.

- Rates of overcrowding are over twice those of the population as a whole.

- In London, Irish-headed households have among the highest rates of poor amenities, especially shared facilities and lack of central heating.

# 6. Health of the Irish in Britain

## 6.1 Limiting long-term illness

There is considerable evidence that the Irish in Britain experience more ill-health than can be explained by their demographic and socio-economic status alone (for a review, see Pearson, Madden and Greenslade, 1991). Data for the period 1970-78 shows that death-rates amongst Irish-born men aged 15-64 were 22% higher than average (Marmot et al., 1984). Although this is partly explained by the concentration of occupations in Social Classes IV and V, the excess remains at 15% when occupation is taken into account. Irish men are the only migrant group whose mortality is higher in Britain than in their country of origin.

Amongst the major causes of death which disproportionately affect Irish men are accidents, suicide and violence (+80%) (Marmot et al., 1984). This reflects employment in the construction industry which has high rates of accidental death because of low safety standards. Suicide is related to much higher incidence of mental illness amongst men born in Ireland. In 1981, men from the Republic of Ireland were admitted to psychiatric hospitals at 3.2 times the rate of the indigenous population and the rate for men from Northern Ireland was 2.5 times greater (Cochrane and Bal, 1989). Deaths from violence are connected to the unsettled lifestyle of single Irish men which exposes them to the dangers of street life.

Higher mortality rates for Irish-born men were also recorded from tuberculosis (+145%) and cancer of the oral cavity and pharynx (+83%) and of the gall bladder and gullet (+76%). Death from liver cirrhosis (+63%), peptic ulcer (+42%) and high blood pressure (+35%) were also in excess of average. All these sources of premature death were higher than in Ireland, suggesting that the migration experience was implicated.

Irish-born women also showed higher levels of excess mortality (+16%), though their relative position was slightly less disadvantaged than that of men. The statistics showed lower levels of premature death than in Ireland, whilst in Britain they were ranked third amongst migrant groups.

Major causes of mortality included tuberculosis (+115%), accidental poisoning (+77%), liver cirrhosis (+59%) and cancer of the lung and trachea (+59%) (Marmot et al., 1984). Irish-born women were also admitted to psychiatric hospitals at much higher than average rates. In 1981, rates per 100,000 for women from the Irish Republic were 1,167 and 834 for women for Northern Irish-born women, compared with 485 for women from England and Wales (Cochrane and Bal, 1990). The most important single cause was depression, accounting for 35% of admissions from Republic Irish-born women and 32% of those from Northern Ireland. Links between depression and women's migrant status and negative experiences living in Britain need further investigation. However, attempts to explore crude measures such as standard mortality rates and psychiatric hospital admission rates in more detail have been limited by lack of data.

A new question was introduced into the 1991 Census, asking: 'Does the person have any long-term illness, health problem or handicap which limits his/her daily activities or the work he/she can do?' This is very broad, self-assessed measurement of health so it can only produce a general picture of health experiences of different groups. The findings are strongly age-related, as limiting long-term illness is likely to be low in young people and substantially higher amongst the older population. Thus the age structure of ethnic/birthplace groups must be taken into account in any analysis.

Because the Irish-born population in Britain is an ageing one (see Figure 3.1), a higher than average rate of limiting long-term illness is not unexpected (17.8% compared with 13.4% for the total White population). Published Census tables do not distinguish by age and origin in the Irish Republic or Northern Ireland. These data are available in the 2% Individual SARS, though the sample size is much smaller. Plotted in Figure 6.1, this shows a slightly greater tendency for Irish-born people to experience limiting long-term illness, especially in middle age (Walter, 1996). Both Republic and Northern Irish-born men aged between 45 and 64 have above-average rates, though Irish-born women differ much less from the average, and exceed it only for the ages 45-59 for Republic-born women and 45-54 for the Northern Irish-born. Apparent fluctuations at the young and old age extremes of the graph could be due to very small numbers.

Although the excess illness rate in the Irish-born population is a small one, it is nevertheless systematic and suggests that reasons for higher rates of ill health amongst middle-aged Irish people needs investigation. Relatively large numbers of the population are involved since these are the 'bulge' years in the age structure. Moreover, the higher overall rate, even if age-related, means that health provision needs to be sensitive to the particular needs of older Irish people.

Other studies have identified higher than average rates of limiting long term illness in the Irish Republic-born population from 1991 Census results. The London Research Centre (Storkey, 1994) found that rates for children in London aged 0-17 were very high, second only to the Black Other Census group. Westminster (11%) and Tower Hamlets (8%) had particularly high rates, whilst Islington and Waltham Forest both had rates above 5%. A peak at ages 0-4 for Irish-born children was unusual. Very small numbers are involved in these samples, but they require further investigation.

Owen (1995) calculates higher rates for the Irish-born population in Britain as a whole, showing that these are more than twice those for non-White Census-defined ethnic groups, and a third higher than for all White people. More than a quarter of households headed by an Irish-born person contain someone suffering from limiting long-term illness, which is well above average for White people, though the average number of ill people per household is lower than for Census-defined ethnic groups. A considerable part of this excess ill-health is explained by the older age structure of the Irish-born population, but Owen calculates that illness rates of the Irish-born are still 5 to 10% above age-standardised rates, with greater differences for men than for women. He also draws attention to higher illness levels in children.

There is a range of evidence indicating poorer health amongst the Irish-born population in Britain. Health is a particularly significant reflection of the range of material circumstances which affect people's lives. However, a fuller analysis is hampered by lack of suitable data, as Pearson, Madden and Greenslade (1991) have shown.

## 6.2 Health status of the second generation

Recent research using the Longitudinal Study to trace people born in England and Wales with at least one parent born in the Irish Republic has pointed to starkly poorer health amongst this group than in the total population (Harding and Balarajan, 1996). Causes of death amongst the sample of 6,308 second-generation Irish people were traced over the period 1971-89. These showed that higher mortality was recorded for most major causes, with significantly greater mortality from all cancers and lung cancer for men at working ages (15-64) and for women aged 60 and over. There was also a significant excess of deaths from respiratory diseases amongst older women, whilst higher mortality from 'other cancers' peaked at ages 35-44.

The authors found that these high rates could not be ascribed to social class differences, and point out that the patterns observed are very similar to those reported for Irish people in the migrant generation. A number of possible explanations are raised for discussion, including cultural factors such as lifestyle, the trauma of migration and negative attitudes towards the Irish in Britain.

This is a very important area for further research, requiring the linkage of all aspects of Irish people's life experiences and structural positions to pinpoint causal factors. As Harding and Balarajan (1995: 1,392) point out:

> *With over two million second generation Irish and growing numbers of a third generation, clearly special consideration should be given to their health.*

Moreover, investigations of longer-standing health deficits in regions of Britain which experienced high rates of Irish immigration in the nineteenth century gives support to the possibility that more distant generations may continue to be affected (Williams, 1994).

Health can be regarded as a significant index of the Irish community's position within British society, and one which can be monitored very effectively over time. It is also a way in which the costs of inadequate provision for a migrant group are ultimately borne both by members of the group themselves and by the wider society in which they settle.

# 7. Ethnic monitoring

## 7.1. Introduction

Monitoring of ethnic groups arises out of recognition of the need to work towards equal opportunities, especially in employment and service provision. The Commission for Racial Equality's statutory *Race Relations Code of Practice for the Elimination of Racial Discrimination and the Promotion of Equality of Opportunity in Employment*, adopted by Parliament in 1984, calls for the use of monitoring recording the ethnic origin of individuals (CRE, 1984).

Because of the overwhelming association of ethnicity and blackness in Britain, the Irish have not automatically been included in ethnic monitoring procedures. Usually, their inclusion has followed strong lobbying by Irish welfare groups, which has been successful only in a receptive political climate. Thus the Policy Report on the Irish Community in London (1984) recommended to the Ethnic Minority Committee of the GLC

> *(i) That the Committee recognise the Irish as an Ethnic Minority Group and to adopt the following definition of Irish for such purposes: persons who come from, or whose forbears originate in, Ireland and who consider themselves Irish.*

> *(ii) That the London Boroughs be requested to adopt the definition of Irish given above for the purpose of ethnic monitoring.*

However by no means all of the London boroughs responded to this recommendation, and many still do not recognise the Irish as an ethnic category. In its instructions for monitoring in a workforce survey, for example, one borough which monitors only in some areas stated:

> *The word 'Black' is an all encompassing term that denotes staff from African-Caribbean, Asian and other ethnic minority origins.*
> (Hounslow: Workforce Survey 1993)

Ethnic monitoring is carried out by a number of bodies, including local authorities, housing associations, the police force and some major employers. For this research project, two types of body, local authorities and housing associations, were selected. Surveys were carried out to assess the extent to which the Irish were included as a specific category in ethnic monitoring, aspects which were monitored and the results of findings.

### 7.2 Monitoring surveys

### 7.2.1 Local Authorities

### 7.2.1.1 Extent of inclusion of an Irish category

A postal survey of 514 local authorities in England, Wales and Scotland was carried out in May/June 1994. The section on London boroughs, where by far the largest proportion of Irish inclusion is found, was partly updated in November, 1995. The final findings showed that 16 out of 33 London boroughs carried out some form of ethnic monitoring which included an Irish category. A further 3 boroughs had recently agreed or planned to so, and 2 were considering adoption, making a total of 64%. Reporting on a separate survey, the *Irish Post* (21/10/95), said the remaining 12 had not expressed an intention of recognising the Irish.

Outside London, recognition of Irish ethnicity was much sparser. Two Metropolitan Boroughs, Manchester and Birmingham, out of a total of 36 (6%) monitored the Irish. None of the 39 County Councils stated that they included an Irish category (response rate 85%), although a high proportion carried out ethnic monitoring (88%). Amongst the remaining 422 local authorities in England, Scotland and Wales, where there was a lower incidence of ethnic monitoring overall (65%) and a response rate of 59%, only 7 (2%) monitored the Irish. One was in Scotland (Tayside) and the remainder scattered in England, mainly in midland and eastern areas (Leicester City Council, Norwich City Council, Colchester District Council, Reading District Council, Gedling Borough Council) together with one in the north (Carlisle City Council). Most monitored a single aspect of employment or service, Norwich City Council, for example, monitoring housing allocations. Only Leicester could provide a report including at least some of the data.

Where adoption of an Irish category had taken place, this was often quite recent. The earliest date mentioned was 1980 by the London Borough of Haringey, where the Irish were included at the start of ethnic monitoring. For most other authorities, however, recognition came in the late 1980s and 1990s, though often at different dates for different aspects of service. In Manchester, for example, the Irish were included in monitoring personnel in 1986, housing in 1988, education in 1991 and social services in 1993.

Amongst those who had adopted an Irish category, there was no standardisation in the description of Irish identity. 'White Irish' was used in some cases, leaving nowhere to record the position of black Irish people. In other cases the 'Irish' category was recorded separately, but subsequently listed with other groups under the heading 'White'. In the social services the usual classification was, 'European - Irish', although Harrow proposed to change this simply to 'Irish'.

### 7.2.1.2 Coverage of monitoring

Even where an Irish monitoring category was adopted by a local authority, it might be extended to only a few of the possible areas of employment or service.

Only two London boroughs (Brent and Southwark) claimed to monitor in all seven areas which were surveyed - personnel, housing, education, social services, environmental services, leisure and council tax benefit. Most others included five or fewer of this list. A particularly significant category was personnel, including both applications and recruitment, which indicates the willingness of the borough to consider the composition of its own workforce, rather than simply comply with directives from elsewhere, as in the case of social services.

Outside London and the Metropolitan Boroughs, coverage was much less complete and mainly limited to personnel or housing, since statutory responsibility for education and social services lay with County Councils.

### 7.2.1.3. Use of monitoring findings

A striking aspect of the survey was the almost negligible use of monitoring results. Most authorities appeared to make no further use of the statistics they had gathered. A few pointed out that recognition had been so recent that results were not yet available. Others referred to reports containing this information, but in most cases the Irish category was not specifically mentioned in the report or had been aggregated with the White category.

Monitoring material was analysed thoroughly by collecting bodies only where a strong local Irish lobby was present and particularly where there was specific Irish representation within the local authority Race Equality Unit, with an Irish Liaison Officer. The most extensive coverage was in Southwark, though even there not all relevant categories were sufficiently sub-divided to allow Irish proportions to be calculated. In employment, for example, data was provided for the social services department, where 7.8% of the staff were Irish. However the breakdown by grade grouped by 'black', 'white' and 'other'. However, more details were provided about employees in residential homes, where the 'Irish' comprised 3.1% of headquarters staff and 12.6% of domiciliary staff (Southwark Social Services, 1992).

In one of the very rare instances of analysis and publication of monitoring results involving an Irish category, the finding was startling. Haringey Women's Employment Project (1987) investigated the structure of women's employment by the council and found that Irish women, who comprised 11.6% of the female workforce, were concentrated in the lowest paid category of 'manual and crafts' to a much greater extent than any other ethnic group (Table 7.1). This powerfully challenges the assumption that the black/white division is the only important dimension of ethnic disadvantage.

### 7.2.2 Housing associations

As a migrant group in Britain, the Irish rely on rented accommodation to a greater extent than the British-born. The sharp reduction in availability of council-rented property has made the Irish more dependent on other forms of provision, such as housing association lettings. Tenure patterns in the 1991 Census show that the Irish-born are over-represented in housing association accommodation (Republic-born women 4.2%, men 4.0%) compared with the total British population (women 2.7%, men 2.4%) (Table 5.1). For the Northern Irish-born the figures are 3.3% and 2.2% respectively.

Access to housing association accommodation is of particular importance to the most disadvantaged Irish-born groups. Analysis of 1992/93 CORE data shows that housing association tenants are poorer than average, more likely to be unemployed and to be paying more than a quarter of their income in rent and to be heavily dependent on state benefits. They are increasingly likely to be referred as homeless from local authorities (Cara, 1994). In 1993/94 this accounted for 47% of referrals, compared with 24% internal transfers from Local Authority accommodation and 15% direct applications.

### 7.2.2.1 Extent of inclusion of an Irish category

A postal survey was sent to the 88 largest housing associations which own over 65% of all housing association homes. The results showed that 51 of the 66 associations who replied (response rate 70%) monitored the Irish as a separate group. However, the major reason for this inclusion was the appearance in 1989 of an Irish category in the CORE (COntinuous REcording) system of collecting housing data. Only a few stated that monitoring had started before this date, for example, the Cooperative Development Services (Liverpool) Ltd HA gave a date of approximately 1984 and Thames Valley HA gave 1985. A number of associations who claimed not to monitor Irish statistics stated 'except for CORE', indicating that for many others this was probably the prime reason for the collecting the data.

In response to requests from associations for advice on making CORE data comparable with the new Census ethnic categories, the National Federation of Housing Associations (NFHA) Quarterly Bulletin (1993) produced a much reduced set of compatible categories which would enable associations to compare their data with the Census. Instead of a two-part classification which recorded both origin (7 groups, including Irish) and skin colour, the new 'best-fit' method included only six groups: White, Black Caribbean, Black African, Black other, Asian and Other, amalgamating the Irish with 'White' in most cases. Clearly, the choice of Census categories is having far-reaching effects on ethnic monitoring, providing both a rationale for the selection of categories and the practical advantage of a baseline of data against which to judge the equity of local distributions.

### 7.2.2.2 Coverage of monitoring

Three possible areas of inclusion were investigated, housing allocations, personnel recruitment and tenant harassment. Almost all associations monitored for the first two and about half also included harassment.

### 7.2.2.3 Findings

There was almost no evidence from the survey that the findings had been used by individual housing associations to examine the equity of Irish access to housing or employment in this housing service. No targets had been set for inclusion of Irish tenants, although this was stated to be the principal purpose of ethnic monitoring procedures.

In only two cases was a report mentioning Irish data provided to us. The Leicester Housing Association Ethnic Monitoring Report in 1993 showed that 0.3% of its lettings were to Irish people, who were then presumably included in either the 'White' or 'Other' categories for the remainder of the analysis. The Swale Housing Association included an 'Irish' category in its employment application form, these being: British/European, Irish, Caribbean, African, Asian (with subdivisions), South East Asian (with subdivisions) and Other. An Irish applicant for a job was duly recorded in an illustrative breakdown of applications given for one advertised post, but the final classification for annual employment applications was white British, white European, African, black British, Asian and Caribbean.

Even where data was initially collected, therefore, the 'Irish' group had often been re-amalgamated on the basis of small numbers. However, there was lack of consistency and clarity about the nature of the aggregation, and it was often unclear where the Irish had finally been placed. Whereas the Raglan HA included the Irish in a 'Mixed/other' category, the Yorkshire Metropolitan HA monitored the Irish separately in allocations and personnel recruitment, but in its quarterly performance reports to district committees grouped all ethnic minority applicants and tenants under a single heading, explaining that 'ethnic minority' includes all applicants/tenants not described as 'British/Euro-white'. Moreover a Merseyside housing association appended the following note to our questionnaire;

> *We collect the ethnic origins of tenants, employees etc. using the ethnic origin categorisation on the NFHA CORE system which picks IRISH as a group. But in our analysis they are grouped under white category. WHY is IRISH to be monitored as a separate group within WHITE?*

Despite this universal aggregation by housing associations themselves, statistical analysis of the complete set of CORE data by the Irish housing association, Cara, showed that disadvantage amongst Irish tenants could be clearly identified. The figures showed an increase of lettings to Irish people from 4.6% of the total in 1990/91 to 5.9% in 1992/93, followed by a slight decline to 4.0% in 1993/4. When ethnic groups were compared by mean weekly income, the Irish had the second lowest earnings (£94), only just above 'Caribbeans' (£93) and well below average (£103). The highest incomes were those of 'Asians' (£106) and 'British/Europeans' (£104). Much higher than average proportions of tenants in the Irish category were unemployed (46%, compared with 37%). Again the 'British/European' group had the lowest rate (35%). The Irish category also included by far the highest proportion of sick or disabled tenants of any ethnic group (9.5%). This compared with an average of 5.3%, the next highest being 'British/Europeans' (5.5%).

All housing association tenants are disadvantaged, low-income groups, and the Irish are shown to be in greater than average need of this type of housing. But the amalgamation of the Irish with 'white British/European' groups in most statistical presentations disguises their low position on indices of income, unemployment and health amongst ethnic minority groups. Frequently they are at the opposite ends of the range from 'White' groups as a whole. But these statistics are no longer even available for analysis as they are not recorded in the reduced CORE records.

## 7.3 Conclusions

The extremely small quantity of data already collected and analysed makes an overwhelming case for the inclusion of an 'Irish' category in ethnic monitoring. In two examples described here, those of female council employees in Haringey and housing association tenants in Britain, Irish people are actually in a worse position than those in all, or almost all, recognised ethnic minorities. These cases illustrate unequal access to resources in both income and housing, and might suggest discrimination. There is no question that Irish people are disadvantaged in other situations which have not been monitored, possibly severely, and that this needs to be acknowledged and included in ethnic monitoring procedures.

However, recognition remains extremely patchy and dependent on strong and persistent demands from well-organised Irish welfare groups. There is some evidence, especially in London (*Irish Post*, 1995), that the rate of acceptance is slowly increasing, especially following the CRE recommendation on inclusion of an Irish category in 1994 (*Irish Post*, 1994). Outside London, and the large Irish-born population centres of Manchester and Birmingham, however, recognition is almost non-existent, and indeed declining as a consequence of the choice of 1991 Census categories. Even where data is collected it remains largely unused. At present no targets are being set to achieve more equitable distributions of funds and no plans formulated to ensure that services are delivered to Irish people in a more ethnically-sensitive manner.

The possibility of ethnic monitoring of the Irish population is clearly provided for under the 1976 Race Relations Act, which defined 'racial grounds' for discrimination as any of the following: colour, race, nationality, and ethnic or national origins. But relevant bodies appear content largely to ignore this category to date.

# 8. Conclusions

The Irish have been the most important source of migrant labour in Britain for two hundred years. They constitute the largest ethnic minority in Britain's workforce and, if migrants and their children are included, the total is about three million, far higher than any non-White Census-defined ethnic group enumerated in 1991. This migrant labour role underlies the demographic and social characteristics outlined in this section.

Patterns of immigration from both parts of Ireland are strongly related to demand for labour in Britain, so that numbers arriving and their areas of settlement reflect the changing labour needs of the economy. The most significant period for immigration in the post-War period was the 1950s when the Irish made the largest contribution to meeting a substantial labour shortage, and migrants arriving in this period remain as a distinctive bulge in the population pyramid of the Republic-born population. They settled predominantly in the Midlands and the South East of England. A second bulge arrived in the mid-1980s, when unemployment again fell sharply in Britain, indicating demand for labour. In this case, a large proportion of the inflow represented a highly qualified 'brain drain' responding to a shortage of professional and skilled workers, particularly in London and the South East, which was met by migration from Ireland and other parts of the world.

The Irish have also remained an extremely flexible source of labour in the secondary, low-paid manual sector of the British economy. Whilst other sources have increasingly been excluded by immigration legislation based on skin-colour criteria, the freedom of movement for citizens of the Irish Republic, as well as those from Northern Ireland, has allowed them to respond quickly to upturns and downturns in the economy. For men this has meant recruitment into the construction trade and general labouring, while high levels of demand for female labour have been in catering, cleaning and domestic service. The majority of the Irish-born population is thus clustered in the lowest socio-economic categories, reinforcing negative stereotypes.

There is a significant difference in the roles of migrants from the Irish Republic and those moving from Scotland and Wales, and also to a considerable extent from Northern Ireland, into England. Much larger proportions of Scottish, Welsh and Northern Irish migrants are located in relatively high social class categories. The South East of England operates as an 'escalator region' for well qualified workers from these internal ethnic groups of the United Kingdom. By contrast, the overall employment patterns of the Republic Irish-born are much closer to those of the African-Caribbean population in Britain.

The Republic Irish-born population is disproportionately clustered in the larger conurbations of Britain, where demand for manual labour has been greatest. They have thus shared problems of poor housing and inner city decay to a greater extent than average for the population in Britain. In addition, their access to affordable housing has been limited because of their migrant situation. The decline of the rented sector, both public and private, since the 1970s has had a more marked effect on the Irish-born than on the indigenous population, since, as both migrants and low paid workers, they have had a particular need for flexible access to cheap housing.

The Irish-born, particularly those originating in the Irish Republic, experience a range of disadvantages compared with the indigenous White population. Census figures show that they remain distinctively concentrated in the lowest social classes, with lower than average rates of upward social mobility. Their housing levels are significantly lower than those of the White population, with less access to tenure as owner occupiers and the worst amenities of any major ethnic/birthplace group in Britain. The health of Irish-born men in middle age is consistently poorer than average.

However, none of these factors is monitored, with the result that disadvantages go unrecorded and no targets for improvement are set. Irish people are also excluded from funding which attempts to redress disadvantage, for example through specific allocations to ethnic-identified housing associations. Yet Census statistics show clearly that there are much greater similarities in the position of the Irish Republic-born and other non-white Census-based ethnic minorities than with the White indigenous population. They belie any beliefs that a rapid assimilation occurs simply on the grounds of 'whiteness'.

This statistical background provides a baseline from which to draw samples for further investigation of issues of disadvantage and discrimination. Census data shows that the Irish population is strongly represented in the conurbations of the Midlands and South East of England. A particularly important group is the 1950s migrants, now leaving the workforce where they have been clustered in manual occupations. Younger migrants from the 1980s, some of whom are highly qualified, are another key section of the population. It is important to recognise variation in Irish people's experience arising from their period of arrival and areas of settlement.

In the following sections of this report, more detailed investigation of the processes leading to disadvantage and the consequences for the Irish population in Britain will extend the analysis to draw on qualitative as well as quantitative data. In Part Two, the focus is on visible evidence of disadvantage and discrimination presented to, and experienced by, Irish community and groups and advice agencies. Part Three will explore the hitherto largely invisible experiences of a cross-section of Irish people in London and Birmingham.

# REFERENCES

AGIY (1995) *Census 1991 briefings*, Action Group for Irish Youth.

Bennett, C. (1991) The housing of the Irish in London: a literature review, *PNL Irish Studies Centre Occasional Papers Series 3*.

Canter, D., Drake, M., Littler, T., Moore, J., Stockley, D. and Balluj. (1989) *The faces of homelessness in London*, Interim report to the Salvation Army, Department of Psychology, University of Surrey.

CARA (1994) Annual Report.

Castles, S. with Booth, H. and Wallace, T. (1984) *Here for good. Western Europe's new ethnic minorities*, Pluto Press, London.

Castles, S. and Miller, M. (1993) *The age of migration: international population movements in the modern world*, Macmillan, London.

Cochrane, R. and Bal, S. (1989) Mental hospital admission rates of immigrants to England, a comparison of 1971 and 1981, *Social Psychiatry*, 24.

Commission for Racial Equality (1984) *Race Relations Code of Practice for the Elimination of Racial Discrimination and the Promotion of Equality of Opportunity in Employment*.

Compton, P. (1991) Migration trends for Northern Ireland: links with Great Britain , in Stillwell, J. Rees, P. and Boden, P.(eds.), *Migration processes and patterns: Volume 2 Population redistribution in the United Kingdom*, Belhaven, London.

Connor, T. (1987) *The London Irish*, London Strategic Policy Unit.

CSO (1994) Annual population and migration estimates 1987-1994, Statistical Release, Dublin, Government Information Services, .

DOE, (1994) Annual statistics on travelling population. *Employment Gazette* (1994) Irish nationals in the British labour market, 102.1. Department of the Environment.

Fielding, T. and Halford, S. (1993) Geographies of opportunity: a regional analysis of gender-specific social and spatial mobilities in England and Wales 1971-81, *Environment and Planning A 25.10: 1421-1440*.

Garvey, D. (1985) The history of migration flows in the Republic of Ireland, *Population Trends*, 39.

GMB (1993) *Divided by degree: an analysis of 1991 census data on race, qualifications and unemployment*.

GLC (1984) *Report on the Prevention of Terrorism Act in London and report on consultation with the Irish community*, Ethnic minorities in London, Greater London Council.

Harding, S. and Balarajan, R. (1996) Patterns of mortality in second generation Irish living in England and Wales: longitudinal study, *British Medical Journal* 312:13891392.

Haringey Women's Employment Project (1987) *Women's employment in Haringey. Facts and Figures.*

Heath, A. and Ridge, J. (1983) Social mobility of ethnic minorities, *Journal of Biosocial Sciences*, Supplement 8.

Hickman, M. (1990) *A study of the incorporation of the Irish in Britain with special reference to Catholic State Education: involving a comparison of the attitudes of the pupils and teachers in selected Catholic schools in London and Liverpool*, Ph.D. thesis, Institute of Education, University of London.

Hornsby-Smith, M. and Dale, A. (1988) The assimilation of Irish immigrants in Britain , *British Journal of Sociology*, xxxix.

Hounslow (1993) *Workforce Survey*, London Borough of Hounslow.

Irish Post (1994) A monitoring breakthrough, 9 April.

Irish Post (1995) Now Greenwich Irish to get recognition, 21 October.

Jackson, J. (1963) *The Irish in Britain*, Routledge and Kegan Paul, London.

Kelly K. and Nic Giolla Choille T. (1995) Listening and learning: experiences in an emigrant advice agency, in O'Sullivan P. (ed) *Irish women and Irish migration, Vol IV: The Irish World Wide*, Leicester University Press.

Kennedy R. (1973) *The Irish: emigration, marriage and fertility.* University of California Press, Berkeley.

Kenrick, D. and Bakewell, S. (1990) *On the verge: the gypsies of England*, Hatfield: University of Hertfordshire Press.

LIWC (1995) *Rights for Travellers*, London Irish Women's Centre.

LRC (1986) *The Docklands Housing Needs Survey 1985*, London Research Centre.

Marmot, M., Adlestein, A. and Bulusu, L. (1984) Immigrant Mortality in England and Wales, 1970-78 , *OPCS Studies on Medical and Population Subjects*, 47, HMSO, London.

NESC (1991) *The economic and social implications of emigration*, National economic and Social Council, Dublin.

NFHA (1993) Comparing CORE and 1991 Census readings for ethnic origin, *NFHA CORE Quarterly Bulletin*, August.

OPCS (1993) *1991 Census Ethnic Groups and Country of Birth Tables*, HMSO, London.

OPCS/GRO(S) (1993) *1991 Census: Supplement to Report on Ethnic Group and Country of Birth* (Table A), HMSO, London.

Owen, D. (1995) Irish-Born People in Great Britain: settlement patterns and socio-economic circumstances, *1991 Census Statistical Paper 9*, Centre for Research in Ethnic Relations, University of Warwick.

Pearson, M., Madden, M. and Greenslade L. (1991), *Generations of an invisible minority: the health and well being of the Irish in Britain*, University of Liverpool.

Prandy, K. (1990) The revised Cambridge scale of occupations *Sociology*, 4.24.

Salt, J. (1989) A comparative overview of international trends and types, *International Migration Review*, 27:2.

Savage, M. (1988) The missing link? The relationship between social and geographical mobility, *British Journal of Sociology*, 39.

Southwark (1992), *Social services report*, London Borough of Southwark.

Storkey, M. (1994) *London's Ethnic Minorities*, London Research Centre, London.

Thomas, R. (1986) The social classification of women, *EOC Research Bulletin*, 10.

Walter, B. (1984), Tradition and ethnic interaction: second wave Irish settlement in Luton and Bolton, in Clarke, C., Ley, D. and Peach, C. (eds.) *Geography and ethnic pluralism*, Allen and Unwin, London.

Walter, B. (1988) *Irish women in London*, London Strategic Policy Unit.

Walter, B. (1989) Gender and Irish migration to Britain, *Anglia Geography Working Paper* 4.

Walter, B. (1996) The Irish-born in Britain, 1991: statistical background, *Anglia Geography Working Paper* 8.

Williams, R. (1994) Britain's regional mortality: a legacy from disaster in the Celtic periphery? *Soc. Sci. Med.* 39:189-199.

# Part Two
# **Survey of community groups and advice agencies**

# 1. Introduction

In its original outline of the research requirements for this study of discrimination and the Irish in Britain, the Commission for Racial Equality included a survey of Irish community groups and advice centres. This forms the second stage of the research being reported on in this document. The aim of the survey of community groups and other advice agencies was to establish the evidence of discrimination as presented by Irish users/clients to these agencies.

This stage of the study is important because it was expected to reveal the range of problems and issues of disadvantage and discrimination which come to the surface in this way.

The CRE anticipated that it would be in the records of these groups and the testimonies of their staff that we could trace the evidence about racist and discriminatory experiences presented by clients who come to the agencies. The majority of the evidence presented in this part of the report, therefore, is based on in-depth interviews with the staff of 24 Irish community groups and other agencies.

Phenomena such as discrimination on the grounds of colour, race, nationality or ethnic or national origins and racial harassment necessitate qualitative research and in-depth interviews. For example, qualitative data is necessary for analysing a phenomenon such as racial harassment as its meaning is couched in the individual incident or experience. It is not a phenomenon which can yield other than its very bare bones to quantitative analysis. The processes of discrimination can also be very subtle, hidden under a blanket of bureaucratic obscuration or an insistence that other factors are determinate.

Quantitative research requires that answers and positions be formulated with some precision, whereas the basis of racism and racial consciousness is ambiguity and contradiction. (For a summary of the problems this produces for research on 'race' see Skellington et al., 1992). Qualitative data, whether based on observation, the clinical or focused interview, or life history makes it possible to confront the special features and subtleties of racism and to view the person or the social process in some larger context or situation (Harris, 1991).

In this research report, we are presenting a variety of forms of data to convey the dimensions and the patterns of Irish peoples' lives in Britain and to explore anti-Irish racism and discrimination.

In this section the emphasis is on qualitative data based on in-depth interviews with workers in a range of Irish community groups and advice agencies. It is they who have had the daily experience of a case-load of Irish issues and they who are daily attempting to gain services for Irish people.

Staff members of these groups are thus in a position to have an overview of the range of problems which their clients experience in Britain and which necessitate both statutory bodies and voluntary organisations addressing Irish needs. The representations by clients (many of whom have already raised their case with other agencies or statutory bodies to no avail) to Irish community groups are, therefore, a crucial linchpin upon which hinges the case that the Irish experience racist discrimination.

## 2. Existing documentation about Irish experiences in Britain

When we commenced the research there already existed, in the reports of various community groups, indications of the main areas in which discrimination might occur: access to social security benefits, racial harassment, mental health issues, housing problems. Also available was material from the small number of local authorities who have processed data about the Irish which they have collected as a result of ethnic monitoring.

In addition, there had been a number of research reports which extrapolated as far as was possible the data about the Irish-born population in Britain from the 1981 census (Walter, 1986; 1989; Connor, 1987). It was not our intention in this stage of the research to duplicate existing work. We began, therefore, by reviewing available research in order to inform the emphasis we would give to the survey of Irish community groups and welfare agencies.

Empirical assessment of the social disadvantages and discriminatory practices experienced by the Irish in Britain is limited at the academic level. No full length text has followed Jackson's (1963) survey, though Lennon, McAdam and O'Brien (1988) provide powerful qualitative evidence of discrimination experienced by Irish women and Hillyard (1993) documents the damaging effects on the community of the Prevention of Terrorism Act. Articles and papers address more specific issues, including migration and settlement (Boyle, 1968; Drudy, 1986; Jackson, 1967, 1986; NESC, 1991; Pearson, Madden, 1990; Strachan, 1991; Walter, 1980, 1986, 1989, 1991), housing, (Bennett, 1991), employment (Hazelkorn, 1990, 1991) health (Raferty, Jones, Rosato, 1990; Pearson, Madden, Greenslade, 1991, Greenslade, 1994) and second generation experience (Ullah, 1985; Hickman, 1990).

Far greater coverage of different aspects of Irish disadvantage is provided by reports produced by local authorities and welfare agencies, particularly during the 1980s in London. Issues addressed include youth (AGIY, 1985-1993; Randall; Kilburn IYAG, 1987; ILEA, 1988; Federation of Irish Societies, 1987), mental health (Brent Irish Mental Health Group, 1986; Finnegan and Harrington, 1988), elderly (Irish Liaison Unit, Haringey, 1988), education (IBRG, 1985; ILEA, 1988, Hickman, 1990), women (London Irish Women's Centre, 1984-93; Walter, 1988, 1989), policing (LSPU, 1988), Travellers (LSPU, 1989) as well as broader coverage (GLC, 1984; Connor, 1987; LSPU, 1987). Reports have also focused on particular boroughs (e.g. Lambeth, 1985; Haringey, 1987, 1991; and Ealing, 1989, 1989).

Outside London far less material appears to be available. For example, in 1986 an unpublished report on Irish experience in Birmingham was presented to the City Council by Dr. Ita O'Donovan, but only in 1992 was a conference called with the aim of disseminating information more widely.

We were aware when drawing up the research proposal that the Action Group for Irish Youth (AGIY) and the Federation of Irish Societies (FIS) had initiated in

81

1993 a study of the service needs of the Irish community in Britain. The study also explored the feasibility of introducing a standardised information system, which would enable each individual agency to collect data for their own monitoring purposes while also feeding into a collective data base.

As we commenced our research, the two organisations were in the process of establishing the Standardised Information System (SIS) for Irish service providers. Our intention was to negotiate access to the first six months' data which the SIS produced, knowing that this would provide the most up-to-date statistical account of Irish clients and their service needs.

Twenty two agencies participated in the initial research on existing information systems and agencies' information needs. A computerised system was then piloted in winter 1993 amongst eleven of the agencies. A report based on both these stages of research was published in 1994 (Kowarzik, 1994).

Subsequently, the SIS has been extended beyond the original eleven agencies and regular quarterly reports are issued which give a breakdown of all the clients approaching the participating agencies and their service needs. London agencies form a majority of the groups who are operating the SIS (having formed 95% of the agencies upon whom the original research report was based).

In the absence of wide scale monitoring of Irish needs by local authorities or voluntary agencies, the SIS information is the only systematic data that exists about the service needs of the Irish community. During the pilot period of two months in 1993 which produced the initial research report for AGIY and the FIS, a record card was filled in about every client who presented to one of the eleven agencies. The main findings of the subsequent report were:

- Over 1,000 Irish people approached the agencies for advice and support in the two months of the pilot period.

- Over 4,000 different services were provided to clients at one or subsequent visits. 59% related to advice services such as housing, employment, welfare rights and health; 25% to support services including repatriation, travel, accommodation and counselling; and 16% to material support services consisting of providing food, clothing, financial support etc.

- of Irish clients were self referrals, only 5% were referred by other voluntary agencies and 6% by statutory agencies.

- have been in Britain for less than a year, over a third of the clients had been resident in Britain for ten or more years, and 5% had lived in Britain all their lives.

- Half the clients fell into the 25 to 44 age group; 43% were women and 57% were men.

- Two thirds of the sample of clients described themselves as unemployed and 29% lived in insecure housing.

- One in eight clients had experienced racial harassment; adding police harassment and arrests under the PTA the proportion of clients who experienced racial harassment increased to one in five.

- Many clients reported health related problems: one in ten reported mental health problems; one in eight men reported misuse of alcohol; 4% of the younger under 25 age group reported drug misuse; and over a third of the 65 and over age group had a disability. (Kowarzik, 1994:1-2)

The London location of the vast majority of the participating agencies affected the sample of Irish clients which produced the above findings in a number of ways. The sample produced significantly fewer older Irish people than the figures in the 1991 Census would have given cause to expect. 9% of the sample population were over sixty five, whereas the Census recorded 27% of Irish-born people of pensionable age, with a slightly lower percentage (23%) for London.

In terms of economic status, the sample population differs from the Irish-born population described in official statistics. Two-thirds of the clients in the study were unemployed compared with 17% of Irish men in London (AGIY 1995).

However, given the underestimation of true levels of unemployment in official data and the fact that it would be unemployed people who would have most cause to seek assistance, the predominance of unemployed people amongst the sample is unsurprising.

The proportion of people in the sample in three types of housing tenure, that is local authority housing, the privately rented sector and housing associations, broadly followed patterns identified in 1991 for Irish-born people. However, two major differences were the low proportions in owner-occupation (4% compared with nearly 60%) and the high proportions (over 30%) who were homeless, living in bed and breakfast accommodation or occupying short life housing.

The first two quarterly reports to be issued after the permanent implementation of the data collection system in participating Irish agencies were for the periods January to March 1995 and April to June 1995. Both these reports confirm the main contours of both the characteristics of the sample population in the original survey and the main service needs of these clients.

## 3. Aims of Stage Two

Systematic data about people who approach Irish agencies for advice, therefore, exists. Consequently, our task in stage two of the research was two-fold: to establish whether the picture of Irish experiences and service needs which emerges from the many community group reports and the SIS data is representative of a more widespread picture beyond London; and to examine in more depth the assessments of Irish service providers of the needs of their Irish clients and the difficulties some clients experience in obtaining appropriate services. We have three aims:

i) to systematise the available evidence;

ii) to establish whether or not there are some contexts in which Irish people might experience either direct or indirect discrimination;

iii) to develop a provisional typology of the possible discriminatory and exclusionary practices which operate in relation to the Irish.

# 4. Methodology of Stage Two

Aware of this existing research and following the guidelines laid down for the research by the CRE, we decided our main focus would be in-depth interviews with staff and community groups and advice agencies. The purpose of these interviews was to identify dimensions of discrimination drawn from issues brought to welfare and advice centres and to explore these further through interviews with centre personnel.

For the reasons given above, we decided in-depth interviews were the best method, given the time and resources available.

We began with a survey of all front-line, advice-giving Irish agencies in our chosen locations in order to develop a database from which to select groups for interview. We surveyed agencies in areas which reflected the different periods of settlement of the Irish population. To this end we chose: London, Birmingham, Manchester and Glasgow. Our selection of these four cities was for the following reasons:

i) London is essential because it was both an important destination for the Irish who migrated in the 1940s-1960s and has been the chief destination for Irish migrants in the 1980s;

ii) the other main destination in England for the 1940s-1960s emigrants was the West Midlands. Birmingham was also the location in the 1960s for one of the few studies of ethnic and race relations which included the Irish (Rex & Moore, 1967), thus in selecting Birmingham, we hoped it might yield interesting points of comparison 30 years on from this very influential study;

iii) Manchester was chosen because it is still a major centre of Irish-born settlement, has an active Irish community, and it is also representative of one of the old areas of highest density settlement for the Irish: Lancashire;

iv) Glasgow was included because Scotland was an area of heavy Irish settlement in the past and over 50% of the Irish-born population in Scotland live in the Strathclyde area (58% of Republic born and 47% of those born in Northern Ireland).

We anticipated that there could be quite different contours of experience for the Irish in Scotland (see Miles and Dunlop, 1986; Walker and Gallagher, 1990). We thus approached stage two of the research differently in Glasgow, and it is dealt with in a separate section later in this part of the report.

## 4.1 Community Groups' Postal Questionnaire

In total, 104 community groups in three cities in England were sent a postal questionnaire in our initial survey. Of these, sixty five returned completed questionnaires (62.5%). Twenty of the postal questionnaires were returned undelivered (19.2%), leaving nineteen groups which failed to respond to the questionnaire (18.3%).

### 4.1.1 Returned Questionnaires

The questionnaire was designed to elicit information about the agency, it's client base and the services it offered. The majority of the sixty five groups which returned the questionnaire target the Irish community as their client base (48 or 74%) and are located in the London area (53 or 82%). Three (5%) of these groups target travellers and gypsies, which includes a significant Irish component. The remaining groups have no particular ethnic group as their intended client base.

The majority of the sixty five groups will accept all age groups and both genders as clients: 80% (52) of these groups accept all age groups as clients; while 86% (56) will accept clients of either gender. Roughly one third of the groups here are community groups, offering a variety of services for their clients (23 or 35%), while nearly another third are front-line groups (19 or 29%).

Both these types of groups tend to have large numbers of clients, often not matched by paid employees: this suggests that these groups are often reliant upon volunteers to provide their services. Indeed, it appears that there is no numerical correlation between the numbers of clients and the number of paid employees.

The range of services offered varies. Forty groups (62%) give advice on benefits to their clients, and forty five (69%) offer a service on housing: however, a lower number (43 or 66%) give advice on social services. Thirty (46%) groups provide a service on legal matters, while twenty four (37%) provide a service dealing with the police and thirty three or 51% provide a service on harassment.

Again, the number of groups which deal with anti-Irish discrimination is only just above half (36 or 55%). Thirty (46%) provide a service/advice on employment.

The average number of employees is 4.7, in comparison with an average of 2,337.9 clients per annum per group. This means that there is a large number of clients to employees.

While there is no correlation between ethnic focus of the groups and the client-employee ratio, it is the case that the groups which have no ethnic group as a target group have a better such ratio. There are a number of groups (18 or 27.7%) which have no paid employees and are, therefore, wholly reliant upon volunteers.

**Services provision and client profiles: Irish community groups and advice agencies**

| Type of Service | % of sample which includes | |
|---|---|---|
| | Postal Survey (N = 65) | In-depth interviews (N = 24) |
| Housing | 69 | 87 |
| Social services | 55 | 78 |
| Police | 37 | 57 |
| Benefits | 62 | 74 |
| Harassment | 51 | 65 |
| Legal matters | 46 | 61 |
| Employment | 46 | 70 |
| Domestic | 37 | 57 |
| Anti-Irish discrimination | 55 | 70 |
| Campaigning | 62 | 65 |
| **Client profile** | | |
| All ages | 80 | 83 |
| Both sexes | 86 | 87 |
| Irish | 74 | 96 |

## 4.2 Stage Two Interviewees: Analysis of Questionnaires.

In-depth interviews were conducted with twenty four community groups, chosen to represent geographical and service area spread. The twenty four comprise just over a third of the groups (37%) which returned completed questionnaires in the postal survey of community groups.

Only one of these twenty four groups does not target the Irish community per se as its client base. Eighteen (75%) of the groups were based in London; three in Birmingham and three in Manchester (in each of the latter two cities we selected all groups who returned a questionnaire and who provided an advice service). The profile of the clients of the selected groups is: nineteen groups (79%) accept all age groups as clients and twenty (83%) accept both genders. The three groups which are gender specific all cater for women, and are all based in London.

What is noticeable is that these twenty four groups provide a wider range of services than the larger group of sixty five (see table A). This suggests that the groups involved in the in-depth survey had a breadth of experience in dealing with the problems of Irish people, across a spectrum of areas. The average length of existence for these groups is ten years (which is one less than the average for the larger group).

As with the larger group, the number of clients per annum is high in comparison with the number of paid employees. The average number of clients is 3,113, with a median of 1,522: both of these figures are higher than the equivalents for the larger analysis of sixty five returned questionnaires. In comparison, the mean number of paid employees in this sub-group is 3, with a median value of 2. The equivalent figures from the larger analysis are 4.7 and 1, but there is higher variance for number of employees in this analysis (383.3 compared to 16 in the sub-set of 24). This suggests that the disparity between employees and clients is much lower in this sub-set of community groups; this may be reflected in the higher rate of services offered by these groups. However, three (13%) of the twenty four have no paid employees: in comparison, of the sixty five groups eighteen (28%) have no paid employees.

# 5. England: findings from in-depth interviews with staff of community groups

The next five sub-divisions of this section of Part Two will present the findings from the in-depth interviews with staff in the twenty four selected groups in England. The data is presented under the following headings: ethnic status and ethnic monitoring, critiques of service delivery by statutory bodies; racial harassment; the criminal justice system; Travellers.

## 5.1 Ethnic Status and Ethnic Monitoring

The postal survey of local authorities and housing associations (reported in Part One, Section 7) indicated the extremely patchy inclusion of an Irish category, especially outside London, and low reporting of findings. We followed this up by interviewing staff of community groups about the impact of exclusion from monitoring on their activities. It is important to recognise that ethnic monitoring is an issue which is still strongly debated.

On the one hand, the CRE has consistently argued for the introduction of ethnic monitoring procedures. Their argument is that only by monitoring and evaluating the implementation of policies and the provision of services is it possible to measure how successfully discrimination is being combated. Also, in this way, it is possible to measure the progress of organisations in creating equal opportunities in recruitment, selection and promotion and of exposing discrimination over time. On the other hand, members of ethnic minority groups have expressed doubts about, and opposition to, the introduction of monitoring practices. They question the need for more evidence in the light of the numerous official and academic reports detailing the range and scope of racism and discrimination in Britain. They are also wary of the use to which such statistical data can be put (Skellington et al., 1992).

Widespread acceptance of the legitimacy of ethnic monitoring procedures is recent. Until the mid-1980s, relatively little statistical data was collected nationally and regularly on an ethnic basis. The change that occurred in the 1980s was largely a consequence of the inner-city disturbances of 1981. Prior to that any progress which occurred on 'race' issues was dependent on the initiatives of individual practitioners and managers. As a consequence there were great variations between and within local authorities. After 1981, however, this changed and the later period also saw the increasing participation of people from black communities in local politics (Connelly, 1990).

By the early 1990s, most agencies and statutory bodies accepted that 'race' equality was an appropriate subject for discussion. Taking one London borough, Haringey, as an example, in fact one of earliest to institute a wide-ranging equal opportunities policy, will illustrate the terms in which 'race' equality has been included in the agendas of local authorities. Haringey's policy document states that equal opportunities involves both a recognition and acceptance that discrimination and disadvantage means some people have not had equal opportunities in access to and receipt of services and in employment. Its equal opportunities policy seeks to redress this imbalance to ensure an equitable outcome in the delivery, and provision, of services.

Haringey's policy document states that it is concerned about the divisive effect of racism, which subjects black and ethnic minority people to negative attitudes and treatment as inferiors, resulting in racial discrimination, racial disadvantage, racial hatred and racial harassment. The ultimate effect of racism is to deny equality of opportunity to black and ethnic minority people. The Council recognises that racial discrimination and disadvantage impacts on different communities in different ways which results in different issues of relevance to the various communities. The Council further accepts its responsibility to identify the needs of different black and ethnic minority groups so as to ensure that services and employment practices are relevant to all black and ethnic minority groups. Haringey outlines its commitment to consultation with those who receive services and affirms that positive steps will be taken to include disadvantaged and discriminated against groups in consultation regarding the identifying of needs, planning and delivery of services to meet these needs. Other councils' policies are variations on this theme, although many are less wide ranging.

This example illustrates that 'race' is now recognised as an important factor that might explain differentiation in patterns of performance or status between different groups of people. In other words, it denotes an acceptance that inequalities between people might be explained by ethnic or racial difference. However, there is often a great distance to be travelled from a stated willingness to consider issues of ethnic and 'race' differentiation to policy formation and implementation in this area. It has been argued that the real spurt in activity, which produced a few good models of race equality, was in the early 1980s. Since then the burden of legislative pressure and the extent of the constraints placed on the role of local authorities has served to undermine initiatives which were taken in that period (Ouseley, 1990)

It is certainly true that 'race' equality policies have continued to be subject to sustained criticism in the 1990s. This has come both from certain elements in the tabloid press but also from researchers and activists who question the impact of 'race' equality strategies, and in particular of ethnic monitoring policies. Some objections stem from the view that ethnic monitoring encourages the perpetuation of differences in areas where ethnic differences are irrelevant. Others (for example, Reeves, 1993) think that the procedure is a 'benign form of discursive racialisation'.

The argument has been made that most ethnic monitoring systems have adopted a form of racial explicitness which is also racially exclusive. Consequently the problem of discrimination is treated in terms of discrete (and static) racial groups rather then in terms of the relationship between them. A presumption of fundamental differences between blacks and whites has, therefore, entered the mainstream as a result of addressing 'race' issues as a discrete collection of problems. This isolates racial disadvantage from the wide range of other disadvantages with which it is inextricably linked and emphasises difference at the expense of needs which might exist in common (Nanton & Fitzgerald, 1990).

By demanding that all ethnic monitoring systems include the Irish as a category, Irish community groups are both endorsing some of these criticisms of the impact of ethnic monitoring and, at the same time, reinforcing the need for such procedures. In most cases, legislation and guidelines to service providers indicate that they should be aware of ethnic issues in the delivery of services. However, given the construction of the discourse of 'ethnic minorities' in this country the term is usually understood as referring to African, African-Caribbean and Asian populations.

This understanding exists despite the fact that no definition of ethnic minority refers solely to visible differences. All the commonly cited definitions include reference to one or more of the following: nationality, religion, language, ethnic origins. We came across no official, written recommendation on race equality policies that service providers should only monitor clients whose skin colour was black. The conflation of the term 'ethnic minority' with skin colour as an operating definition, therefore, needs to be explained by other means. Many would argue that in practice it is a self-evident conflation because there is undisputed evidence that it is populations who are visibly different who experience the most racism and discrimination in British society.

This is an understandable position at one level because of the systematic racism and discrimination which innumerable research reports have described as the experience of different collectivities of mainly British citizens who have migrated from the New Commonwealth and Pakistan, and their British born children. The critiques and political struggles that the experiences of these groups produced have necessarily focused on exposing and resisting a variegated racist discourse and diverse set of discriminatory practices directed at black people.

However, the conflation of the category 'ethnic' with that of visible difference means that ethnic monitoring procedures are not an efficient means of tracing and estimating the size of ethnic minorities in Britain. Because most ethnic monitoring systems are based on a 'colour axis' this means that all respondents are forced into a categorisation of their ethnicity in terms of 'colour'. The differentiated groups, that is those that are recognised as ethnic minorities, are usually those of a visible difference. The majority ethnicity (or what is taken to represent the majority ethnicity) is usually defined as 'white'. Ethnic monitoring systems, therefore, monitor skin colour to the extent that they monitor anything efficiently.

Our research reveals that there is an almost universal call by Irish community and advice groups for ethnic monitoring of Irish needs. The disadvantages for the Irish, and the problems created by the lack of monitoring of their needs as a community are issues referred to again and again by the Irish community and welfare groups interviewed for this stage of the research. The reason for this lies in the obverse of the situation that confronts the various groups of people in

Britain who are primarily positioned in terms of visible difference. The Irish, because they are the same colour as those who are taken to be the indigenous population, are assumed to fall into that category of people, 'whites', who cannot experience racism and discrimination. This fundamental assumption underlies most of the difficulties which Irish organisations have when raising issues about possible Irish disadvantage or discrimination with other voluntary agencies and in particular with various statutory bodies. A number of the agencies we questioned referred to the lack of monitoring of the Irish as a form of indirect discrimination.

One of the chief consequences of the absence of the Irish from discussions about ethnic minorities is that information about the Irish has to be culled from a variety of unsatisfactory sources. In particular, the Census only provides consistent information on those born in Ireland. The absence of a question on parental birthplace (except in 1971) and the absence of the Irish from the ethnic category question means it is not possible to provide detailed information on those of Irish descent (as dealt with in Part One of this report). An agency in London dedicated to facilitating the access of Irish people to 'decent, affordable housing' cited the extent to which Irish groups have to monitor their own needs as indicative of the way in which the specificity of the Irish as an ethnic group is not taken seriously.

The lack of monitoring of the Irish by the vast majority of local authorities (see Part One, Section 5.2.1) means that the Irish are not accepted as a group of people whose different pattern of performance and status compared with the indigenous population (white British) could be related to issues of ethnic or racial equality. Where a local authority does monitor for the Irish, usually after considerable pressure from local Irish community groups, this does not in itself solve the problem of recognition of Irish needs. However, in the view of all the groups we interviewed, monitoring is the baseline without which it is impossible to obtain any serious consideration of the issues Irish organisations raise. This is because inclusion in all ethnic monitoring systems would represent acknowledgement that some Irish people could experience problems as regards equal opportunities in access to and receipt of services and in employment.

We asked Irish groups what impact if any being monitored had if they were in a local authority that included the Irish or if they were a national group or a London city-wide group if they could comment on the general effects of monitoring where it did take place. The responses ranged from details of the positive impact of monitoring to criticisms of the erratic implementation of the monitoring of the Irish to flat declarations that there had been no impact.

Of the twenty three groups who answered this question, six thought there had been a beneficial impact, seven thought there had been no impact usually due to the local authority not processing the data on the Irish (see Part One, Section 5.2.1.3), or not following through with policies that took on board Irish needs. Ten groups thought the monitoring of the Irish by local authorities had an erratic impact.

The six groups who answered positively to the question about the impact of ethnic monitoring, gave examples either of funding they had received from the local authority or examples of support they had for their work from council officers. Examples of positive responses from the local authorities were: opening a wing of a residential home as a specifically Irish wing; consulting the local Irish organisations when drawing up community care plans; meetings with social services to establish how service delivery to the Irish community could be improved.

The largest number of groups (ten) thought ethnic monitoring produced an erratic impact. This was for the following reasons:

i) either because the response they received when raising Irish issues still seemed determined by the individual or department they were dealing with;

ii) or because the Irish were monitored for some services and not for others;

iii) or because, although the Irish are monitored, there is a confusion about how policies should be implemented with many assuming that in practice reference to ethnic groups meant black people;

vi) or because there was no consistency in monitoring policies and it was hard to obtain an across-borough or Council picture.

Thus even when the Irish are monitored a link is not necessarily forged between the data collected and service provision. In some councils, for example, the link is made in one area of provision but not in others. This worries agencies when the future is contracted service provision. It is vital from their point of view to ensure an Irish dimension to those developments. A number of groups emphasised that any impact that monitoring policies had was still largely due to the efforts of the Irish groups in the area to constantly raise issues and pressurise the local authority. The verdict of the groups was that monitoring of the Irish needs to be systematic, consistent and comprehensive across all local authorities, statutory bodies and voluntary agencies.

In addition, it is of prime importance that data collected on the Irish be processed as a distinct category in any published or internal papers on ethnic data. Evidence was reported to us of census enumerators directing Irish people in 1991 to the 'white' category in the ethnic question rather than if they wished to the 'Other' category, which gave them the opportunity to write in that their ethnicity was Irish. Similar examples of 'strong direction' were reported to us as occurring in the newly introduced ethnic monitoring within the NHS. Incidents of when Irish people tick 'Other' and enter Irish, it is then crossed out and the 'White' box is ticked for them by staff. This is in direct contravention of the fact that ethnic monitoring is supposed to be by voluntary self-identification.

Even when this does not occur and the Irish are able to tick an 'Irish' ethnic category, this does not ensure that the subsequent presentation of data will retain that distinctiveness. To take but one example, this is demonstrated in Birmingham Council's Community Care Plan 1995/6. In the section of the plan which deals with community care for older people, a table is given of the ethnic breakdown of Birmingham's population aged 40 and older. The ethnic categories listed in the table are: White, Black Caribbean, Black, Black Other, Indian, Pakistani, Bangladesh, Chinese, Asian Other, Other. The invisibility of the Irish is thus reinforced by a local authority which prides itself on having been one of the earliest to include the Irish in ethnic monitoring, that is, since the mid-1980s. For all people concerned with delivering services for older Irish people in Birmingham it is particularly problematic because, as the 1991 census shows, the Irish are the ethnic group with the highest proportion of the population who are over 60 years old. In no respect does Birmingham's community care plan either acknowledge this, or highlight that specific provision might be appropriate.

Since this research was commissioned in 1994, the CRE has recommended that an Irish category be used in all ethnic monitoring. In August 1995 it published and circulated its list of recommended classifications with an Irish category added. One consequence is that the Shelter training form now includes an Irish category where previously it did not do so. Shelter makes it clear on its monitoring form that it uses the classifications recommended by the CRE. Some of the Irish groups we interviewed in late 1994 and early 1995 had commented to us that Shelter did not include the Irish. Given Shelter's role in identifying important housing issues this is, therefore, a significant development.

The point of gaining recognised ethnic minority status and of inclusion in ethnic monitoring is not primarily about ensuring that there is exact equality of outcomes for given populations. Most evidence suggests, contrary to popular belief, that members of ethnic minority groups under-claim. The distribution of resources remains therefore unequal. What is paramount is the policy of equal opportunities. In other words, recognition of the Irish as an ethnic group and subsequent ethnic monitoring of the Irish is essential to ensure that prejudice, disadvantage and discrimination do not coalesce and lead to unfair exclusion from access. From the perspective of these Irish groups we interviewed, the campaign for recognition of the Irish as an ethnic group, and for inclusion within monitoring procedures, is a claim for equal treatment albeit within an imperfect system for distributing resources. The constraints on resources, at a time of substantial cuts, makes it even more essential that statutory bodies and voluntary agencies guarantee equality of access and fairness in the initial treatment of clients and assessment of their claims.

## 5.1.1 SUMMARY

- Ethnic monitoring is a controversial procedure. Arguments in favour include its value in measuring success in combating racism and progressing towards equal opportunities. Arguments against include the assumption of fundamental differences which isolate racial disadvantage from other forms of disadvantage and divert attention from common needs. But, by the 1990s, it has become increasingly accepted.

- Although definitions of 'ethnic' include nationality, language and national and ethnic origins (Race Relations Act 1976), it is widely assumed to refer exclusively to black/white differences.

- There was an almost universal call from Irish community groups for ethnic monitoring to include the Irish. Disadvantage and problems for the Irish because of lack of monitoring was frequently referred to by the agencies.

- The problem that the Irish are assumed to fall into the category 'whites', who cannot experience racism and discrimination, underlies the difficulties Irish organisations have when raising issues. Lack of monitoring was seen as a form of indirect discrimination in itself.

- A major consequence is lack of information about the Irish, which has then to be culled from a variety of unsatisfactory sources.

- The Irish have to monitor their own needs, which is an index of the lack of seriousness with which these are treated.

- Non-recognition of Irish need meant that it was an uphill struggle for agencies to obtain services for their clients. The vast majority of Local Authorities did not accept that the Irish were a group whose patterns of disadvantage compared with the indigenous population could be related to issues of ethnic/racial inequality. Groups felt that monitoring was a baseline without which it was impossible to gain serious consideration of the issues they raised.

- Where monitoring was included, its impact varied. In a third of cases, there was no impact as the material was not used. In over half, the impact was erratic, depending on individuals and departments. Nevertheless a few cases of positive benefits could be identified, including funding received and consultation over services.

## 5.2 Critiques of Service Delivery to the Irish-born population by Statutory Bodies

### 5.2.1 Denial of Irish specificity: the consequences for policy formation and service delivery

The overwhelming view of Irish organisations that the Irish should be recognised as an ethnic group and that there needs to be monitoring of the Irish in Britain stems from the immense difficulties they have in raising Irish issues in the context of service delivery. In this section, using examples drawn from the in-depth interviews, we explore the link between Irish invisibility in official discourses and the consequences this has in practice for Irish people and the Irish agencies acting on their behalf. The interviews revealed that the denial of Irish specificity is manifest in: the absence of the Irish from local authority plans for service provision; in their absence from the issues dealt with in the training of local authority staff; and in a general lack of awareness of Irish cultural differences or specific Irish needs. For these reasons, the groups we interviewed, although well aware of examples of good practice when they do occur, are convinced that equality of access and fairness in the initial treatment and assessment of claims does not necessarily exist for Irish people.

In interviewing twenty four organisations we received more comment about the absence of the Irish from the plans of voluntary bodies and statutory organisations and about the denial of the cultural differences and other specificity's of Irish people than any other issue. In all the questions we asked, whatever their focus, there was some comment about this central difficulty from at least some of the groups. The denial of Irish needs and the refusal to countenance that there could be an Irish dimension to a range of social issues was, in the view of many of the people we interviewed, an ingrained predisposition of the professionals they encounter. This situation appears to result from the anomalous position of the Irish and from taken-for-granted attitudes that the Irish do not merit separate attention.

### 5.2.1.1 Statutory Bodies: absence from plans and lack of consultation

The absence of the Irish as a distinct grouping in local authority plans or in their consultation mechanisms stems directly from a reluctance to recognise the Irish as an ethnic group and as a group for whom this ethnicity might form the basis of differential experiences and treatment. A small number of the examples we were given of this will be used to convey the problematic context this creates for Irish organisations when they raise Irish issues.

i) Housing

A survey of London boroughs into the monitoring of Irish applicants carried out by CARA Irish Housing Association in 1993 showed that of:

> ... 16 boroughs who recorded applicants of single homeless by ethnicity, only 9 monitored the Irish applications as a separate group and only 4, Brent, Camden, Islington and Haringey could give actual figures.

As our own monitoring survey of major housing associations showed, an Irish category was included in CORE Housing Statistics between 1989 and 1993, but there was almost no evidence that any use was made of the data (see section 5.2.2.3). If the authorities who monitor the Irish do not collate and publish that data, it makes it very difficult for Irish community groups who are trying to address and raise the profile of proven Irish need to raise issues and make the case in a particular local area. One other consequence is that other statutory bodies and voluntary organisations can resist including the Irish on their own agendas and in their own monitoring.

It was argued closely by two of the Irish housing associations we interviewed that the mainstream housing associations (HAs) do not want to know, and arc not interested in, the Irish community and that they do not develop programmes catered to provide for Irish need as they do for other ethnic minority groups. One Irish agency which does not deal specifically with housing commented that:

> There are problems with referrals. We have major battles to get accepted for nominations by HAs. We are always asked the question: Why the Irish? We are only grudgingly accepted. We don't get the referrals we should and we think that we don't get our fair share of the quota. We have to fight to get the Irish prioritised.

A seminar in 1988, organised by the Association of London Authorities and the London Boroughs Association on homelessness, highlighted the low proportion of housing association compared with local authority lettings which were allocated to priority homeless people, many of whom in the cities are black or from ethnic minorities (Mullins, 1989). This particularly impacts on the Irish who in numerous surveys have been shown to be disproportionately represented amongst those who are homeless or who are sleeping rough (see for example, O'Meachair & Burns, 1988; O'Flynn & Murphy, 1991, various reports of the Brent Irish Advisory Service). In 1994, the Irish at 15% of total users, comprised the largest single ethnic minority using Severe Weather Shelters (Cara, 1995). In the view of the Irish HAs, therefore, the reluctance of statutory and voluntary bodies to recognise specific Irish need makes the task of Irish HAs even more of an uphill struggle than it is for others.

There are 2,400 HAs in Britain. Within the Irish community despite its size, there are only three registered associations. One of the Irish housing associations has been refused recognition by the Housing Corporation on the grounds that there is no need for another Irish association. Irish associations were excluded from the ethnic minority strategy of the Housing Corporation between 1986-1996. This programme was designed specifically to assist minority groups and it covered 60 groups set up by other ethnic minority communities to address the disadvantages their communities face in housing. One Irish HA commented to us:

*They [the Housing Corporation] say things to us that they wouldn't dare say to black housing groups. They don't see the Irish as an ethnic group - they don't take the idea seriously. And there is no recognition of Irish housing need.*

Under Section 56 of the 1988 Housing Act, the Housing Corporation has a duty to eliminate unlawful discrimination and promote equality of opportunity. This extended the provisions of the 1976 Race Relations Act from local authorities to the Housing Corporation (Mullins, 1989). It is in the light of these responsibilities that the Irish HAs are critical of the provision being made by the Housing Corporation for the Irish in London. Part One of this report detailed the extent and type of disadvantage in housing that Irish people experience. In London alone 17% of the Irish population are concentrated in private rented accommodation, with its insecure tenure, poor conditions and vulnerability to harassment, compared with 10 per cent of the remaining population.

In the 1995-6 Approved Development Programme (ADP) for London announced by the Housing Corporation the allocations to meet the needs of Irish people were disappointingly low in the view of the Irish HAs. Only two of the Irish HAs received an allocation from the Rent Programme, this amounted to 0.43% of the London Programme and will produce only 11 homes for Irish people in the whole of the London region during this period. One of these two Irish HAs received an allocation to produce 13 homes for Irish people in Birmingham, this appears to be the only allocation outside London which addresses the needs of the Irish community. There was an allocation to the third registered Irish association under the Rough Sleepers Initiative. During the period 1990-1995 registered HAs in London accommodated 17,436 single adults under 30 years old of which 624, or 3%, were of Irish origin. This provision has to be compared with the estimate that the single Irish homeless represent around 15% of all homeless people (An Teach, 1996).

Given the level of housing need among Irish people in London, all three Irish associations interviewed (which included two of the three associations registered with the Housing Corporation and one which is not registered) stressed how inadequate these allocations are in the light of proven need. Their representations to the Housing Corporation met the response that the overall 1995/6 Allocation has suffered drastic cuts due to the governments tight fiscal policies and this produced the small allocation to Irish HAs. One of the Irish HAs carried out an analysis of the allocations to Irish associations in each of the previous two better funded years: 1993-4 and 1994-5. In these two years the allocations to Irish HAs represented 0.29% and 0.26% of the London Programme respectively. Thus, for the past three years, the Housing Corporations allocations to Irish HAs have been consistently less than 0.5% of the budget and in fact, in the years the overall budget was higher, Irish HAs received a smaller percentage of the Allocation.

Obviously, cuts in the budget of the Housing Corporation make matters difficult all round, but at the same time they reinforce the need to examine questions of access and make it even more important that they be resolved. Since we completed these interviews, the Housing Corporation has changed the framework within which it addresses 'black and minority ethnic' (to utilise the Housing Corporation terminology) housing needs. The emphasis has switched from channeling specific funds to the sixty or so ethnic minority groups recognised for this purpose to an emphasis on the improvement of the performance of all providers in responding to the priority housing needs of black and ethnic minority communities.

This means that, instead of supporting particular organisations, the Housing Corporation will meet needs regardless of who the provider is. Understandably, some black HAs have protested about this as comprehensive information on such needs does not yet exist and because they think it will threaten the existence of smaller associations and imperil specific housing provision. For Irish organisations the need to have the Irish generally recognised in terms of ethnic minority status becomes all the more important. Also, given the Housing Corporation's disappointing past record in meeting Irish needs, it is essential to ensure that in future procedures for assessing need, the Irish are not in the disadvantageous position they have been until now. Encouragingly, for Irish HAs and others giving housing advice the Irish are referred to in the 'enabling framework' twice, representing a degree of recognition of them as a 'minority ethnic group'.

ii) Community Care plans

The Community Care Act, 1991, gave local authorities a leading role in purchasing community care. Under the legislation local authorities have to: provide a community care plan, meet community need and the onus is on the local authority to consult with local communities. In this context, the definitions of 'community' that the politicians and officers of a particular local authority are operating with become crucial. We received varying reports from Irish organisations about the extent to which the Irish community had been consulted in the preparation of community care plans. There was no particular pattern, some authorities who had included the Irish in ethnic monitoring for a number of years were amongst the most remiss in terms of consultation with the Irish over community care. Other authorities who have included and recognised the Irish as an ethnic group held extensive consultations with local Irish advice agencies.

One large Irish community centre in London reported that the community care plan of the borough included no mention of the Irish in its section on black and ethnic minorities despite the Irish being the largest ethnic minority in the borough. This had happened the previous year and comments made by the organisation then had not been taken on board. Their view was that the Irish are not really acknowledged as forming an ethnic group despite their inclusion in ethnic monitoring by the particular London borough. In another example, an Irish community organisation pointed out that there had been extensive consultations with Asian and African-Caribbean groups in the formation of the boroughs community care policy. However, there had been none with the Irish. They also stated that they had a small percentage of the contracts issued for care of the elderly compared to the numbers of Irish elderly in the borough.

On the other hand, a large Irish advice aentre in another part of London commented that in their case there had been very successful consultations with the local authority concerning community care. The authority listened to what the Irish community (the largest ethnic minority in the borough) had to say and fed it into their community care plan. They were well aware that this situation was not necessarily replicated in other authorities, even those that already monitor the Irish. The completely ad-hoc basis upon which the Irish have been included in or not included in the consultations about the formulation of community care plans is completely unsatisfactory and discriminatory in the eyes of the Irish groups we interviewed. The needs of the largest ethnic minority group are not being considered in any systematic way.

iii) Health Authorities

An Irish women's organisation in London told us about, and furnished documentation on, their participation in research conducted by the Medical Campaign Project, funded by the City and East London Family Health Service Authority, about health and homelessness in Hackney (Medical Campaign Project, 1992). This was a study of the single homeless and their access to primary health care. On being approached to participate in the research, as an organisation to which homeless people go for advice, the Irish agency readily complied. The report was published in October 1992. In the section of the report dealing with the community groups that had been consulted there was separate and specific mention of the following; the Black British/Caribbean groups; Asian groups; Vietnamese and Chinese groups; and Turkish and Kurdish groups. There was no reference to the Irish in Hackney. This was despite having included an Irish agency in the research. It also ignored the fact that solely on the numbers of the Irish-born (therefore not including anyone of Irish descent), the Irish, according to the 1991 census, constitute the second largest ethnic minority group in the borough.

Agencies in other London boroughs also reported exclusionary practices in relation to health services. One north London agency reported that there is no specific provision for the Irish elderly with dementia in the borough they serve, whereas there are specific dementia units for other ethnic minority groups. The member of staff interviewed declared that there appears to be 'complete exclusion of the Irish from Enfield and Haringey Health Authority structural planning, although the Irish elderly have the highest headcount of any ethnic minority in the region'.

Another agency that specifically deals with problems Irish people may have in relation to HIV/AIDS argued that the Irish are not taken seriously in relation to funding by District Health Authorities. This is despite the group having produced a number of research reports and having pointed up the specific and different context in which Irish people may contract the disease. Their view was that the case for the Irish has to be argued very loudly, louder than for other ethnic groups, despite the high incidence of HIV among the Irish. Their reports argue that Irish HIV issues are specifically Irish, often very complicated and very different to HIV issues in much of the rest of northern Europe, for example (PIAA, 1993).

There seemed to be more patchy contact between Irish agencies and the health authorities compared with their regular approaches to statutory bodies dealing with housing and benefits issues. Nevertheless, a number of them expressed concerns, especially in relation to mental health issues, even if they were not directly involved in taking up these issues on a daily basis for their clients. These concerns usually centred on incidents clients told them about while actually coming to the Irish agencies about other matters. The view was that Irish needs were even more marginalised within the health service than elsewhere. This was thought to apply in particular to already vulnerable groups: those with alcohol use problems, Travellers and the mentally ill. These fears on their clients' behalf have been reinforced over the years by the research which has been completed about the lack of cultural sensitivity towards Irish people with alcohol use problems and the very high rates of admission to hospitals of Irish people with mental health problems (see Cochrane, 1977; Cochrane & Stopes-Roe, 1979; Norman, 1987)).

iv) 'The numbers game'

The lack of, or inadequate consultation with, Irish agencies and the absence of the Irish from council or borough-wide plans was nearly always linked in the interviews to an account of how, given their numbers in the local population, or other category for whom need has to be proven, the Irish do not obtain their justifiable quota of allocated resources. Many groups commented at length on this subject. Because of the lack of importance attached to considering Irish needs (even in boroughs or cities which recognise the Irish as an ethnic group), the absence of systematic monitoring and the un-systematic way in which these needs are addressed, Irish groups feel that they are forced back on quantitative arguments.

They must rely on comparing the percentage the Irish form in the population with the actual amount of resources allocated and the actual provision of specific services for the local Irish population. In the face of the denial that the Irish have specific needs, or may be subject to unequal and racialised treatment these arguments are constantly pressed especially in relation to funding issues. They have to demonstrate unequal outcomes in order to raise the crucial issue for their clients of possible racialised treatment and unequal access to services. Given how debates about equal opportunities are framed currently, in the view of our interviewees there is no other space open to them.

### 5.2.1.2. 'The battle' to raise Irish issues/non-recognition of anti-Irish racism

Many of the staff of Irish organisations were of the view that nothing happens unless the Irish constantly assail the authorities with the case for the inclusion of Irish interests in planning services etc. One person referred to 'the battle' as a form of indirect discrimination. This level of petitioning is not only necessary because of the generally constrained context of public funding but within that framework the groups we spoke to were convinced they had to work harder, for longer, to obtain recognition of Irish need and the provision of appropriate services for their clients. The battle is necessary because of the non-recognition of the existence of anti-Irish racism and the hostility that sometimes exists to any raising of Irish issues.

One Irish women's group in London raised a number of concerns. The agency has encountered condescending, dismissive and hostile responses on different occasions when raising the needs of Irish women with a number of voluntary organisations and statutory bodies. They have taken up the issue in writing in certain cases. On one occasion the Chair of a prominent grant dispensing organisation commented, at a meeting of the organisation, that the Irish agency was one of the few groups who worked with Irish Travellers, who he viewed as one of the most discriminated against groups of people. These comments were greeted with boos from one political grouping at the meeting (the agency staff present were of the impression that they would not have booed references to black groups in the same way).

Another Irish group has encountered similar opposition in the following manner. The local Conservatives issued a leaflet opposed to the amount of money the local council spent on grants each year to various groups and organisations. A majority of these grants were to ethnic minority groups, for example, five were to Asian groups. However, it was the one grant to an Irish organisation which was singled out for comment as a 'complete nonsense'. The project staff commented that the Irish group were being used as a surrogate for attacking all the ethnic minority grants, but it is the Irish group which can be attacked in print with a low risk of inciting subsequent flak. The attack on grants to Irish groups is a surrogate for attacks on any ethnic minority group having access to what are viewed as privileged resources.

A particular issue of concern raised by a number of the groups was staff training for service providers. Their view was that either there is an absence of any consideration of the Irish within the training or the content which is included is very contentious. For example, the Irish HAs stressed that, as far as they knew, unlike other ethnic minority groups, there is no training to enable staff in HAs or in housing departments to spot Irish housing need. One borough-wide Irish community group in London reported their worries about the training that social workers generally receive and the attitudes which some trainees might possess. This group takes students from social work courses on placement. Recently, one of these students wrote a case study based on her time at the Irish organisation in which she identified one problem faced by clients as being anti-Irish racism. The college selected the student's project to be seen by the external examiner who wrote: 'The Irish experience discrimination, but it is not racism'. The Irish group contacted the CRE who faxed the college that the Irish were covered by the 1976 Race Relations Act; the college took it up with the examiner. The group agreed to continue to take students for the college as they want to raise the consciousness of social workers about Irish issues.

The same organisation also reported that, when they used to do training sessions for a nearby University's course for community workers (who were mostly black men), the response from the trainees was always the same: 'The Irish don't experience racism'. There was a complaint from one student about the training session because of its subject matter, that is objecting to it being about the Irish. The university supported the idea that the issues had to be raised and now includes Irish issues in the curriculum. In both these examples the educational institution had an Irish dimension to their courses and under pressure about this remained committed to the practice. But, in the view of the Irish agency, these examples beg the issue of the general training of social workers. How many courses make any reference to an Irish dimension? Would statements that imply the Irish cannot experience racism because they are white routinely go un-questioned?

A study of alcohol and the Irish, funded by the Department of Health, and carried out in the London Borough of Brent in 1994 had this to say about the training of alcohol workers in Brent:

> *Whilst some of the alcohol workers had received race awareness training in the last 12 months, none of this training included an Irish component. The fact that not one of the alcohol workers in Brent had received recent awareness training on anti-Irish racism is appalling. The potential impact of this on the quality of service provision for Irish people may well be disastrous.*
> (McCollum, 1994)

The report recommended that those engaged in the planning and organising of training programmes for staff should incorporate and develop in to training schedules a rolling programme of awareness interventions on Irish issues and the experience of being an Irish migrant in Britain.

The absence of any content or reference to the Irish in vocational training or in up-date courses means that, when Irish issues are raised, they are greeted within a range from bafflement to outright hostility. If service providers and other professionals lack a conception of there being an Irish community or lack an understanding of how the specificity of Irish migration and settlement in Britain can be a problematic situation for different groups of Irish people, this can have direct consequences. It could influence not only the first point of contact Irish clients have with service providers but it amplifies the difficulties that Irish organisations have in raising issues of Irish concern. An Irish worker in Manchester described how, when Irish issues were raised, especially by someone speaking in a Mancunian accent, at meetings with other professionals or council officers, there is often an uncomfortable silence. People, in her view, are looking for the stereotype or wondering why this particular individual is raising Irish issues.

Two agencies referred in particular to hostility coming from some black professionals in service provision positions. The message from some of the black professionals that these interviewees have worked with is that there is no way that the Irish can compare their experience to that of a black person. Such a view in the opinion of these staff reinforces the notion of a hierarchy of racism and discrimination. This can exacerbate white/black divisions which are generated and legitimised by a myth of white homogeneity in the first place.

These examples of black professionals denying the existence of anti-Irish racism have to be set against another reality stressed by other groups. In a number of the local authorities where Irish organisations have made the most headway in gaining recognition for the existence of the Irish as an ethnic minority group and of the existence of anti-Irish hostility and discrimination, it is the receptiveness to this perspective of strategically placed African-Caribbean and Asian councillors and officers which has often been crucial. Without their recognition of common, but by no means identical, problems there would be fewer authorities and statutory bodies addressing Irish issues than currently exist.

Finally in this section, we include reference to some evidence which was submitted to us by an Irish community group in Sheffield. This is interesting in this context because it indicates that Irish people can face similar problems in areas where the Irish constitute a very small proportion of the population as well as those in which they form a higher concentration. The Sheffield Irish Peoples' Forum has documented in detail not only the attacks on Irish people in recent years in the city but the difficult process and variety of obstacles they faced in getting the Labour council to recognise what was happening. It is worth quoting from their documentation, prepared for Sheffield Council and submitted to us for consideration in the light of this investigation. Sheffield is a city with a very small Irish-born population, however, the pattern of attacks on Irish people and the responses these attacks elicit is very similar to evidence we collected in, for example, parts of London.

The Sheffield Irish Peoples' Forum (we are referring to this group by name as they were not part of our interview sample) was set up in 1991 following repeated attacks on Irish children in a local area of the city. What follows is drawn from their account of what happened when they drew the attention of Sheffield City Council to these incidents. The response of the Council's Community Safety Unit was: '... there is nothing we can do, our remit is to only work with black people and they are the only ones who suffer racism and discrimination'. The Race Equality Council in the city also informed a member of the Forum that 'there was nothing that could be done'. There followed a series of representations to the Family and Community Services department and the Equality Services Committee. The latter committee agreed to put a paper prepared by the Forum, *Race Discrimination: the Irish Community, Law and Policy*, on the agenda in January 1994 but, because of the 'unique' issues involved, the Forum were told that the approval of the Council Leader would have to be sought. This was the beginning of a series of obstacles and objections placed in the Forum's way before they eventually succeeded in having the Irish recognised as an ethnic group in September 1995.

A particular motif of many of the incidents reported in Sheffield was the assumption by officials to whom incidents were reported that any Irish person who experienced harassment must have some association with the IRA. This attitude was also encountered by the Forum when making the above representations to the council, they were told that the Irish people making complaints had to show that they were 'law abiding and not terrorists'. In the view of the Forum, therefore, not only was it denied that Irish people could experience racism and discrimination but this was communicated to the agency and individual complainants in terms that stereotyped all Irish people as terrorists.

This was seen in particular by the politicians involved as a legitimate basis upon which to resist intervening and recognising when a specific group of people were being harassed because of their ethnic/national origins. The Race Equality Officer who attended meetings between the Forum and the councillors stated that on the basis of what he/she witnessed that they had 'never seen a group so vilified'.

All the examples presented in this section have illustrated the many circumstances in which anti-Irishness is denied and give rise to the 'battle' groups have to engage in to raise issues on behalf of their clients.


### 5.2.1.3. Implications for a culturally sensitive service

Since the late 1970s, there have been many calls for service providers, especially in social services, to be 'ethnic sensitive' or 'culturally sensitive'. The idea behind these calls is to draw attention to and counter the easy tendency for the cultural worlds of others to be deemed irrational, ignorant and problematic. Ballard writing about ethnic minorities and social services in 1979 describes the process as:

> *Practitioners coming into contact with a new ethnic group for the first time step across an 'ethnic boundary' into a world with its 'internal ethnic rules and logics', which the practitioner needs to understand before he can tell whether an item of behaviour is normal or aberrant. Instead of regarding distinctive minority patterns as pathological, bizarre, or just plain wrong, they could be more usefully seen as coherent systems, and properly tapped might even become resources for social services agencies. The provision of 'ethnically sensitive' services should be a normal part of good professional practice, and might also throw a new, and more positive, light on much that currently appears problematic.*
> (Quoted in Ely & Denney, 1987)

In the context in which this injunction to be culturally sensitive was being written in the 1970s, the expectation was that service providers would know when they were dealing with a 'new ethnic group' by the colour of their skin. The problem that Irish people encounter and Irish organisations report is the opposite, although it results in the same demand for a culturally specific service.

Because of the myth of homogeneity and the assumption that all whites share the same ethnicity, that is, there is no basis upon which some one who is white is disadvantaged on ethnic grounds or can be subject to racism, claims to the contrary by the Irish are greeted with incredulity or hostility. The demands made by Irish community groups for a culturally sensitive service for Irish people are a direct challenge to these constructions of whiteness. These challenges by Irish groups are intended to peel away the mask of invisibility with which the debate about ethnic minority groups has cloaked the Irish and render the specificity of their position as migrants in Britain visible.

To illustrate this, one London-based group made a general point that was echoed by a number of other agencies. Citing the example of a number of Irish elderly people in the borough who know little English, the staff pointed out that assumptions are made by service providers that all Irish people speak English equally well. It is also assumed that Irish people know all about the welfare system and other systems which exist in Britain. The Irish who have migrated from the Republic of Ireland are not viewed as coming from a foreign country and therefore no allowance is made for their ignorance of procedures which readily becomes evidence of Irish stupidity, and thus a stereotype becomes reinforced.

Paradoxically, this is the reverse of situations where the Irish are perceived as foreign and their passports are demanded as proof of identity in order to claim benefits or housing (see next section). The Irish appear to be subject both to processes of inclusion and exclusion, the common feature of each process being that depending on the context either can be disadvantageous.

A number of Irish groups in different contexts explained their anxiety that assessments of clients and their needs were made by professionals who assumed that there was no need to take into account any specific circumstances when dealing with an Irish person because of their whiteness. For example, the process by which individuals are assessed under the terms of the Housing (Homeless Persons) Act 1985 part 111, is, in the experience of one Irish group specialising in this area, inadequate to protect some of the most vulnerable sections of the Irish population in Britain. The group has:

> ... on a number of occasions presented individuals who have been subsequently accepted as vulnerable, to the Housing Needs Division, only to be informed that the individual will have to remain 'roofless' until the medical aspects of their case have been assessed by the District Medical Officer. This policy, written or informal, contravenes the Act which protects the vulnerable and is not in line with the Homeless Code of Guidance issued by the Department of Environment. (Patterson and McGlackin, 1993)

The agency is concerned that, should this policy continue in the borough concerned, then it will continue to place some of the most vulnerable members of the community in situations where a serious risk to their health and safety exists. In their view, with the movement to community care, it is essential that a joint assessment panel approach to the assessment of vulnerable people's needs is followed. This should involve social services and such a joint assessment panel would advise on a persons social and health needs as well as housing needs.

The role of assessments is, therefore, crucial in the view of this and other agencies. Another Irish agency directly concerned with young Irish mothers and their children reported that in their experience social workers have very little understanding of Irish issues and this is particularly apparent in their ignorance of Irish family values and culture, especially as they may impact on single mothers. Other community groups made similar references. A report on alcohol and the Irish concluded that ethnic-specific services should be considered for Irish people (and other ethnic minorities) by purchasers and providers in any discussion about service provision for people with alcohol problems. Many of the respondents in the survey had been presenting to an Irish advice agency with problems directly or indirectly related to their alcohol use. When the subject of alcohol use was broached, it was evident that respondents were reluctant to be referred to a non-Irish agency but were extremely receptive to receiving a counselling service from an Irish agency.

Another example illustrates the problems which ensue when there is a failure to recognise the Irish as a migrant population. A London-based agency makes the case for specific attention to be paid to the needs of Irish people with HIV infection based on arguments that recognise the impact of migration on health and reflect the different epidemiology of HIV/Aids in Ireland compared to England and Wales and most of the rest of northern Europe. The pattern of HIV infection in the Republic of Ireland is similar to that of southern Europe and Scotland, with a predominance of infection among Intravenous Drug Users (IDUs), with a corresponding increasing incidence of perinatal transmission and of transmission by heterosexual intercourse. The pattern of infection in England and Wales conforms with that of northern Europe in general where the epidemic predominantly affects homosexual men but the proportions of infected drug users and of heterosexuals are gradually increasing.

When individuals migrate from an area with one epidemiological pattern to an area with a different one there can be a number of consequences: i) migrants may not have been exposed to the same health education programmes as people in the country of destination; ii) within the migrant group there may be specific needs which are not catered to in the country of destination; iii) mobility itself may affect health behaviour. All three of these factors apply to Irish people living in Britain who are affected by HIV/Aids. The consequences of the different epidemiological patterns, combined with the serious material disadvantage many Irish migrants experience in Britain, could result in a significant population at risk of HIV infection. Irish people living in Britain may not be able to find services appropriate for their needs. Networking between agencies in the two countries is seen by workers to be of paramount importance in order to co-ordinate appropriate service development (PIAA, 1993:2).

A number of agencies commented that, in the absence of cultural sensitivity towards the Irish, the presence of an Irish professional on, for example, a social work team often became the crucial random factor upon which success in advancing a client's case might depend. We were given a number of examples of instances where a client only received appropriate service provision once the agency acting on their behalf got a case transferred to a team which included someone Irish. If there are no Irish people on a team, then there is frequently less sympathy and understanding of the cultural needs of Irish people. There was also evidence that, when statutory bodies work regularly with local Irish groups and consult them about Irish clients, then service provision becomes more sensitive. However, other groups felt that sometimes local authorities had a tendency to shift all Irish clients their way and thus evaded dealing with Irish clients themselves.

One group cited a voluntary sector organisation, the Stockwell Project, as both exceptional and exemplary in the policies it adopted towards Irish needs. In this case a crucial factor seems to have been the presence of Irish staff in the organisation. There is a danger of essentialism here which was recognised by the people making the comments. The implication being that the mere presence of any Irish person would make a positive difference, this homogenises all Irish people as a category, and is obviously not necessarily the case. However, in the face of the widespread battle to raise Irish issues, the conclusion of many of the agencies is that the chances of success are raised, although not guaranteed, if there are Irish staff in a voluntary organisation or in a service provider position.

### 5.2.1.4 Stereotyped Responses and Exclusionary Practices

A lack of monitoring of the Irish, an absence of recognition of Irish needs and ignorance of Irish culture and of the specificity of Irish migrant experiences does not exhaust the catalogue of responses of service providers to demands that there be an Irish dimension in their provision. The substantiated doubts the Irish agencies hold about the treatment their Irish clients sometimes receive are compounded by the evidence the groups have collected of the stereotyped responses and exclusionary practices operated by many service providers in relation to the Irish. The groups interviewed reported a range of racialised and stereotyped responses to Irish people/organisations on the part of professionals involved in welfare and social services, both in voluntary and statutory bodies. The stereotypes most often operationalised are those of the Irish: as drunks, as stupid, and as fraudsters.

In two London boroughs Irish organisations gave us details of council employees whose anti-Irish attitudes had been the subject of complaint by either the organisation concerned or one of its clients. In one case, the employee in question was moved from a front-line position in the DSS; in the other instance the person was eventually sacked. What these examples show is that in two instances when a case was pressed, the local authority (both were what in the context of this report would be viewed as amongst the more 'Irish aware') recognised that racist remarks had been made by their employees and that they had a responsibility to take some action. This was not, however, the response described to us in the majority of cases. These two examples were of very explicit remarks, whereas often racist responses are more subtle and often not perceived in this way at all by the perpetrators or their line managers.

A number of groups said that the most common stereotypes that they had come across from, for example, housing officers or social workers, were those of the Irish being 'a bit thick', 'feckless' and 'pulling a fast one'. The operation of these stereotypes means that the seriousness of the issues facing the Irish people they deal with is not taken on board.

Below we examine, first, examples of stereotyped responses from service providers and, second, examples of exclusionary practices that may operate in respect of Irish applicants.

i) Stereotyped responses

a) Irish as drunks

A number of Irish agencies commented on the pervasiveness of the stereotypes about the Irish, being stupid or drunks, and how they operate in all institutional situations. Consequently, some groups commented that, if an Irish user drinks, all services for that person will be targeted at the alcohol use. There will not necessarily be an examination of their problems: alcohol may be covering for poverty or abuse. A Birmingham agency reported that the fact the Irish are the biggest users of alcohol services in the city generates the reaction 'that's what we'd expect'. The stereotype of the Irish as inveterate drinkers is so ingrained that a worker at one London advice agency described how statutory bodies he has approached to ask for support for the organisation assume that the project runs ceilis and that he is the barman.

A Manchester group while reporting good responses from the council in connection with, for example, obtaining 'hard to let' properties for new young Irish migrants commented on how this could coexist with stereotyped reactions in other contexts. The stereotype of the 'drunken Paddy' means that if Irishmen are harassed no-one believes them. Again, they report that the stereotype of the drunk is to the forefront in health professionals' responses to the health needs of older single Irish men.

An agency in London, which employs an alcohol worker, reported that the attitude of one large hospital serving their area towards what the hospital calls Irish 'Alkies' was: take them in, dry them out and discharge them. The stereotype view is that there is nothing else to be done with them: hopeless cases. A south London agency described how a woman, under stress because of her husband's drinking, was told by her GP: 'What do you expect? He's Irish'. Another specific gap, pinpointed by an Irish HA was the lack of specific services for Irish drinkers. The agency gets a lot of referrals from alcohol groups, about a third to one half of their clients have drink problems, because there is nowhere else specific to send them to ensure they get a culturally specific service.

Doherty (1993) in his study of alcohol service provision in London found that the particular experiences of Irish people were not recognised and providers were not geared towards providing a culturally sensitive service to Irish users. Despite 23% of clients approaching alcohol service providers belonging to the Irish community these services had not accorded to the Irish the growing recognition which they were giving to the need to reflect the cultural experience of African-Caribbean and Asian communities in their service provision. As a result, Irish agencies are a vital first contact for people with an alcohol problem.

This is confirmed in a study by Harrison and Carr-Hill (1992; see also Kennedy & Brooker, 1986) which reports that Irish people misusing alcohol found Irish agencies more helpful in dealing with their problem than mainstream alcohol or counselling services. Their study in particular related the evidence that exists of higher than average consumption of alcohol by Irish men in Britain to the problems associated with migration. Their study suggests, after a comparison with the situation in Ireland, that Irish people develop a drinking problem after migrating to Britain where settling means overcoming many hurdles. There are significant differences in alcohol use between those living in owner occupied or rented housing and those living in hostels or other transient housing, who were more likely to drink extensively. There is evidence of a correlation between health problems and regular alcohol consumption and the possible effect on the user's economic and social life. Those with a drinking problem are more likely to receive low income, are more likely to have social and relationship problems, and are more likely to suffer ill health. Further research is necessary to examine what alcohol may be masking in the lives of some Irish people in Britain.

b) Irish as fraudsters

Automatically suspecting Irish people of fraud is a response often manifest at the first point of contact with an Irish client. The groups interviewed provided many examples of how these suspicions were conveyed through what were viewed by them as unreasonable requests for identification by various authorities.

A key moment for any individual when applying for benefits or for housing is the first encounter with staff in a front-line situation. It is at this point that critical 'gate-keeping' strategies or exclusionary practices operate. Many of the concerns of Irish agencies about access of Irish people to benefits were summarised in a report *Identity Crisis* (AGIY, 1993). This report highlighted a number of barriers to benefit for Irish people particularly problems with proving identity. The main findings were that

i) over 25% of Irish applicants were refused Income Support

ii) 1-in-6 claims are referred to the fraud investigators

iii) 30% of cases delayed as Benefits Agency questioned the validity of the ID offered by Irish customers

iv) 86% of those providing one form of ID were asked to provide supplementary ID

111

v) 38% of Irish customers asked to provide the full Irish passport as proof of ID

vi) Official Register's copy of an Irish birth certificate given no status by the Benefits Agency.

The report concluded that the findings demonstrated that the Irish experience of the benefits system pointed to unequal treatment, denial of rights of access to benefits, unreasonable delays in payment and an unsatisfactory level of 'customer service'. The Irish agency which produced this report subsequently held a conference to which the Benefits Agency, Irish welfare organisations and non-Irish agencies who work with Irish people were invited. There was some discussion with the Customer Service Branch of the Benefits Agency about how the Agency should address the issues and they agreed that there should be staff training about Irish issues and concerns.

In our interviews we discovered substantial evidence from the Irish agencies to suggest that Irish people were accorded differential treatment. These include, for example, asking for a number of forms of identification or insisting on a passport when it is unnesssary for any Irish person to be in possession of a passport to travel to England and therefore many do not possess one. A number of agencies reported that other Irish IDs are often not accepted and in some cases applicants are simply told to go away or that their birth certificates are false. Irish applicants have had the following said to them on presentation of birth certificates: 'You bought that on the boat coming over' or 'Irish ID is very dodgy'. Irish people producing birth certificates as a form of ID to benefits officers have been greeted with: 'You can buy these in Camden Irish Centre'. A benefits officer said to a woman trying to obtain child benefit: 'It's going to take longer if you are Irish'.

The experience of groups, therefore, is that many Irish people making claims are immediately suspected of fraud and this presumption underpins the demands made on many Irish people to produce specific, often multiple, forms of ID for a benefits officer. People are most frequently told: 'You shouldn't have come over here, you should go home'. In the agencies' view the stereotype which operates is 'Irish people are on the fiddle' and hearing an Irish accent is sufficient to trigger this response in a claims officer.

One London agency has observed that in the provision of housing Irish people are subject to overlong interviews and assumptions are made that they 'must' have certain documentation (the most common example is a passport), and a 'mind-set' is demonstrated that cannot see how another society might function. These are not universal practices, certain DSS offices were regularly identified as being more likely to respond in this way to Irish applicants than other offices. However, they are discriminatory practices and were cited by a wide range of the Irish agencies we spoke to.

Erratic implementation of procedures can lead to many problems. In virtually every case of questioned identification taken up by Irish agencies, the individual was subsequently awarded the benefits for which they were correctly claiming in the first place. No doubt there are many people refused benefits who do not subsequently seek help from an Irish agency or other advice bureaux and therefore never receive benefits to which they are entitled. The attitude of some DSS officials, as reported by the agencies, was to prevent Irish people receiving their due benefits and the discretion which exists in requirements for the presentation of ID appears to be one of the main exclusionary practices utilised by DSS officials and others to regulate, control and minimise Irish applicants for benefits or housing. A number of the London agencies commented that since the DSS had moved to Glasgow there had been a better service when following up clients difficulties but this did not necessarily lead to an improvement in the first encounter with a DSS official in a local office.

The finding that a significant majority of the Irish community and advice groups we interviewed described Irish clients experiencing difficulties over ID when making claims for benefit or applications for housing is a very important one. In particular, the regularity with which passports are asked for as identification was criticised. Irish passports are expensive and unless departing on a foreign holiday or moving elsewhere in continental Europe or the United States for work there would be no reason why any Republic of Ireland citizen would be in possession of a passport on arrival in Britain. It is also noteworthy that a small number of the examples reported to us involved people who had moved from Northern Ireland being asked for a passport to prove their identity when claiming benefit in Britain.

We draw attention to this finding because the assumption is that only groups of people who have been targeted by the immigration and nationality laws of the past 30 years are persistently asked for identification, and, in particular, asked for passports as a means of identification. In 1985, a major report about racism and the social security system concluded that: 'It is rarely white people who are asked to produce their passports, but mainly people who are black or of other ethnic minority origin' (Gordon & Newnham, 1985:26). The Irish are of 'other ethnic origin' but they are also 'white'. The above statement, like so many others, is written as if to be a member of an ethnic minority is to be 'black'.

With justification, this 1985 report on racism in social security, carried out for the Child Poverty Action Group, pointed out the discrimination inherent in the fact that over half the black people living in Britain have been born in this country but they were still likely to be asked to produce their passports as identification. However, this does not obviate the fact that other ethnic minority groups, including those that are white, can be subject to a similar procedure.

The current demands that Irish people can face for a passport as ID are contrary to the legal framework established in 1948 which specifically designated that citizens of what became the Republic of Ireland were not to be treated as 'aliens' (this decision as indicated in the Introduction of the report was in part taken to ensure long-term access to Irish migrant labour, see Hickman, 1998 forthcoming). The demands for Irish passports also contravene a DHSS directive of 1987 which stated to staff that Irish citizens are not obliged to present passports when making social welfare claims. This directive was issued after months of lobbying by Irish social workers in response to complaints that many Irish people were being mistreated when making welfare claims. The directive reminded staff that Irish citizens can move freely between the Republic of Ireland and Britain and *Passports should not be a precondition for payments* (*Irish Post*, 28.2.1987:13).

Many of the worst problems are undoubtedly experienced by newly-arrived Irish migrants in Britain. In the view of two of the agencies this is in part because most do not know the system and the difficulties apply especially to applications for benefits and housing. However, there were a number of examples given to us of people who, having returned to Ireland (possibly because of family sickness or on becoming unemployed in Britain), then experienced all the same difficulties of proving identity again on their return to Britain. In these experiences lie the contradictions of being from a country which provides the main source of migrant labour for the British economy. In particular, if an individual is from the Republic of Ireland, and even occasionally from Northern Ireland, they are at risk of being subject to or encountering treatment which is a product more of established racialised myths and stereotypes about Irish peoples presence in Britain rather than an assessment of their entitlement to what they are claiming. As we commented earlier there is considerable evidence that groups who are identified as being 'scroungers' are amongst those least likely to utilise services or to claim their full benefit entitlement. These issues are explored more fully in Part Three, Section 4.3.1.

ii) Exclusionary practices

a) Housing allocation practices

If an individual approaches a local authority for housing they are going to have their claim assessed in terms of three main criteria:

Are they homeless?

Are they in priority need (this means do they have young children, are they vulnerable for any reason, are they elderly)?

Are they homeless 'intentionally'?

It is only when a local authority accepts that a person is homeless, and that they are in priority need, and that they are not intentionally homeless that they have a legal duty to offer the person somewhere to live. Homelessness is described as someone having no accommodation in England or Wales or Scotland. In addition, someone is counted as homeless if it was probable that their occupation of accommodation would lead to violence from someone else living in it, or to threats of violence from someone else living in it and likely to carry out the threats. Accommodation is not counted if it is not seen as 'reasonable' to continue to occupy.

Intentional homelessness is caused when someone deliberately does, or fails to do, something and because of this they stop occupying the accommodation which was available and which it would have been reasonable for them to continue to

114

occupy. 'Available' for occupation means that the property must be available for the individual and for any person who might reasonably be expected to reside with them (eg. spouse and children). The category 'intentionally homeless' lends itself to a variety of interpretations. The DSS or Homeless Persons Units in using the classification are supposed to be careful to check that this applies not 'through any fault of their [the clients] own'.

In the current era of heavily restricted resources, all people making applications to local authorities for housing are being rigorously questioned. The community groups interviewed described some of the ways in which these processes specifically impact on Irish people. The newly arrived are particularly susceptible to the ruling that they have made themselves 'intentionally homeless'. They are also the group least likely to challenge the decision, even though there may be little or no evidence that the officers verified or understood the context in which the individual became homeless.

Agencies reported cases where 'leaving Ireland' in and of itself is taken as a definition of a person making themselves intentionally homeless. A south London agency cited one of their clients who was asked by Southwark Homeless Persons' Unit why she did not return to Ireland. After a long struggle they gave her accommodation. However, the view of the HPU was that she had made herself 'intentionally homeless' because she had left a house in Ireland. The clients of this Irish south London agency were reported as usually perceiving themselves as at the bottom of the pile, below the English and black people, when it came to having their needs addressed.

We were provided with other examples of Irish people failing to access housing or benefits on initial application which caused concern to the agencies. A case which received considerable publicity while we undertook this research was of a family from Northern Ireland who were forced to flee their home because of intimidation and violent threats to the family. They travelled to Luton and applied to the council for housing, to be informed that by leaving Northern Ireland they had made themselves 'intentionally homeless'. One person was refused benefit after returning from Ireland, although she had successfully claimed before. On this occasion her ID was questioned. Two women were refused housing allowances and were declared intentionally homeless. They were offered travel permits to return to Ireland by Camden Council. They had been declared intentionally homeless because, after a check of their housing status in Ireland, the mother of one woman was established to have a Corporation flat. In some cases, Irish people have been refused benefit under the Habitual Residency Test, this is not supposed to apply to citizens of the Irish Republic (Adler, 1995). These decisions are problematic in the context of labour migration.

One of the women's organisations we interviewed has detected a changed pattern of treatment of the Irish. In the early 1980s, Irish people were often likely to get issued with travel warrants to return to Ireland. The early 1990s has seen a pattern emerge of the Irish declared 'intentionally homeless'. In the late 1980s there was considerable publicity about the policy of the London Borough of

Camden to send all Irish people claiming housing assistance back to Ireland on the ground that they had made themselves intentionally homeless by leaving Ireland. In the face of the opposition that this policy engendered the council's housing management sub-committee extended the decision to cover other categories also, so that they would not appear anti-Irish. Irish community groups are of the view that decisions which declare someone to be intentionally homeless should be subject to ethnic monitoring. This would reveal whether there is a discriminatory pattern or not. Until that is introduced, many of the groups continue to suspect discriminatory treatment of the Irish in this context.

One of the three Irish housing associations in London, said Irish people are being actively discouraged from going on local authority housing waiting lists. Another London housing association, also reports what it views as discriminatory practices in the way in which Irish people are 'put off' at housing office receptions. The organisation is only able to obtain two move-on places a year from hostels. Local authorities play a key role in defining need and acting as gatekeepers to permanent accommodation. They currently provide nearly half the nominations of Irish-born people to housing associations. Single Irish people often go through a revolving door of being on the streets, then in temporary accommodation and then back on the streets again, with little or no prospect of a permanent solution to their housing problems' (CARA, *Monitoring of Irish applicants for housing: a survey of London Boroughs 1994*).

There is general concern over the small numbers of Irish people putting themselves on lists for council housing whose needs, therefore, go unrecorded. CARA's research into single women verifies this with very few single Irish women registering and, in fact, being actively discouraged from doing so. In practice this results in CARA having serious problems getting nominations from some local authorities who claim they do not have any single Irish people on their lists.

Currently, the London boroughs are accepting nominations from housing associations to rehouse about 500 single people a year. Between 1991 and 1993 approximately 62% of the nominees were from ethnic minorities but only 7.8%t were Irish compared with 29.8% Black and 21.4% Cypriot (An Teach ,1996).

The solution to this 'Catch 22' situation involves two related strategies according to Irish HAs. First, there urgently needs to be a standardised monitoring policy in local authority housing departments on ethnicity and gender which includes an Irish dimension, and covers emergency housing and general housing advice (CARA, 1994; An Teach, 1996). This data should be collated, analysed and fed into strategies on improving access to housing for ethnic minority groups.

Second, all local authorities, not just those in areas of traditionally high Irish settlement, need to develop links with Irish agencies to establish a greater understanding of the issues involved and information on vulnerable sections of the community. These developments are all the more needed in the context of community care and its strategic importance when local authorities identify priorities for Special Needs Housing.

b) Other examples of exclusionary practices

Particular groups of Irish people seem to experience difficulties in obtaining health services from general practitioners. The main categories appear to be: Travellers, the homeless and drug users. The three categories of Irish people mentioned here would in all likelihood encounter problems in accessing services if they were not Irish.

The point, according to agencies commenting on this matter, is that if a drug user, or a homeless person or a Traveller is Irish then the response they elicit is often compounded by the service providers categorisation of them as an 'Irish drug taker' etc. This is an example of where a number of facets about a person are influencing their chances of access to services which they require and have a right to.

Many people experiencing difficulties in accessing services are subject to multiple categorisation thus rendering their chances of obtaining what they need as lower than they otherwise would be.

One London advice centre cited a case they took up of a client with mental health problems who was desperate for treatment. A staff member of the agency went with the client to see a GP, who threw both of them out of his office. The client then got into trouble, exacerbated by lack of treatment, and is now in a secure unit. Another agency thinks that discrimination especially affects people with mental health problems because their health problems are seen to be because of their Irishness.

In other circumstances encounters can be rendered more difficult because of stereotyped responses. One agency reported an incident where different doctors commented to an Irish woman who was having her fifth child: 'You Irish breed like rabbits'.

Another aspect of gate-keeping policies practised by local authorities in certain areas is that of routinely referring Irish applicants to the local Irish agency. A large Irish community organisation in London described 'a blanket policy' of sending Irish applicants to the Centre by the local DSS and HPUs rather than fulfil their statutory duty by, for example, giving clients accommodation or an emergency payment.

The workers expend considerable resources equipping clients with the appropriate information and in helping them complete their forms in order to maximise their likelihood of being successful in a housing application. This can involve: liaising extensively with various agencies in the Republic of Ireland and Northern Ireland, including social services, housing authorities, schools, hospitals, solicitors, Garda/police, General Registrar's offices, private landlords.

These investigative efforts are undertaken in order to provide clients with the concrete and written verification of details outlined in any HPU application. In the view of the agency, it is their efforts on behalf of their clients which have resulted in comments at the offices of local statutory bodies to the effect that birth certificates: 'can be bought at the Irish Centre'.

Much of what has been described in this section of the report indicates that many Irish people when either claiming benefits or seeking assistance in housing and in other situations can find themselves to be the object of a combination of racialised commentary and challenges to their right to be in the country. Stereotyped responses towards the Irish appear to operate as one of a number of gate-keeping practices utilised when dealing with Irish applicants for housing, benefits or other forms of support.

### 5.2.2. SUMMARY

- Widespread denial of specific Irish needs and refusal to countenance an Irish dimension to a range of social issues constitutes a serious form of discrimination against Irish people.

- This denial appears to be an ingrained view of many professionals in the service delivery field.

- An Irish dimension is absent from plans and consultation processes of statutory bodies. This leads to serious under representation. For example:

  - only 3/2400 Housing Associations are linked with the Irish community, compared with 60 for 'recognised' ethnic groups. In 1995/96 Irish housing associations received only 0.43% of the Housing Corporation's Approved Development Budget for London.

  - no systematic inclusion of an Irish dimension in Community Care plans drawn up by local authorities.

- A 'battle' is always needed to secure recognition of Irish issues

  - Irish agencies have to assail the authorities before any notice is taken.

  - there is considerable opposition from people who cannot understand why the Irish are not in an identical position to the white British-born.

- Very low awareness of the specificity of problems of migration and settlement in Britain for Irish people and of cultural differences in their background exists among statutory service providers. Training programmes (e.g. for social workers, health workers) rarely include an Irish dimension.

- Arguments that anti-Irish racism cannot be compared with that experienced by black people reinforce the notion of a hierarchy of discrimination and accentuate a framework of competition for scarce resources. They strengthen black/white divisions and allow the Irish to continue to be attacked in print as a surrogate for attacks on all ethnic minority groups.

- Stereotyped responses and comments from service providers and other workers mean that Irish issues are often not taken seriously. For example, drink problems among Irish men are seen as a reason for denying other forms of help, and Irish people are more readily suspected of fraud when they make benefits claims.

- Statutory authorities use gate keeping practices to exclude Irish people from equal access to services. For example, Irish people are actively discouraged from applying for Local Authority waiting lists and are more likely to be classified 'intentionally homeless'. Certain groups of Irish people have greater difficulties in access to GP health care because their 'Irish' label compounds other aspects such as drug use, homelessness and travelling lifestyle.

### 5.3 Racial Harassment

In 1987 the CRE produced a working definition of racial harassment:

> *Racial harassment is violence which may be verbal or physical and which includes attacks on property as well as on the person, suffered by individuals or groups because of their colour, race, nationality or ethnic or national origins, when the victim believes that the perpetrator was acting on racial grounds and/or there is evidence of racism.*

In giving this definition the CRE stressed that the victim's perception of racism may be crucial. However, the CRE also explained that:

> *... the main focus and perspective behind any definition of racial harassment must be that it is an issue where white people are responsible for attacking, in one way or another, people from black and ethnic communities.*

Whereas the CRE's definition of racial harassment clearly encompasses the type of incidents which Irish organisations reported to us, this latter point implicitly assumes that the only people likely to be subject to racial harassment are black people. This definition can lead, therefore, to confusion because it fails to clarify the full range of groups who might experience racial harassment. This has generated extreme difficulties for Irish organisations in their attempts to get particular attacks on Irish people recognised for what they and their clients think they are.

For many years people argued that there should be central monitoring by the Home Office of the extent and nature of racial attacks. This is now being done but the definition used is not that of attacks on people because of their colour or ethnic origin, that is attacks motivated at least in part by racism, but of 'racial incidents' in which the victim and the assailant are of different ethnic (in practice perceived different racial) groups and where a racial motive is either suggested by the victim or inferred by a police officer. Other research has commented that this means that attacks on white people, where the offender is alleged to be black, can be and are recorded as 'racial incidents' even if these are, in reality, criminal acts and there is no evidence of racial hostility but simply an allegation by the victim or the officer to whom it is reported. The specific racist basis of many white attacks on black people is therefore denied and racial violence is redefined as just another aspect of inter-racial crime (Skellington, 1992).

The likelihood of attacks on Irish people, which are motivated, at least in part, by the Irishness of the individual, being counted as 'racial incidents' is very low. Counting 'racial incidents' is perceived as counting violent acts between blacks and whites. A further problem with this form of monitoring which impacts generally and has specific implication for attacks on Irish people is that, even if the motivation for an attack was better conceptualised, a racial incident is usually taken to be an attack on an individual or group or their property. This behaviouristic definition fails to take into account more subtle, but no less intimidatory expressions of harassment: racist graffiti or other written insults; verbal abuse; disrespect towards differences in music, food, dress, or customs;

120

deliberate mispronunciation of names; mimicry of accents; exclusionism (Cashmore, 1994).

Most estimates of racial harassment based on independent research indicate that racial harassment is a greater phenomenon than official statistics show and that a considerable proportion of it is of this more subtle variety. For example, a report of the Policy Studies Institute found that of those who experienced racial harassment 60% had not reported it to the police and in addition suggested that the incidence of racial harassment was probably 10 times that suggested by a Home Office report in 1981 (Brown, 1984). It is particularly the subtle or 'low level' form of racial harassment which is under reported (Nanton and Fitzgerald, 1990).

As indicated, below, in the examples of racial harassment of Irish people that community groups reported to us, the issue of under-reporting and non-recognition of those attacks is of as great a concern as the nature of the attacks themselves. The racial harassment of Irish people we give examples of in this section, all took place in some form of public arena, that is, the harassment emanates from another party beyond the immediate confines of the individual's home and excludes their work place (details of harassment at work emerged in Stage Three of the research rather than here, because of the high number of unemployed, self-employed, home-worker and retired people who utilise the agencies).

Nineteen out of twenty four groups reported a least one category of racial harassment. The proportion of clients reporting harassment to those nineteen groups ranged from 5% to 100% of the clients presenting to an individual group (100% existed in the case of an agency dealing specifically with Travellers). All nineteen of the groups reporting racial harassment reported examples of clients being subject to verbal abuse. Nine organisations reported examples of both verbal abuse and physical attacks. The other ten agencies reported verbal abuse and other forms of harassment. Except in the case of the four agencies who only dealt with women clients, all agencies reported harassment as occurring to both men and women, although sometimes in different proportions. The four agencies with women-only clients all reported racial harassment. Six agencies reported that younger (under 35 years) people were more likely to be harassed, while the other agencies said incidents involved their clients of all age groups.

### 5.3.1 Types of abuse/attack

When Irish people are racially harassed, their treatment usually involves name calling of various kinds. This is most common in the case of verbal abuse but may take the form of letters sent to them or graffiti on their property. The most common abusive terms used on the basis of incidents described to us were: 'Irish bastard', 'Irish gay bastard', 'dirty Irish bastard', 'Irish pig', 'Irish bitch', 'Irish slag', 'Irish dog', 'IRA scum'. Verbal abuse was also reported which referred to the Irish having large families (breeding like rabbits, etc).

Physical attacks were usually on the person but sometimes on their property. The latter involved: damaging the possessions of people in hostel accommodation; trampling on washing; paint attacks on people's houses or flats; excrement through doors. The physical attacks on Irish people (apart from those already described above) included: bullying of Irish children because of their accent; a bottle broken over the head of an Irish woman in south London; a woman shot with an airgun in north London. All these attacks were accompanied by racist verbal abuse.

The documentation of racial attacks and harassment of Irish people in Sheffield already referred to above included evidence of: physical attack and verbal abuse of Irish families and elderly people by neighbours; physical attack and verbal abuse of Irish people in entertainment venues and at public functions in the city; and harassment of children in schools and of students in higher education institutions.

On the basis of the evidence of these nineteen groups the two most common sources of harassment for Irish people are their neighbours and the police. Fifteen agencies gave details of neighbour harassment and thirteen of police harassment. The other two sources occasionally named were far-right political organisations and the statutory authorities. Neighbour and police harassment was reported in each of the three cities we surveyed in England. Individual experiences of these forms of harassment are illustrated in Part 3, section 5 of this report.

### 5.3.2 Neighbours

In the case of harassment by neighbours three types of housing situations seem to be particularly associated with attacks on Irish people: private multi-occupancy households; hostel and other temporary accommodation, for example, bed and breakfast; and council housing estates. Two agencies in London stressed that a significant proportion of their housing caseload was the consequence of harassment incidents: 33% of the case load of one London-based Women's group and between 66-75% of the housing cases dealt with by a south-London Irish group. A number of agencies reported that Irish people, who come to them, wanting re-housing, often give harassment as a reason.

The point about harassment from neighbours is that it demonstrates that there is no difficulty in identifying Irish people. In these as in other contexts, alternative criteria to colour lag only marginally behind the latter as a signifier of difference. Accent is the chief signifier of Irishness to neighbours but it is not the only one. For example, an Irish agency in south London reported that women who had put claddagh knockers on their doors, subsequently had graffiti daubed on the doors such as: 'Irish bitch', 'Irish slag', 'Get out'.

Irish people approach the Irish agencies about harassment usually after they have been unable to persuade the local authority of the merits of their case. A number of examples will illustrate the situation some Irish people can find themselves in:

On a London council estate a Bengali family and their Irish neighbour were both subject to harassment by the same group of local youths, calling them names and throwing stones at them. Both households complained to the council. The Bengali family were moved because it was considered a clear case of racial harassment, but the neighbourhood office did not even record the Irishman's complaints. He was subsequently threatened with arson by the youths and he left his flat. The council then declared that he had abandoned his flat and brought his troubles on himself. Eventually, he was rehoused after going to an Irish agency who intervened on his behalf but he was only allocated temporary accommodation.

A case dealt with by an Irish women's agency involved a woman living on a council estate who had her car badly vandalised and 'IRA scum go home' daubed on her door. The local housing office were not receptive to her complaints because there were no witnesses to the damage to her car and they defined it as a typical neighbour dispute despite the graffiti on her door.

A common context in which these difficulties with councils occur is when attempts are made by Irish people to obtain re-housing when they are being attacked by their neighbours. The resistance on the part of Council officers to recognising attacks on Irish people as racist appears to be widespread.

One London based group gave details of one of their clients, a woman with three children, who was physically attacked by her neighbours because she was Irish. She tried to get rehoused by the council with no success and then was attacked again as were her children. Finally she was moved after considerable intervention with the Council from the agency.

Southwark Irish Forum have documented attacks on Irish people in their area and the difficulties which have been faced in gaining recognition from the council or race equality officers in recognising that attacks could be racist (see reports in *London Irish News*, 22.6.90 & 12.7.90)

In some cases, however, the local authority does recognise the harassment for what the Irish people experiencing it believe it to be: racial harassment.

On a council estate in north-west London an Irish family were harassed by families on both sides. The local authority in this case recognised it as anti-Irish abuse, the incidents had started during the last bombing campaign in Britain, but it had not decided, at the time we were informed of the case, on who to rehouse.

Another incident concerned a woman who was woken in the night by taunts: 'IRA queer bitch, 'IRA scum', 'Hang IRA scum'. Also BNP stickers were stuck to the building. The woman was from Northern Ireland. In this case after an Irish agency intervened on her behalf the council agreed that the incident be given racial harassment status and she was rehoused.

These were the two examples we were told about where recognition was given. Interestingly, both these successful complaints involved incidents connected to Northern Ireland.

In private multi-occupancy households, the agencies report that it is frequently elderly single Irish men who encounter hostility. In those areas where Irish housing projects exist harassment is often a reason given by elderly men for wanting to move into the new project. Harassment in hostels and other temporary accommodation can affect young people and families and on council estates. It seems to especially affect women, single mothers often being specific targets. These contexts suggest that, in many instances, an Irish person is subject to multiple-categorisation in derogatory terms and thus becomes a more likely object of harassment.

### 5.3.3 Police

Police harassment falls into two main categories: that which is targeted and frequently, although by no means always, connected in one way or another with the situation in Northern Ireland (examples of targeted police harassment not directly connected with Northern Ireland include: attacks on people leaving Irish pubs and attacks on Irish homeless); and harassment which is part of a more general response of police officers once they discover that someone they have stopped, picked up, or in some other way come into contact with, is Irish. This section will focus on the targeted harassment which is unconnected with Northern Ireland and that harrassment which occurs more randomly.

All evidence about police harassment connected with Northern Ireland and the operation of the Prevention of Terrorism Act (PTA) is dealt with in a separate section below. The main reason for this is our wish to make clear one aspect which emerged from the interviews: that the harassment that Irish people might experience from the police is not necessarily directly connected to Northern Ireland. Much of it, as indeed with much that takes place in the implementation of the PTA, appears to be generated by more general racialised attitudes towards Irish people and consists of examples of racial harassment as defined by the CRE.

We were given many examples by the thirteen groups who reported police harrassment, the following are some of them:

The view of one large Irish centre in London is that: 'The Police often vent their anger on Irish people on the street'. Recent incidents, prior to the time of our interview included: an Irishman beaten up by the police in the local High Street, he was pulled from his bicycle and abused and assaulted by police officers who made direct and abusive reference to his Irish background, this was witnessed by a third party, and the case is now going to court; an Irish squatter attacked by the police was too scared to make a complaint, he has now been repatriated to Ireland by the centre; an attack by the police on the Irish residents in a local shelter for homeless people.

Another London Irish centre was of the view that the police completely over-react to Irish drunk cases; alternatively Irish people who are injured or ill in public spaces are often assumed to be drunk. One particular incident was

124

mentioned by many of the London agencies and there was considerable publicity about it in the pages of the *Irish Post*. This was the case of Richard O'Brien. Mr O'Brien died during the Easter weekend, 1994, after police officers were called to a disturbance at a venue in Walworth, south London. He was not involved in the fracas and was waiting outside for his wife when the police arrived. Eyewitnesses told the subsequent inquest of how he was arrested and then restrained by officers who carried him face down to a police van and put him inside. His wife who was also put in the van alleged that one officer shouted: 'we can't get the fat Paddy in'. Mr O'Brien died later in police custody. The inquest jury took less than half an hour to reach a unaminous verdict that he was unlawfully killed.

Sir Montague Levine, one of Britain's most senior coroners concluded the inquest by condemning police restraint techniques as 'appalling'. Deborah Coles of the charity Inquest commented that the inquest on Mr O'Brien was 'one of the most shocking cases I have ever sat through and an indictment of the way in which the police treat the Irish community' (*Irish Post*, 18.11.95). A spokesman for one Irish community group afterwards called for British police forces to include the Irish in ethnic monitoring of crime statistics, the Irish Embassy to be immediately notified where Irish people died in custody or in prison, and the abolition of the Prevention of Terrorism Act.

Another agency reported an incident where an Irishman was stopped by security guards in a shop and accused of shoplifting. They badly treated and abused him. When he complained about their treatment of him to the police on their arrival, the police arrested him and held him for five or six hours. Eventually he was let go and not charged; he had been innocent of any offence. In Manchester the main Irish centre's view was that the police are more likely to harass Irish people in what are viewed as the 'rough areas'.

One agency dealing solely with Irish women's issues reported that a frequent circumstance in which women are harassed by the police is when they are stopped for traffic reasons. They described individual incidents where Irish women on being stopped have been subject to racist remarks. In one case, a woman was unreasonably kept in a police station overnight and subject to racist remarks. When she protested the police threatened to charge her, and she made a counter-complaint. After she was released, without charge, a Police inspector visited her home to persuade her to drop the complaint, which she did.

### 5.3.4 Politically-motivated attacks

Some racial harassment of Irish people is directly politically motivated. The examples we were told about nearly always involved the BNP or invoked the BNP. Apart from the example quoted above, these incidents have involved: an Irishwoman living in Tower Hamlets who complained about a neighbour's rubbish. The neighbour's boyfriend threatened to break her windows, called her a 'fucking Irish bastard' and threatened that her flat would be bombed by the BNP. She complained to her landlord, who did not take it seriously. Also in south-east

London, an Irish gay man was attacked by the BNP. Slogans, like 'Irish Gay bastard', were sprayed on his flat and it was smashed up.

### 5.3.5 Attacks on Irish agencies

Part of any account of the racial harassment experienced by the Irish must be details of the abuse and attacks which Irish agencies and/or their workers have experienced. This can take the form of abusive phone-calls, for example, after bomb attacks. Some have received threatening material through the post, for example, BNP newsletters. Individual centres have been physically attacked. For example, after Ireland qualified for the last world cup and England was out of the competition, a window was smashed in a north London agency's premises. There have been a number of attacks on the offices of one Irish Women's organisation. A housing scheme of one of the Irish HAs was attacked and physically defaced, with slogans such as: 'Go home Irish scum'. One consequence of this is that the agency no longer specifies that its schemes are specifically for Irish people on the signs outside the buildings. Burning rags have been put through the letter box of another agency in a north-London borough. Individual workers have been attacked or verbally abused. We were told of examples where Irish workers employed to pursue Irish interests in a statutory body have been subject to sustained harassment and the undermining of their efforts to develop services for Irish people.

### 5.3.6. SUMMARY

- The CRE working definition of racial harassment (1987) included attacks against individuals or groups because of their 'colour, race, nationality or ethnic or national origins'. However, a subsequent clause stressed that the main concern was with 'white' attacks on 'people from black and ethnic communities'.

- Monitoring of racial harassment in practice records violent acts between whites and blacks, regardless of motivation and intention. More subtle forms of harassment, which are also intimidatory, are excluded, for example, graffiti, verbal abuse, disrespect towards cultures, mimicry of accents.

- For all these reasons racial harassment of Irish people is underreported and largely unrecognised.

- However 19/24 community groups recorded reports of harassment from clients. Most frequent forms were by neighbours and the police.

- Verbal abuse was most common, taking the form of name-calling e.g. 'Irish bastard', 'Irish gay bastard', 'dirty Irish bastard', 'Irish pig', 'IRA scum'. It was also expressed in letters and graffiti, and could be accompanied by physical attacks on the person or property. The latter include damage to possessions in hostels, trampling on washing, paint attacks on property, excrement through letterboxes and bullying Irish children about accents.

- Neighbour harassment was greatest in multi-occupancy households, hostels and temporary accommodation, and on council estates. Irish people approached Irish agencies after Local Authorities refused to take action.

- Police harassment falls into two main categories. One is specifically targeted in relation to Northern Ireland and the operation of the Prevention of Terrorism Act. However, the other, which is much more widespread, may be part of a pervasive set of anti-Irish attitudes in the British police force. Many instances were reported to agencies of police attack and abuse of Irish people triggered by hearing Irish accents or names. The recent inquest into the death of Richard O'Brien illustrates a level of apparently acceptable anti-Irish violence by the police which is only occasionally brought to light.

- Far-right political violence, involving the British National Party, is targeted against Irish people.

- Irish agencies reported attacks on their premises and workers, including abusive phone calls, smashed windows and graffiti. These are reported in the Irish Post, generating anxiety in the Irish community, but do not reach the British press.

## 5.4. The Irish and the Criminal Justice System

The Irish are usually ignored in the context of studies of ethnic minorities and the Criminal Justice System. This was frequently mentioned by the people we interviewed for Part Two of the research. Many of them were convinced, usually on the basis of accounts given to them by clients, that this was an area in which there was possibly discriminatory treatment of the Irish.

Under the Criminal Justice Act 1991, the Secretary of State is required to publish such information as he or she considers expedient to help people working in the administration of justice to 'avoid discriminating against people on the grounds of race and sex or any other grounds'. The first report was published in 1992. Throughout the report, ethnicity is defined in terms of colour. The Irish are not considered. In 1988 the CRE funded a large-scale study of the way ethnic minorities are dealt with by the criminal justice system. Comparisons were made between black, Asian and white defendants and, again, there was no consideration of the position of the Irish. The study was carried out in five areas of the English midlands which have large Irish communities. Inevitably, as with other studies, the omission of consideration of the Irish almost certainly distorted the findings. As even a small proportion of Irish people among the 'white' defendants would have led to an underestimate of the real difference between the treatment of black and Asian groups and the remaining 'white' defendants in the study.

A number of studies provide the evidence that there might be issues of differential treatment to be investigated concerning the Irish and the criminal justice system, quite apart from the operation of the Prevention of Terrorism Act. For example, a secondary analysis of the second Islington Crime Survey published in 1992 examined data relating to Irish people. It found that in a large number of areas of police activity - stop-and-search, search of a vehicle, charges following a stop and search - members of the Irish community were more likely to be subject to these activities than non-Irish whites but less likely than members of the black and Asian communities (Woodhouse et al., 1992; see also Southwark Council, 1992).

Other studies, also carried out in London, provide suggestive evidence that: Irish people are disproportionately stopped by the police; are disproportionately the victims of street crime (experiencing street victimisation more than any other ethnic group); are over represented in remands into custody; and are more likely to be jailed than other ethnic groups (see O'Meachair et al., 1994; Young, 1994; Islington Street Crime Survey, 1995; Middlesex Probation Service, 1989/90).

A study which considered sentencing by the origin of the defendant in magistrates courts, found that the Irish received sentences that were the most adversely removed from the recommendation in the probation report. It found that more adult Irish males received immediate sentences of custody than either non-Irish Europeans or African-Caribbean's: 44% Irish as against 28% non Irish. This study has never been published amid many rumours that its Irish content was unexpected. Written by Barbara Hudson, it was an investigation of social enquiry reports in Middlesex in 1989 (Murphy, 1994).

In 1991 the first National Prison Survey was undertaken in England and Wales. It included no mention of the Irish but recorded that 19.4% of prisoners were Catholic which may be indicative of the fact that Irish people are disproportionately represented. Cheyney in a recent report on foreign prisoners, stated that when the needs of foreign prisoners are mentioned that Irish prisoners are never included: 'When foreign prisoners were discussed during the course of this project, it was a common reaction to suggest that the research should not be concerned with prisoners from Ireland' (Cheyney, 1993:5).

Some of the people we interviewed thought there was a widespread resistance to discussing issues about the Irish and the criminal justice system. Undoubtedly, some of this reluctance is explained by the over-determination of all issues connected with the Irish, policing and the courts by Northern Ireland and the Prevention of Terrorism Act.

### 5.4.1 Prevention of Terrorism Act

Most of the Irish community groups we interviewed discussed their concerns about the Prevention of Terrorism Act at some stage in the interviews. It should be noted that our interviews did not include a direct question about the Prevention of Terrorism Act. The issue was raised frequently by the community groups at their own behest.

In the aftermath of what became known as the Birmingham pub bombing in November 1974 the Prevention of Terrorism Act (PTA) was rushed through parliament. At the time there was considerable shock and outrage about the 21 deaths caused by the bomb. The British state, as in the case of any state, has a duty to protect its citizens as best it can. The government's response was to introduce to parliament legislation, the stated aim of which was the prevention of terrorism.

The PTA enacted considerable new powers to control the movement of people between Ireland and Great Britain. The Act provides extensive powers to establish a comprehensive system of port controls and a process of internal exile which gives the Secretary of State the power to remove people who are already living in Great Britain to either Northern Ireland or the Republic of Ireland.

In the 22 years during which it has been implemented the PTA has given rise to increasing concern. It was repeatedly raised with us by the community groups that there is little evidence that it has led to the prevention of terrorism. There is, however, in their view, increasing evidence that racialised stereotypes and problematising discourses about the Irish have led to the toleration of a range of civil liberties abuses sustained by Irish people in Britain through the operation of the PTA. We are heavily in debt to one academic researcher, Paddy Hillyard, of Bristol University, for much of what we record in this section of the report.

Although the legislation was extended in 1984 to cover international terrorism the port powers were devised, and have principally been applied, to control Irish people travelling between Britain and Ireland (Hillyard 1993). In Hillyard's view, and this was also the view of most of the community groups interviewed, the Prevention of Terrorism Act is:

*... a discriminatory piece of law in that it is directed primarily at one section of the travelling public. In effect it means that Irish people in general have a more restrictive set of rights than other travellers. In this sense, the Irish community as a whole is a 'suspect community'.*
(Hillyard 1993:13)

The evidence suggests that the use of the powers is targeted at two particular groups: principally young men living in Ireland and Irish people living in Britain. The introduction of the Prevention of Terrorism Act created a dual system of criminal justice in Britain. Of the 7,052 who had been detained under the Act by the end of 1991, 6,097, or 86%, have been released without any action being taken against them (Hillyard 1993).

130

People are suspects primarily because they are Irish. The usefulness of the PTA has always hinged on the fact that it can suppress political activity, build up information on Irish people and intimidate the whole Irish community (see Lennon et al., 1988, pp. 194-200). It fuels anti-Irish racism, with the oft repeated injunctions of the police after various incidents to 'Keep an eye on Irish neighbours and watch out for Irish accents'.

One of the Irish community groups we interviewed for the research specialised in assisting Irish people picked up under the PTA. The organisation has a network of solicitors throughout the country who are briefed on the PTA and can be contacted if someone is picked up under the Act. The organisation is also approached by people who have been picked up and want to take up issues about the treatment they have received. Consequently, in recent years, the group has developed campaigns to give publicity to examples of harassment of people under the Act. They reported to us that between 1984 and 1992 over 1,000 people were stopped and examined at ports and airports.

These figures hide the major impact of the port powers on the free movement of passengers as they record only those stoppages which lasted longer than one hour. Stoppages of less than one hour do not have to be recorded in the official statistics. The latter constitutes the mass experience of the PTA by Irish people (Hillyard, 1993).

These stoppages can vary from a few minutes where home address, destination, and purpose of visit are collected to occasions which are very frightening and intimidatory experiences for people (involving, for example, strip searching) The former type of stoppage, if not necessarily frightening, both represents massive surveillance of the Irish population and is part of the apparatus which reinforces the adoption of a low public profile amongst the Irish in Britain.

In addition there is considerable hidden surveillance passing through ports and airports between Britain and Ireland. In 1978, it was recorded that 30,000 people had their names checked out on the records held by the National Joint Unit at Scotland yard. This increased to 100,000 in 1989 and then dropped to around 80,000 in 1990. No figures have been published for subsequent years (Hillyard, 1994).

The events in Northern Ireland and bombing campaigns in Britain during the past quarter of a century have often been responded to in the media and more generally in a manner which associates all Irish people as potential terrorists or members or supporters of the IRA. Many groups referred to what was viewed as the blanket categorisation of 'the Irish' as having a unique association with violence and terrorism and they think that the operation of the Prevention of Terrorism Act has been a significant element in encouraging the perception of all Irish people as a suspect community.

The wide powers of examination, arrest and detention, the executive powers to proscribe selected organisations, the range of specific offences under the Acts, the power to issue exclusion orders and a whole new range of provisions covering seizure and investigation, have all played their part in making the Irish living in Britain, or Irish people travelling between Ireland and Britain, a suspect community.

This community is treated in law and in police practices very differently from the rest of the population. To the extent that the legislation is principally directed at Irish people, it is an example of institutionalised racism. (Hillyard, 1993: 258-9)

Hillyard's study of the Prevention of Terrorism Act argues that not only have the Irish been constructed as a suspect people, but the Act has also criminalised Irish people living in Britain. He is using the term 'criminalised' in the sense of describing how certain categories of people are drawn into the criminal justice system simply because of their status and irrespective of their behaviour. Evidence for this was also provided by a number of the community groups interviewed.

The impact of the legislation was seen in two ways in particular. It reinforced in a uniform way the tendency of Irish people to 'keep their heads down'. The corollary of this is that when Irish people do get together they are frequently seen as 'IRA'. This constant linkage of any Irish person or all Irish people with the IRA has in part been possible because the Irish have been a hidden, unrecognised community who in particular have kept a very low profile and silence about Northern Ireland.

There is evidence that the police have systematically over the years used the Act to arrest and harass people who were active politically regardless of any evidence that they had any connection with terrorist activities. The extent to which the existence of the legislation has both exposed Irish people to blanket stereotyping and, simultaneously, constrained not just political activities but many cultural activities is hard to underestimate. This view was put to us repeatedly in our interviews with community groups.

The operation of the Prevention of Terrorism Act by the police, as well as other evidence of harassment of Irish people, gives rise to concern that the legislation and its implementation reinforces a climate within the police service in which racialised stereotyping of the Irish is not uncommon.

One agency reported that, when contacting the police by telephone on behalf of a client, the police officer who dealt with the matter told the agency staff member an anti-Irish joke. An official complaint was lodged after the incident. It is the licence that the police officer concerned felt free to exercise in telling an anti-Irish joke, even to an Irish organisation, which is the striking feature of this example. Although the research on the Irish and the criminal justice system is not extensive, that which does exist gives rise to serious concern about the possibility that more widespread anti-Irish discriminatory practices might exist in this arena.

132

### 5.4.2. SUMMARY

- The Irish are ignored in most studies of ethnic minorities and the criminal justice system despite well-publicised cases of miscarriages of justice. The limited research available suggests, however, that the Irish may well be subject to unequal treatment in policing and court practices.

- The Prevention of Terrorism Act has reduced the civil liberties of Irish people in Britain, but this is tolerated because of racialised stereotypes. The Irish in Britain are a 'suspect community'. The PTA has operated to intimidate the community as a whole.

- Mass experience of the PTA is stoppages at ports and airports of under one hour, which are not recorded in official statistics. They vary from brief questioning to frightening experiences, such as strip searching.

- The impact of the legislation is seen in two ways. First, it reinforces in a uniform way the tendency of Irish people to 'keep their heads down'. Second, when Irish people do get together they are seen as 'IRA'. This constrains group activity of all kinds, including social and cultural events.

- The PTA appears to reinforce racial stereotyping of the Irish by the police service.

## 5.5. Travellers

Irish Travellers are one of a number of groups who fall under the definition of 'Gypsies' given in the 1968 Caravan Sites Act. Gypsies were defined as including 'persons of nomadic habit of life, whatever their race or origin but does not include members of an organised group of travelling showmen or of persons engaged in travelling circuses, travelling together as such'. The OPCS has suggested that the category 'Gypsies' includes Romany Gypsies, Irish Travellers, Long Distance Travellers, Gypsies who rarely travel and new Age Travellers (Green, 1991). As was shown in Part One (section 3.1.5), however, statistics on numbers in all these groups are highly inaccurate. The prejudice, discrimination and ill-treatment that Travellers experience has been well documented elsewhere (LIWC, 1995).

Our concern in the interviews with Irish community groups was to establish whether the experience of Irish Travellers was significantly different from the rest of the Irish population and whether the discrimination that the Travellers experience is due primarily to their way of life or to their Irishness.

The distinction is often made between 'real' gypsies on the one hand and Travellers on the other hand. The latter, as a number of groups we interviewed commented, are often assumed to be Irish, and may be referred to as 'Irish Tinkers'. One group, dealing specifically with gypsies and Travellers, reported that some 'real' gypsies discriminate against Irish Travellers and we were told that the National Gypsy Council has equated Irish Travellers with a 'hooligan element'. However, in other instances alliances have been made between gypsies and Irish Travellers.

It is noteworthy that there are very few 'No Gypsy' signs, but what exist in great profusion are 'No Travellers' signs. New Age Travellers are also differentiated from Irish Travellers. New Age Travellers are not liked either, but this is not based on a national antipathy.

In all but one case the agencies interviewed were of the view that the experience of Irish Travellers was markedly worse than the experience of other Irish people. However, most of the agencies consulted estimated that both their Irishness and their way of life were responsible for the negative experiences of Irish Travellers. This seemed to be borne out by the extent to which Irish Travellers are distinguished from other Travellers and gypsies.

The differentiation that takes place between Irish Travellers and other gypsies and Travellers often revolves around the Irish Travellers being designated as dirty and as unruly troublemakers. It is Irish Travellers who are likely to be depicted as 'dirty smelly thieving tinkers'. Tinkers are not thought of as 'real' gypsies.

This articulation of their Irishness with their way of life means that Irish Travellers experience a double discrimination. They could also be said to be doubly discriminated against in the sense that they experience hostile treatment from Irish people as well as from other people living in Britain.

It would seem that Irish Travellers are at the bottom of the Irish hierarchy both in the perceptions of many British people and of many Irish people themselves (see McVeigh, 1992 for an account of the hostility of the Irish to their compatriots who have a travelling lifestyle). The reading and writing difficulties that Travellers often have means they are susceptible to being classified as stupid and quite often accused of fraud and often depicted as cunning liars. These are stereotypes which can be applied to the Irish as a whole, as are the epithets of 'bog Irish' and 'dirty Irish'.

This hostility of Irish people in Britain towards Irish Travellers is also propelled, in the view of those we interviewed who work with Travellers, by the need to distance themselves from the negative stereotypes about the Irish which are part of British culture and the fact that these stereotypes are applied most systematically to Irish Travellers.

As one agency staff member put it, the experience of Irish people in general and Irish Travellers in particular is linked as if it was 'a gradient with a steep drop at the end'. Differentiation is, undoubtedly, made between the 'decent' or 'respectable' Irish and 'the Travellers'. The impact of this, was in his view, that it acted as a mechanism of control over other Irish people who fear that they will be classified as the 'dirty Irish'.

Many agencies commented on the extra difficulties that Travellers have in gaining either benefits or housing. Little allowance is made by statutory bodies for their culture and lifestyle and the difficulties that they may have in satisfying the regulations and documentary requirements which afford access to the services which the Travellers need. For example, Travellers often have difficulties proving their identity.

The one document they are most likely to possess is a baptismal certificate. However, this is rarely sufficient to fulfil the documentary requirements because benefit staff view these as an example of an easily forged document.

Most agencies were convinced that automatically suspecting Travellers of fraud was seen to be a completely acceptable attitude by staff dealing with benefit and housing applicants.

Travellers meet hostility in most contexts. For example, one Irish agency in London tried to get a Traveller woman fleeing domestic violence with her children accepted by the local women's refuge. The refuge refused, saying: 'these people wreck the joint'. On being challenged by the Irish worker about this attitude, the refuge did then change it's decision and accepted the woman.

Irish Travellers were described as regularly having difficulties in: getting their children into schools; in obtaining car insurance; in accessing the health service; in the courts; and in obtaining housing.

The latter is particularly contentious as many Travellers are forced to seek housing because very few local authorities have ever fulfilled their obligations to provide sites under the 1968 Caravans Act. However, while few sites are provided there is also a dearth of assistance given to Travellers in making the

135

transition to a settled way of life. The scrutiny to which Irish Travellers are subject was viewed by some agencies to be an instrument for making the Travellers feel uncomfortable and thus a means of encouraging them to move on and out of their area.

The chronic shortage of legal halting sites and facilities bring Travellers into conflict with the law. The legislation set out in the new Criminal Justice Act will make the position of Travellers worse. The new Act removes the duty from local authorities to provide designated sites and will also withdraw central government funding. The Criminal Justice and Public Order Act, 1994, and its effects on Travellers was mentioned specifically a number of times by the groups interviewed. The Act is seen as the beginning of the end for the Traveller because it will legitimise the discrimination that already exists. The view of the agencies who most regularly dealt with Travellers' concerns was that the repeal of the 1968 Caravan Act and the Criminal Justice Act are going to have a disastrous effect on travelling people and especially the children (LIWC, 1995).

### 5.5.1. SUMMARY

- A distinction is popularly made between 'real gypsies' and Travellers, who are often assumed to be Irish. 'No Travellers' signs are widespread and Travellers are stereotyped as dirty and as unruly troublemakers.

- Most agencies believed that the negative experiences of Irish Travellers stemmed both from their Irishness and their way of life.

- Travellers also experience double discrimination by receiving hostile treatment from Irish people as well as other residents in Britain. Settled Irish people feel the need to distance themselves from the anti-Irish stereotypes which are most systematically applied to Irish Travellers.

- Travellers experience extra difficulties in gaining benefits and access to housing. Identity documents are often seen as forgeries. Other difficulties concern school places for children, treatment in courts, car insurance, healthcare and lack of assistance in making the transition to a settled way of life.

# 6. Scotland

## 6.1 The Irish in Scotland

Scotland is the site of an historically very important migration of Irish people but it is also the part of Britain with the most rapidly declining numbers of Irish-born in its population. In 1991, the Irish-born at 49,184 represented a mere 32.8% of their equivalent number in 1881. The population decline has been especially sharp since 1981 (-19%). Nevertheless, Scotland was included in the research because of the past heavy settlement and because we thought it was important to ascertain the extent to which the issues regarding racism and discrimination towards Irish people which emerged in stage two of the fieldwork in England were mirrored or not in Scotland.

We approached stage two of the research differently in Scotland. The main reason for this is that we discovered no specifically Irish organisation dispensing a front-line service of advice to Irish people in Glasgow. It could have been concluded that the non-existence of such organisations indicated the absence of problems or the lack of need for ethnic specific advice for Irish people in Scotland. Our own knowledge of Scotland (based on previous visits and garnered from sources such as Bradley, 1993, Devine, 1991, Gallagher, 1987, Walker, 1995) suggested, however, that the situation was not that straight-forward. In particular, it seemed important to explore two phenomena: the extent to which contemporary anti-Catholicism in Scotland is implicitly anti-Irish; and the extent to which sectarian discrimination is still a significant factor in modern Scotland.

## 6.2 Methodology

The resources of this research project did not extend to more than one visit to Scotland. For reasons given earlier, we intended to carry out interviews in Glasgow alone, in the event a short period of time was also spent in Edinburgh. In the absence of the type of Irish organisations to interview in the same manner as in other British cities we adopted a different approach in Glasgow and Edinburgh.

We began by approaching both academic- and community-based contacts that the researchers had in Glasgow. This process suggested a range of individuals and of organisations to approach for interviews. In the event we interviewed personnel from four different race equality organisations in the two cities as well as a number of academics who were either of Irish descent themselves or whose specialist research area was either the Irish in Scotland or ethnic minorities in Scotland. In addition, we were able to interview a number of people who are members of the small number of Irish cultural and political organisations that exist in Glasgow and Edinburgh.

The interviews were semi-structured as no attempt was being made to conduct systematic comparisons as in the case of the sample in England. The following topics were discussed with interviewees as appropriate: the relationship between anti-Catholicism and anti-Irishness; what forms anti-Catholicism currently takes; what forms anti-Irishness takes; examples of prejudice and/or structural discrimination in the workplace, education, housing, claiming benefits; the police and community relations; whether anti-Irish jokes are widespread in Scotland; people's views on the Monksland controversy; and details of how the PTA operated in Scotland.

We would like to stress two aspects of this study of Scotland:

i) that when asked about the Irish in Scotland the overwhelming majority of those we interviewed, regardless of whether they personally had any Irish connections themselves or not, assumed this was a reference to people of Irish Catholic descent;

ii) that we did not carry out a systematic survey and the discussion below is necessarily tentative but may be useful in suggesting some areas of concern for people of Irish Catholic descent in Scotland today; and more generally that sectarianism continues to be a factor in Scottish society in certain contexts.

## 6.3 The historical significance of anti-Irishness and anti-Catholicism in Scotland

Orangeism first came to Scotland after 1789, brought over by soldiers of the Scottish Fencibles sent to Ireland to quell the United Irishmen's rebellion. It took hold in the western and central industrial lowlands where it gave expression to anti-Catholicism and provided a 'fraternal organisation in which men who lived a hard and unrewarding life, often new to the impersonality of the town and the factory, could develop their sense of self-worth and self-confidence' (Bruce 1990:233). With massive Irish Catholic immigration the local lodge became a vehicle of social exclusion and enabled Protestant workers to reinforce their grip on jobs which carried higher economic rewards or greater security than those available to the immigrants. Ties were close between Scotland and Ulster, including between Irish and Scottish Presbyterianism. This meant that Protestant migrants from Ireland became part of the majority community more easily in Scotland than elsewhere in Britain. It was Irish Catholic migrants who were constituted as a social and political threat.

Miles and Dunlop (1986) argue that the political and ideological consequences of reactions to 19th-century Irish migration to Scotland resulted in the institutionalisation of a cultural signification within the process of the reproduction of class relations in Scotland. This constituted an important part of the context within which classes were formed. Thus, the predominant mode of differentiation in the Scottish working class has remained that between Protestants and Catholics. Relations between Protestants and Catholics are referred to as 'the sectarian problem'. Their view is that religious affiliation may be the principal factor in this differentiation but the idea of 'race' has also been articulated consistently by various factors. Underlying the religious signification in their view, therefore, lies a secondary process of racialisation.

Amongst the institutional mechanisms which sustain this process of signification and racialisation is the segregated, denominational system of education. Separate schools are important for reproducing religious and cultural differentiation. The 1918 Education (Scotland) Act had resolved the problem of incorporating the large Irish Catholic population of Scotland within a national system but did so by the means of full state funding for segregated education. It attracted widespread opposition in the inter-war years. For example, in 1923 the Church of Scotland published a report on the Act with the title, *The menace of the Irish race to our Scottish nationality* (Miles & Dunlop, 1986:27). The presence of the Irish and the increasing influence of the Catholic Church were problematised as a threat to the unity and homogeneity of the Scottish people. Since then, both the activities of militant Protestantism (see Miles & Dunlop, 1986) and the rivalry of Celtic and Rangers (see Bradley, 1993, Murray, 1984) have reproduced this primary cleavage within the Scottish working class. For example, the articulation of religion and national identity is evident at every Celtic and Rangers match. It has been reported that at Rangers matches the songs take the form of oaths against the Pope and the IRA; whereas at Celtic matches the songs are against the Queen and the UDA (McCann, 1988:44).

Miles and Dunlop are arguing, therefore, that the language and tenets of anti-Catholicism in Scotland this century (especially in the first half of the century) have frequently utilised notions of Irish Catholics as an alien 'race'. Further, they point out that what distinguishes Scotland is the absence of a racialisation of the political process since 1945 (primarily it is argued because of low inward migration of New Commonwealth migrants), in the way that occurred in England, rather than an absence of racism per se. Nor was discrimination absent as a phenomenon. In the 1940s and the immediate post-war period, it was still hard to obtain jobs as a Roman Catholic, especially in the skilled trades, for example in Singer Sewing Machine shops. Catholics tended not to pursue jobs as engineers, firemen, technicians, printers and quantity surveyors because of the received wisdom that these were areas of employment where it was very difficult for Catholics to gain access (Gallagher, 1987). Areas like the BBC were also almost totally closed to Catholics until the late 1950s (Radio Scotland, see below). This was an era when support for Rangers was characterised by a celebration of Scottishness which was underpinned by a strong unionism or loyalism (Walker, 1990).

Many academic accounts have commented on how the profusion of 'No Irish need apply' or 'No Catholics' signs created a ghetto, tribal loyalty amongst Irish Catholics in Scotland. This came out clearly in the oral history testimonies in a Radio Scotland programme about Irish Catholics in Scotland (*Paddy Tampson's Bairns*) broadcast in 1995. As Bernard Aspinwall of Glasgow University commented on the programme, without Irish immigration the Catholic Church would have been infinitely smaller and infinitely more respectable. Hostility to Irish Catholics had been generated for centuries as part of a Presbyterian cultural nationalism that underpinned Scottish identity. Down the years this ideology has been reinforced by the influence of freemasonry in Scotland which facilitated collective discrimination against Catholics (Finn, 1990).

Most contemporary discussions about sectarianism both in the media and in academic accounts of Scottish society firmly place it as a phenomenon which has been declining rapidly since the 1960s. Many signifiers are pointed to in demonstrating the veracity of this analysis. For example, the Pope's visit to Scotland in 1982 went off peacefully. He attracted 300,000, the biggest ever crowd in Scottish history, to Bellahuston Park. During his visit he constantly emphasised that Roman Catholicism was an authentic and integral part of the traditions of Scotland and commentators credited his visit with completing the rehabilitation of the Catholic Church in Scotland (Gallagher, 1987). Sectarianism is also seen as having been undermined by shortages in skilled labour during the 1960s. The discriminatory practices of many employers therefore became counter-productive. Catholics who benefited from the post-war welfare and education reforms, being a largely working class community, eventually did well in the expansion of the service sector.

Consequently, as Walker (1995) comments, until recently the assumptions of many were that sectarianism had become largely defunct, confined now to the arena of football. However, both our own interviews and some recent events suggest that there continues to be some salience in assessing the continuing impact of this cleavage in Scottish society. This was suggested in 1994 with the emergence of the political scandal known as 'Monkslandgate': the alleged corruption and malpractice's of the Labour-controlled Monksland District Council. The Council was charged with religious sectarianism: that Catholic Labour councillors had favoured their co-religionists in matters of employment and patronage and this had resulted in the heavily Catholic-populated areas of the district receiving grants and investment at the expense of others. The media described this as 'Catholic Coatbridge' benefiting at the expense of 'Protestant Airdrie' (Walker 1995).

Monksland District Council fell within the constituency of the late John Smith. The Monksland East by-election took place on 30 June 1994 and in the course of a fierce campaign many charges of sectarianism were exchanged particularly between the Labour and Scottish National parties. An article in the *Scotsman* (28.6.94) commented that sectarianism was thought to be a long dead aspect of Scottish politics but that the by-election had brought it to the surface and had explosively shown that it was a live issue in voters' minds. The same report included the findings of an opinion poll a couple of days before the election. This showed that of the Catholics surveyed in the constituency 85% intended to vote Labour and among the Protestants, 65% said they were backing the SNP and 24% Labour. The newspaper concluded that religion, rather than social class, age or home ownership was the clearest identifier of how people were likely to vote.

Walker comments that the SNP was quite clearly the beneficiary of a massive protest vote as a 16,000 Labour majority just survived but was reduced to a 1,640 majority over the Nationalists. The SNP did well in the Airdrie area as people there felt discriminated against:

> *Since the 1960s the perception among many Protestants in certain areas has been one of local Catholic politicians looking after their own community. To a long history of Catholic grievances were added those of some Protestants who felt marginalised in a rapidly-changing society in which the Catholic community profile enlarged. In terms of identity, the Catholics could appear to have maintained a coherence and a vigour in the midst of social, economic and demographic changes which had weakened to a large extent the Protestant self-image, particularly among the working class* .
> (Walker, 1995:182)

The articulation of religion and national identity in Scotland has made impregnable a considerable proportion of the Labour vote since the 1920s. Many people of Irish Catholic descent who vote Labour do not do so solely on class grounds. It has been argued that, certainly in the past, many would have feared an SNP victory as it could give expression to the anti-Catholicism and anti-Irishness with which Scottish nationalism has been associated (Miles and Dunlop, 1986). The articulation of religion and national identity in explaining Catholic support for Labour is illustrated by a recent study of football fans in Scotland. Celtic fans, who are predominantly of an Irish Catholic heritage, exhibited: the lowest support for the SNP, the strongest support for the Labour party, a high degree of support for a united Ireland and the weakest support for the Scottish national team, with over half giving their allegiance to the Republic of Ireland team (Bradley, 1993).

## 6.4 Presentation of Interview Data

Many of the people we interviewed commented on both the similarities and differences between the situation in Scotland compared with England. One over-riding similarity between Scotland and England is that, in the former just as in the latter, ethnic minorities are considered to be 'black', principally the term is used to refer to Asians in Scotland. Racism is viewed not only as a black/white issue but also by many people as an English problem rather than a Scottish one. A number of the professionals working in the race equality field stressed that this was a perspective they often encountered and it made their work very difficult.

Many of those interviewed thought, on the other hand, that many Scottish people were very aware of the sectarian divisions in the society but thought of this as something totally different. Sectarianism involved religion and was political and therefore was completely distinct from racism. It should be emphasised that by no means all the people we interviewed held this view, it was their assessment of how things were generally viewed in Scotland.

One Irish worker in a race equality organisation described how, as the Irish are white, they are assumed not to be subject to racism, although it was acknowledged by her fellow workers that they might be subject to prejudice.

This, however, was not viewed as the concern of a race equality council. She commented that 'tons of money is spent on anti-racist training which regenerates this perspective'. It is also apparently argued that, because very few Irish groups affiliate to the race equality councils, this must mean they do not have any problems.

In the interviewee's opinion based on working in the race equality field, there would be no reason why any Irish group would affiliate when the concerns of the council are entirely presented within a framework of dealing with the racism and discrimination experienced by black people in Scotland. Also any Irish person who did approach a race equality council would not necessarily receive a constructive response. An example was given to us of an anti-Catholic local councillor, who made speeches against 'papists', who also sat on the Executive of a race equality unit. Three separate interviewees referred to this example as being detrimental to the work of the particular race equality unit.

Contrasted with this lack of connection between Irish issues and the race equality units in Scotland is that Irish people do approach the CRE in Edinburgh with complaints about the treatment they have experienced. The legal officer of the CRE in Scotland provided details of the small number of cases which have been brought to her attention in the last three years. This contrasted with none in the previous two years. Cases have included complaints about less favourable treatment or racial abuse in public settings such as hotels. Or complaints about unfair dismissal or failure to hire on racial grounds. She commented that it was only in the last couple of years that there had been any public profile for the fact that the CRE dealt with Irish cases. In particular she thought the publicity that the Trevor McAuley case stimulated in 1994 had significantly raised the profile of an Irish dimension to the CRE's work. She was quite clear that, if an Irish person was treated in a disadvantageous way because of their Irishness, then it was covered by the 1976 Act.

The officers of the Race Equality Unit of Glasgow District Council were specifically told by senior officers when the unit was set up that they were not to deal with issues related to Protestant versus Catholic sectarianism. The justification for this was that sectarianism was about religion and therefore did not come under their remit which was to deal with issues of racism involving visible difference. Glasgow District Council's equal opportunities policy states that: 'there shall be no discrimination on the grounds of colour, race, nationality, ethnic or national origin, religion, social background, marital status, sex, age or disability'. Religion is therefore included in the policy, as are ethnic and national origins. It was not clear, however, how anyone would raise issues of discrimination on any of those three counts if they were not perceived as falling into the category of 'visibly different'. The view was expressed to us by one of the race equality officers that the 1976 Act should be extended to include religious discrimination. In this officer's view it was arguable not only because of the position of Irish Catholics in Scotland but because of the prejudice and discrimination that Jews in Scotland experience.

The differentiation of religious discrimination from racism is a critical part of the discourses in Scotland about ethnic cleavages in Scottish society. This emerged strongly from our interviews. Either the interviewee held that view themselves, or if not, they informed us it was a dominant view and gave reasons why they viewed it as problematic. The differentiation of sectarianism from racism depends on an understanding of racism as a phenomenon solely concerned with visible difference. However, recognition of the existence of cultural racisms means that any group which has been located in ethnic terms can be subjected to 'racism' as a form of exclusion (Anthias & Yuval-Davis, 1992). Given that anti-Catholicism can be generated quite autonomously from any ethnic identification, the point at issue becomes the relationship between anti-Irishness and anti-Catholicism in Scotland.

One academic we interviewed at Glasgow Caledonian University summed up the relationship in Scotland as: 'anti-Catholicism is the peg on which to hook anti-Irish attitudes'. He saw anti-Catholicism as implicitly anti-Irish in Scotland and this could be demonstrated in the linkages made in the slogans and abuse which were still common at football matches and in the calls of marching bands which he remembered vividly from growing up in rural Ayrshire. Another interviewee saw Catholicism and the Irish as 'totally intertwined' in public consciousness in Scotland and could not imagine how they could be separated. Frequently in the interviews people referred to football as a site of both these phenomena.

In particular, a number of people, usually those who were critical that understandings of racism in Scotland did not include sectarianism, commented on the fact that the British National Party (BNP) organises in Scotland on the basis of anti-Catholic and pro-Unionist views. This is a far more fruitful basis for the BNP to drum up support than the white/black dichotomies utilised elsewhere. The latter are used, however, but usually linked to statements which are implicitly anti-Irish. Slogan used include: 'Hang the IRA, Keep Britain White' or 'Keep Ulster British, Kick Blacks out of Britain'.

The Community Relations Council in Glasgow informed us of their concerns about fascists organising in the city, this has been going on around Ibrox (the Rangers' ground) for over ten years. There are constant linkages being made between Protestant sectarianism and fascism. In the view of a leading officer of the Council, the Rangers/Celtic matches are the potential flash point for a big racial incident in Scotland. An academic at Glasgow Caledonian University who has studied the membership of far-right groups in Scotland pointed out that in Glasgow the memberships of the UDA and the BNP are synonymous. John Tyndall had been invited up to speak at meetings on St. Andrews Day for a number of years in the recent past. His research indicated that the meetings have attracted a lot of extreme members of the Orange Order. Mostly they are men and primarily in two age groups: 16-22 years and 50-60 years.

These comments were made as part of more general assessments given to us of the continuing influence of the Orange Lodge in Scotland. An academic whose specialist area is the Orange Lodge pointed out that there are still hundreds of

Lodge branches in Scotland and that their membership is in excess of that of the Labour party. A school teacher we interviewed described how in the area in which his family lives on Glasgow's south side there are Orange Lodge bands marching in streets, with often sizeable Catholic populations, every week of the year. Many of the Catholics, in his view, living in these areas viewed this as, at best, a provocative practice.

Walker (1995) in explanation of these trends argues that resentments over loss of identity, or feelings of insecurity about identity in the context of a perception of a powerful Catholic presence, could draw some towards the militant Protestantism of Loyalist flute bands and paramilitary style groups (discountenanced by the Official Orange Order) which take their inspiration from Northern Ireland. In some ways this is also the case on the Catholic side where republican bands and 'Connolly Societies' attempt to bring about a closer identification among Scottish Catholics with the Nationalist minority in Northern Ireland.

This highlights the potential influence of events in Northern Ireland on Scottish society. The picture which emerged from across the range of interviewees was of there being a general consensus in Scotland to maintain as much distance as possible between what was happening in Northern Ireland and Scotland. Efforts to ensure this insulation have been expended by a variety of authorities. For example, one Glasgow-based academic described how the police have kept 'a deliberate lid' on all sectarian attacks in recent years because they are fearful of the Northern Ireland situation spilling over to Scotland. On Radio Scotland recently, a broadcaster interviewed for the programme on Irish Catholics described what he viewed as the very restrained reporting of Northern Ireland in the Scottish press and the way in which this had contributed to the insulation of Scotland from events across the water.

Few people would disagree that it is desirable that the equivalent crisis which has characterised Northern Ireland for the past three decades should not erupt elsewhere. On the other hand, not all the people we interviewed contemplated the practices of insulating Scotland from Northern Ireland with unqualified approval. It enabled the notion that sectarianism has faded in Scotland to go unchallenged in the public sphere. One of the unfortunate consequences in their view was that it resulted in the level of harassment that Irish Catholics can experience in Scotland going unrecognised. In the view of a small number of our interviewees, the Monksland scandal would not have received the publicity it did if the situation had been reversed. That is if it had been an example of the practice of Protestants discriminating against Catholics.

One consequence of the Northern Ireland situation was reported by everyone we spoke to who had any Irish connections or contacts: the 'heads down' approach of most Irish Catholics about anything political, in the broadest sense of the term. The officer of the Community Relations Council described how attempts are made to include the Irish in various multi-cultural festivals but it has proved difficult to get people to participate for two reasons. One is because anything ethnic is presumed to be just for black people. The other reason is because in her experience Irish people 'keep their heads down' because they are terrified of being called 'IRA' and think anything Irish might be seen that way. She noted however that this did not mean people had erased their culture or political beliefs, it was public expression of them that had been inhibited.

The operation of the Prevention of Terrorism Act in Scotland has obviously contributed to this low profile of Irish Catholics as it has in the rest of Britain. We were told that everyone in one Irish political organisation in Edinburgh has been on the receiving end of the attention of the police. One member of the organisation we interviewed is stopped every time he goes to Ireland by plane, but has never been charged with any offense. The implication that a number of people drew from this is that you have to be prepared for a significant degree of surveillance and interference if you get involved with Irish politics.

All references to Irish Catholics in this account are, as indicated earlier, to Catholics of Irish descent. Most are probably second, third and fourth generation. This represents a major difference compared with our account of England. As most people are descended from migrants of an earlier era when identification with the Catholic church was strong this has remained as an essential element in the ethnic culture and identity to a significantly greater extent than in England. Consequently, recent research in Scotland indicates that there is a continuing attachment to Catholic schools amongst this community and a belief that religious discrimination still operates in the field of employment (Bradley, 1996).

Every person we interviewed who was an Irish Catholic or had significant contacts with or academic knowledge of Irish Catholics in Scotland stated that they either suspected there continued to be discrimination in employment or that they knew others who had cause to believe it. In a survey carried out in 1990 almost half the Catholic church attenders believed that Protestants rather than Catholics would be favoured in the workplace; nearly three quarters of Celtic fans believed so with about the same figures for other Irish bodies surveyed. One third of Rangers fans but only 10% of Church of Scotland attenders also thought that Protestants would be likely to more advantaged than Catholics in employment (Bradley, 1993).

In our interviews certain occupational sectors were singled out as the most likely sites of continued discrimination in access to employment or promotion. Banks and the police force were mentioned by everyone, the view was that they should be investigated for their policies in hiring but especially in promotion. One recent example was given to us of a young woman working for a bank who was told that with her (very Irish) name she would not have a hope of promotion. A number of people commented that they thought in general that white collar and management jobs were more likely sites for these practices today compared with manual jobs in the past. If this was true it could be a response to the greater social mobility of Catholics in the past 30 years.

There is no doubt that there is less discrimination in Scotland than there used to be. What is far less certain is that discrimination on the basis of religion, a signifier of ethnicity, has been eradicated to the extent many academic accounts

146

assume. Name and in particular schooling continue to be efficient signifiers of this cleavage in Scottish society. Name can indicate Irish origin and schools indicate a Catholic (usually of Irish descent); the reverse also applies for the Protestant in Scotland. This is another difference with England where it is accent above all else which is the identifier of Irishness, with a range of secondary signifiers, including names.

Walker (1995) would caution against reading too much into the evidence about continuing sectarianism in Scotland. This is because Protestants and Catholics do not lead the rigidly segregated lives which are a feature of the situation in Northern Ireland. Also Lanarkshire, the area in which the Monksland East constituency is situated is the historical cock-pit of sectarian friction in Scotland and is in no way typical of large parts of the country. Thus he concludes that Scottish civil society is relatively healthy and its political culture now largely inimical to sectarianism at least at national level. Scotland is a much less isolated society than Northern Ireland and its level of interaction with the rest of Britain forms a counterweight to any local sectarian squabbling.

That said, it was noticeable that a majority of the people we interviewed, in particular, those of Irish Catholic descent and some of those working in the race equality field who had become concerned about these issues, welcomed the fact that we had included Scotland in this report and felt that there were issues that warranted further investigation.

## 6.5 SUMMARY

- There is a long history of substantial Irish migration to Scotland, much greater in the past than in the post-1945 period. The main area of settlement was Lanarkshire and greater Glasgow.

- As a consequence there has been an important cultural dimension in the reproduction of class relations in Scotland. The predominant mode of differentiation has been that between Protestant and Catholics, referred to as 'the sectarian problem', but this is associated with a process of racialisation.

- 'Sectarian' differences are sustained particularly by segregated denominational schooling and football allegiances.

- Sectarianism is seen as distinct from racism in Scotland, the latter being firmly associated with black/white issues. Irish experiences are not seen as appropriate to the work of the race equality units, though a few cases have been brought to the CRE in Edinburgh recently.

- However, the BNP argues on anti-Catholic/pro-Unionist lines in Scotland rather than black/white ones. Orange Lodges are also numerous and bands march regularly in the streets of Glasgow's south side.

- Fears of a 'spillover' from Northern Ireland have led to attempts to distance Scotland from events there. This has reinforced the adoption of a low profile by Catholics and non-recognition of any continuing harassment.

- All evidence points to less sectarian discrimination in Scotland than before the 1960s, however, there is less certainty that discrimination on the basis of religion, a signifier of ethnicity, has been eradicated.

- There is evidence suggestive of the continued salience of sectarian discrimination. In the Monksland scandal (1994) the Labour District Council was accused of favouring Catholic co-religionists. Belief that anti-Catholic discrimination exists in certain sectors of employment was widespread amongst interviewees. Sites mentioned included white collar and management jobs such as banks and the police service. Promotion was seen as an area particularly in need of investigation.

# 7. Conclusion

Part Two of the Report has presented the findings of the in-depth interviews with staff in Irish community and welfare groups and it has sought to bring together much of the available published evidence about discrimination and the Irish. The data that the groups gave us primarily concerns three contexts in which Irish people may experience discrimination: in accessing services from statutory bodies and voluntary organisations; incidents involving racial harassment; and experiences in the criminal justice system.

There was also considerable, to some extent, separate reference to the contexts in which Irish Travellers experience discrimination. From this evidence, therefore, it is possible to conclude with some general points that may help to develop a provisional typology of the possible discriminatory and exclusionary practices which operate in relation to the Irish.

This research reveals that there is a universal call by Irish community and advice groups for ethnic monitoring of Irish needs. Indeed, the lack of monitoring itself is viewed by a number of agencies as a form of indirect discrimination. The lack of monitoring places many obstacles in the path of Irish community and welfare groups who try to gain recognition from service providers of the needs of their Irish clients.

The reason for these difficulties lies in assumptions made about Irish people because they are the same colour as those who are taken to be the indigenous population. The Irish are assumed to fall into that category of people, 'whites', who do not experience unequal opportunities in access to and receipt of services and in employment due to ethnic differentiation or racial discrimination.

The absence and invisibility of the Irish in official discourse has had profound implications for Irish organisations in their efforts to address the needs of Irish people in Britain. Visibility and invisibility are socially constructed and can change over time.

Our analysis indicates that the invisibility of the Irish as a ethnic minority group forms a significant aspect of a myth of cultural homogeneity encompassing the whole of the British Isles. This myth developed as part of the British State's response to immigration in the 1950-60s.

The  myth of homogeneity consists of the following notions: that all the heterogeneous cultures, regions and nations of the United Kingdom form a homogenous whole; that the Republic of Ireland as part of the British Isles is broadly within this same cultural domain; and that racism and discrimination are only experienced by people who are visibly different.

The in-depth interviews with the professionals who staff Irish community groups make it clear that the lack of monitoring of Irish needs and the difficulties, hostility and incredulity that groups experience when raising Irish issues all stem from these basic assumptions about the parameters and contours of what constitutes a ethnic minority group in Britain.

The interviews contain more comment about the absence of the Irish from the plans of voluntary bodies or statutory organisations and the denial of the cultural specificity of the Irish than any other issue. Many statutory bodies appear to be involved in a wide-scale process of marginalising the Irish, the consequence of which is to reinforce Irish invisibility as a ethnic minority group.

This research therefore strongly indicates that the denial of the specificity of Irish needs and the refusal to countenance that there could be an Irish dimension to a range of social issues is an ingrained predisposition of many professionals working in voluntary agencies and statutory bodies.

This is a discriminatory practice and ignores the fact that there have been successful cases brought by the CRE that have established that Irish people are subject to racial discrimination.

Our evidence suggests that there are four discriminatory and exclusionary practices which operate in relation to service provision for Irish people. All four practices are predicated on the denial of Irish specificity as described above:

i) The absence of Irish issues in the plans for service provision of statutory bodies and voluntary organisations; this is compounded in many cases by a lack of consultation with local Irish groups;

ii) The non-recognition of the existence of anti-Irish racism leads to a 'battle' in most contexts to raise Irish issues;

iii) The lack of provision of a culturally sensitive service for the Irish in Britain by service providers;

iv) The existence of stereotyped responses to Irish clients by service providers, the most common being assumptions that the Irish are drunks, feckless and fraudsters; these stereotypes can lead to specific exclusionary practices.

Racial harassment of Irish people was an area of considerable concern, in particular because it seems to be underreported and largely unrecognised. What the incidents reported to the community groups indicate is that the Irish are sufficiently differentiated from other people to be the specific object of harassment by various groups, in particular by their neighbours and the police.

Attacks are accompanied by verbal or written abuse which singles out the Irishness of the person being attacked and often links it to other derogatory terms. These attacks were reported in all parts of the country. This evidence highlights further the necessity for racial harassment not to be perceived solely as a 'black and white' issue.

Racial attacks and harassment are a means of control and discipline over a whole community. If only a limited number of people are experiencing attacks this does not negate their significance. Such attacks are likely to be reported in the *Irish Post*, and local newspapers, and this can generate anxiety.

150

The same attacks are less likely to be reported in the British national press, which makes it harder to gain recognition for what is happening. This is an area which underscores the differences between on the one hand the Scots and the Welsh who live in England, and on the other hand the context in which the Irish who have migrated to England live.

It is very difficult to produce an overall picture of the Irish and the criminal justice system in Britain because there is relatively little research on the subject. This is a direct consequence of the invisibility of the Irish in official discourses and consequent lack of ethnic monitoring.

However, as in other areas the relative absence of evidence cannot lead to the assumption that there are no anti-Irish discriminatory practices operating in the general administration of the criminal justice system. This is especially the case given the evidence presented of racial harassment of Irish people by the police and the civil liberties abuses which are inherent in the operation of the PTA.

Many of the Irish community groups were particularly concerned about Irish Travellers. The inadequate provision of sites, the poor conditions on many existing sites and the lack of awareness and information about Travellers are perceived as serious problems. The barring of Travellers from pubs, launderettes and other facilities is considered to be acceptable in society at large.

In recent years discriminatory legislation has heightened the difficulties Travellers encounter in trying to pursue their traditional way of life and maintain their culture.

We were interested to explore regional variations in Irish experiences. In England, the main findings were consistent in all three cities in which we interviewed the staff of community groups.

However, there were some specific differences. For example, the greater availability of housing stock in Manchester resulted in fewer problems in access to housing than in London and the easier contact with the local authorities in Birmingham and Manchester, compared with London, was partly facilitated by each of the former cities having a single local authority.

The greatest variation within Britain was, as expected, between England and Scotland. This was marked by the absence of any Irish welfare group in Scotland providing an advice service for Irish people.

The history of Irish migration and settlement in Scotland and the decline in the Irish-born population accounts for this variation. In particular, the extent to which religion acts as the signifier of the major structural difference in ethnic origin in Scotland.

Historically, there has been considerable discrimination against Irish Catholics. On the basis of a brief exploration of these issues in Glasgow and Edinburgh there is sufficient cause for concern to suggest that further research is necessary to establish whether sectarian discriminatory practices still exist.

# REFERENCES

AGIY (nd) *A Guide to London for Young Irish People*, Action Group for Irish Youth, London.

AGIY (1988) *Irish Emigration: a programme for action*, Action Group for Irish Youth, London.

AGIY (1991) *Data and Information on the Irish in Britain*, Action Group for Irish Youth, London.

AGIY (1992) *The Challenge Now: review '92*, Action Group for Irish Youth, London.

AGIY (1993) *Racial Attacks and Harassment of Irish People*, Action Group for Irish Youth, London.

AGIY (1993) *Identity Crisis: Access to Social Security and ID Checks*, Action Group for Irish Youth, London.

Adler, M. (1995) The habitual residence test: a critical analysis, *Journal of Social Security Law*, No 2.

An Teach (1996) *Housing young Irish people in London*, An Teach Irish Housing Association, London.

Banton, M. (1983) Categorical and Statistical Discrimination, *Ethnic and Racial Studies*, Vol. 6, No. 3, July.

Bennett, C. (1991) The Housing of the Irish in London, *Irish Studies Centre Occasional Papers Series, No. 3*, University of North London Press, London.

Bradley, J. (1993) *Religious Identity in Modern Scotland: Culture, Politics and Football*, Ph.D thesis, University of Strathclyde.

Bradley, J. (1996 forthcoming) Profile of a Roman Catholic Parish in Scotland, in Devine, T.M. (ed.), *St Mary's Hamilton: a Social History 1846-1996*, John Donald, Edinburgh.

Boyle, K. (1968) The Irish Immigrant in Britain, *Northern Ireland Legal Quarterly*, Vol. 19, No. 4.

Brent Irish Mental Health Group, (1986), *The Irish Experience of Mental Health in London*, BIMHG, London.

Brown, C. (1984) *Black and White Britain*, Heineman Educational, London.

Bruce, S. (1990) The Ulster Connection, in Walker, G. & Gallagher, T. (eds.), *Sermons and Battle Hymns. Protestant Popular Culture in Modern Scotland*, Edinburgh University Press, Edinburgh.

Cara (1994) *Monitoring of Irish Applicants for Housing: A Survey of London Boroughs*, Cara Irish Housing Association, London.

Cara, (1995) *Limited Opportunities: Economic Disadvantage and Access to Housing for Sngle Irish Women*, Cara Irish Housing Association, London.

Cashmore, E. (1994) *Dictionary of Race and Ethnic Relations*, Routledge, London.

Castles, S. with Booth, H. & Wallace, T. (1984) *Here for Good. Western Europe's New Ethnic Minorities*, Pluto Press, London.

Cheyney, D. (1993) *Into the Dark Tunnel*, Prison Reform Trust.

Cochrane, R. (1977) Mental illness in migrants to England and Wales: an analysis of mental hospital admissions, 1977, *Social Psychiatry*, Vol. 12, No 1.

Cochrane, R. and Stopes-Roe, M. (1979) Psychological disturbance in Ireland, in England and in Irish emmigrants to England: a comparitive study, *Economic and Social Review*, Vol. 10, No 4.

Connelly, N. (1990) Social Services Departments: the process and progress of Change, in Ball, W. & Solomos, J. (eds.), *Race and Local Politics*, Macmillan, London.

Connor, T. (1985) *Irish Youth Research Report*, AGIY: London.

Connor, T. (1987), *The London Irish*, London Strategic Policy Unit, Greater London Council, London.

Deakin, N. (1972), Changing official perspectives of cultural pluralism in Britain, in Eppel, E.M. (ed.), *Education for Cultural Pluralism*, World Jewish Congress - Cultural Department, London.

Devine, T.M. (ed), (1991) *Irish immigrants and Scottish society in the nineteenth and twentieth centuries*, John Donald, Edinburgh.

Doherty, K.P. (1993) *The Response of London Alcohol Services to the Needs of Irish People with Alcohol Problems*, dissertation, October.

Drudy, P. J. (1986) *Ireland and Britain since 1922*, Cambridge University Press, Cambridge.

Dummett, A. (1973) *A Portrait of English Racism*, Penguin, London.

Egan, K. (1995) *Limited Opportunities. Economic Disadvantage and Access to Housing for Single Irish Women*, CARA, London.

Ely, P. & Denney, D. (1987) *Social Work in a Multi-Racial Society*, Gower, Aldershot.

Federation of Irish Societies (1987) *The Irish Community: the missing component in planning and provision of multi-cultural education*, FIS: London.

Finn, G.P.T. (1990) In the Grip? A Psychological and Historical Exploration of the Social Significance of Freemasonry in Scotland, in Walker, G. & Gallagher, T. (eds.), *Sermons and Battle Hymns. Protestant Popular Culture in Modern Scotland*, Edinburgh University Press, Edinburgh.

Finnegan, P. and Harrington, F. (1988) *Factors in the Genesis of Stress and Mental Health Amongst the Irish in Britain*, Irish Mental Health Forum, London.

Gallagher, T. (1987) *Glasgow: The Uneasy Peace*, Manchester University Press, Manchester.

Gordon, P. & Newnham, A. (1985) *Passport to Benefits? Racism in Social Security*, Child Poverty Action Group, London.

Greater London Council, (1984) *Policy Report on the Irish Community*, GLC Ethnic Minorities Unit, London.

Green, H (1991) *Counting Gypsies*, Office of Population Censuses and Surveys, London.

Greenslade, L. (1994) Caoineann an lon dubh: towards an Irish dimension in 'ethnic' health, *Irish Studies Review*, No. 8, Autumn.

Haringey Council, (1987) *The Irish in Haringey: an assessment of need and a programme for action*, Haringey Council, London.

Haringey Council, (c. 1991), Equal Opportunities: the Irish dimension. An agenda for change, Haringey Council, London.

Haringey Council, (1992) *The Irish in Britain - A Profile of Discrimination and Prejudice*, Report of the Race Equalities Unit, London.

Harris, C. (1991) Developing Research Agendas for the Future, paper presented to the *Conference: Racism and Migration in Europe in the 1990s*, Centre for Research in Ethnic Relations, University of Warwick, September 20-21st.

Harrison, L. & Carr-Hill, R. (1992) *Alcohol and disadvantage amongst the Irish in England*, Federation of Irish Societies, October, London.

Hazelkorn, E. (1990) Irish immigrants today: a socio-economic profile of contemporary Irish emigrants and immigrants in the UK, *Irish Studies Centre Occasional Papers Series, no. 1*, PNL Press, London.

Hazelkorn, E. (1991) Irish labour and British capital: evidence from the 1980s, in Galway Labour History Group (eds.), *The Emigrant Experience*, Galway Labour History Group: Galway.

Hickman, M.J. (1990) *A Study of the Incorporation of the Irish in Britain with special reference to Catholic State Education: involving a comparison of the attitudes of pupils and teachers in selected Catholic schools in London and Liverpool*, Ph.D thesis, Institute of Education, University of London.

Hickman, M.J. & Walter, B. (1995) Deconstructing Whiteness: Irish women in Britain, *Feminist Review*, No. 50, Summer.

Hickman, M.J. (1998 forthcoming) Reconstructing deconstructing 'race': British political discourses about the Irish in Britain, *Ethnic and Racial Studies*, Vol. 21, No.2.

Hillyard, P. (1993) *Suspect community. People's experience of the Prevention of Terrorism Acts in Britain*, Pluto Press, London.

Hillyard, P. (1994) Irish people and the British criminal justice system, *Journal of Law and Society*, Vol. 21, No. 1, special issue on *Justice and Efficiency?*, The Royal Commission on Criminal Justice.

Hyman, M. (1989) *Sites for Travellers*, London Race and Housing Research Unit, London.

Inner London Education Authority (1988) *Working Party Report on Irish Perspectives in Education*, ILEA, London.

IBRG, (1985) *Irish Perspectives on British Education, report of a second national conference*, Irish in Britain Representation Group, London.

Irish Liaison Unit, (c. 1988) *The Social Situation of Irish Elderly in Haringey: a research report of the Irish Liaison Unit*, Haringey Council, London.

Jackson, J.A. (1963) *The Irish in Britain*, London.

Jackson, J. (1967), *Report on the Skibbereen Social Survey*, Human Sciences Committee, INPC, London.

Jackson, P. (1987) *Migrant Women: the Republic of Ireland*, Commission of European Communities, Directorate-General for Employment, Social Affairs and Education: Strasbourg.

Kells, M (1995) Ethnic Identity amongst Young Irish Middle Class Migrants in London, *Irish Studies Centre Occasional Papers Series, No. 6*, University of North London Press, London.

Kennedy, J. and Brooker, C. (1986) The Lundbeck Leader: Irish drinkers in south Camden, *CPN.I*, March/April.

Kilburn IYAG, (1987) *Research Report*, Kilburn Irish Youth Action Group: London.

Kowarzik, U. (1994) *Developing a Community Response: the service needs of the Irish community in Britain*. A Charities Evaluation Services Report, commissioned by AGIY and the FIS, Action Group for Irish Youth and the Federation of Irish Societies, London.

Lennon, M, McAdam, M. and O'Brien, J. (1988) *Across the Water. Irish Women's Lives in Britain*, Virago, London.

LIWC, (c. 1984) *Irish Women: our experience of emigration, Report of the first London Irish Women's Conference*, London Irish Women's Centre, London.

LIWC, (c. 1985) *Living in England, Report of the second London Irish Women's Conference*, London Irish Women's Centre, London.

LIWC, (c. 1986) *Report from the London Irish Women's Conference*, September 1986, London Irish Women's Centre, London.

LIWC, (c. 1987) *Annual Report 1986*, London Irish Women's Centre, London.

LIWC, (c. 1987) *Irish Women: our lives, our identity*. Report of the 1987 London Irish Women's Conference, London Irish Women's Centre, London.

LIWC, (c. 1990) *Annual Report 1988/9 and Irish Women Today: a conference report*, London Irish Women's Centre, London.

LIWC, (c. 1993) *Roots and Realities: a profile of Irish women in London*, London Irish Women's Centre, London.

LIWC, (1995) *Rights for Travellers*, London Irish Women's Centre, London.

London Race and Housing Research Unit (1990) *Travellers in Camden: Anywhere but here*, London.

London Strategic Policy Unit, (1987a) *Travellers and Welfare Benefits*, LSPU, London.

London Strategic Policy Unit, (1987b) *Hearts and Minds, Anam agus Intinn: the cultural life of London's Irish Community*, text by Liz Curtis and Claire Keatinge, LSPU Recreation and Arts Group with Format Photographers: London.

London Strategic Policy Unit (1988) Policing the Irish Community, *Police Monitoring and Research Group, Briefing Paper no. 5*, LSPU: London.

McCann, E. (1988) The Glasgow Celtic Story, *Magill*, May.

McCollum, S. (1994) *Alcohol and the Irish in the London Borough of Brent*, Brent Irish Advisory service, London.

MacEwen, M. (1991) *Housing, Race and the Law*, Routledge, London.

MacGearailt, G. (1985) *The Irish in Lambeth: a report*, IBRG Lambeth branch: London.

McVeigh, R. (1992) The Specificity of Irish Racism', *Race & Class*, Vol. 33, No. 4.

Mason, D. (1990) Competing Conceptions of 'Fairness' and the Formulation and Implementation of Equal Opportunities Policies, in Ball, W. & Solomos, J. (eds.), *Race and Local Politics*, Macmillan, London.

Medical Campaign Project (1992) *Health and Homelessness in Hackney*, City and East London Family Health Service authority, London.

Middlesex Probation Service (1989/90) *Unpublished Research into Social Enquiry Reports*, London.

Middlesex University (1995) *Islington Street Crime Survey*, London.

Miles, R & Dunlop, A. (1987) Racism in Britain: the Scottish Dimension, in Jackson, P. (ed.), *Race and Racism*, Essays in Social Geography, Allen & Unwin, London.

Mullins, D. (1989) Housing and Urban Policy, *New Community*, Vol. 16, No. 1.

Murphy, P. (1994) The Invisible Minority: Irish Offenders and the English Criminal Justice System, *Probation Journal*, Vol. 41, No. 1, March.

National Campaign for the Homeless (1990) *Guidelines for Accommodation Policies in relation to Travellers*, London.

National Economic and Social Council (1991) *The Economic and Social Implications of Emigration*, Dublin.

Nanton, P. & Fitzgerald, M. (1990) Race Policies in Local Government: Boundaries or Thresholds, in Ball, W. & Solomos, J. (eds.), *Race and Local Politics*, Macmillan, London.

Norman, A. (1987) Down and out in Britain, *Community Care*, 12 November 1987.

O'Meachair, G. & Burns, A (1988) *Irish Homelessness: The Hidden Dimension*, CARA Irish Homeless Project, London.

O'Meachair, G, Webb, B. & Young, T. (1994) *Report of the Islington Police and Irish Community Consultative Group*, London.

Ouseley, H. (1990), in Ball, W. & Solomos, J. (eds.), *Race and Local Politics*, Macmillan, London.

Pearson, M. and Madden, M. (1990) Socio-economic characteristics of the Irish in Britain, *Occasional Papers in Irish Studies, no. 3*, Institute of Irish Studies, University of Liverpool, Liverpool.

Pearson, M, Madden, M, & Greenslade, L. (1991) Generations of an Invisible Minority: the health and well being of the Irish in Britain, a preliminary survey, *Occasional Papers in Irish Studies, No. 2*, Institute of Irish Studies, University of Liverpool, Liverpool.

PIAA (1993) *Assessing the Impact of HIV on the Irish Community in Britain: an examination of current issues and service provision*, Positively Irish Action on Aids, London.

Phillips, D (1987) The rhetoric of anti-racism in public housing allocation, in Jackson, P. (ed.), *Race and Racism. Essays in Social Geography*, Allen & Unwin, London.

Raferty, J., Jones, D. R. and Rosato, M. (1990) The mortality of first and second generation Irish immigrants in the UK, in *Social Science and Medicine*, Vol. 31, No. 5.

Randall, G. (1990?) *Over Here: young Irish migrants in London*, Action Group for Irish Youth, London.

Scarman, Lord (1981) *The Brixton Disorders, 10-12 April 1981*, Cmnd 8427, HMSO, London.

Skellington, R. with Morris, P. (1992) *'Race' in Britain Today*, Sage in association with The Open University, London.

Southwark Council (1992) *Crime, Policing and the Irish Community*, London.

Strachan, A. (1991) Post-war Irish migration and settlement in England and Wales, 1951-1981, in R. King (ed.) *Contemporary Irish Migration*, Geographical Society of Ireland Special Publications (6), Dublin.

Taylor, S. (1992) *The Irish in Britain - A Profile of Discrimination and Prejudice*, Report of the Race Equalities Unit, Haringey Council, London.

Ullah, P. (1985) Second-generation Irish Youth: identity and ethncity, *New Community*, Vol. XII, No. 2, Summer.

Walker, D.J. & Redman, M.J, (1977) *Racial Discrimination*, Shaw & Sons, London.

Walker, G. (1995) *Intimate Strangers*, John Donald, Edinburgh.

Walter, B. (1984) Tradition and ethnic interaction: second wave Irish settlement in Luton and Bolton' , in C. Clarke, D. Ley and C. Peach (eds.) *Geography and Ethnic Pluralism*, Allen and Unwin: London.

Walter, B. (1986) Ethnicity and Irish residential distribution, *Transactions of the Institute British Geographers*, Vol. 11, No 2.

Walter, B. (1988) *Irish Women in London*, London Strategic Policy Unit, London.

Walter, B. (1989) *Irish Women in London. The Ealing Dimension*, Ealing Women's Unit, London.

Walter, B. (1989) Gender and Irish Migration to Britain, *Geography Working Paper, No. 4* (June), Anglia College of Higher Education, Cambridge.

Walter, B. (1995) Irishness, gender and place, *Environment and Planning: Society and Space*, Vol. 13.

Woodhouse, T, O'Meachair, G, Clark, N. & Jones, M. (1992) *The Irish and Policing in Islington: A Report to Safer Cities*, Islington Council, London.

Young, J. (1994) *Policing the Streets-Stops and Search in North London*, Centre for Criminology, Islington Council, London.

# Part Three
# Survey of individual experience of discrimination

# 1. Rationale

This stage of the research was designed to extend the investigation of experiences of discrimination to a cross-section of the total Irish-born population in Britain. Those seeking help with problems from Irish agencies are likely to have the most acute need, the opportunity to use the agencies' services, knowledge of their existence and a willingness to come forward. Evidence from the second stage of the research shows, however, that widespread denial of the specificity of Irish needs, associated with anti-Irish attitudes amongst the British population, makes it unlikely that services are available to, or are used by, all those in need of them. Moreover, the unacknowledged character of anti-Irish racism may have more widespread indirect effects on the Irish-born population which also limit access to resources on equal terms with the white majority society.

Specific reasons why Irish community groups and other welfare and advice agencies may not see the full range of evidence about discrimination experienced by the Irish community include:

(i) the poor previous experiences of those subject to discrimination when presenting for advice, either because of anti-Irish racism or because of denials than discrimination towards the Irish can exist;

(ii) the tradition of unwillingness to utilise state agencies, and because of specific experiences in the labour market, for instance the construction industry;

(iii) lack of knowledge of the existence of Irish groups, or their absence from areas without either established community organisation and/or large Irish populations.

It was decided therefore to carry out a pilot study based on in-depth interviews with a sample representing the range of demographic and socio-economic characteristics of the Irish-born population identified in the first stage of the research. This follows the general lines of the methodology used by the PEP/PSI research (Daniels, 1968; Smith, 1977; Brown, 1985) which has done so much to establish and highlight the extent of discrimination and disadvantage experienced by Asian and African-Caribbean groups.

A national survey of the Irish in Britain would ideally produce a picture of a complexly-structured community. It would be possible to identify many layers and levels within the community which the length of the period of Irish immigration to Britain and the specificity of the racism requires. The major dimensions which would be represented in the survey would include age, social class, period of emigration, place of origin in Ireland (North or South, rural or urban), gender, religion, generation and national identity.

In this instance, however, very limited resources were available, sufficient only for a pilot study. This was carried out over two two-month periods and included 88 respondents. It is hoped that a much more comprehensive survey will follow up the issues which are highlighted here, drawing on this experience.

Because of the importance of the two major post-war immigration waves of the 1950s and the 1980s, Birmingham and London were chosen for this preliminary investigation. Birmingham was a major area of settlement of 1950s migrants who now form the largest section of the Irish-born population in Britain. London has attracted large-scale Irish settlement throughout the period and has become the principal focus of migration in the 1980s and '90s.

The main objective of the pilot study was to establish whether sufficient evidence existed to suggest:

(i) a significant degree of hidden racism and discrimination not signaled in the agency reports;

(ii) that groups other than, or in different proportions to, those who present to agencies may experience racial disadvantage and discrimination;

(iii) further elaboration of the particular experiences of discrimination Irish people experience in specified areas, including housing, employment, access to social security benefits, and interaction with the police and health services;

(iv) the extent to which the experiences of discrimination and disadvantage reported to agencies is replicated in the Irish population as a whole.

# 2. Methodology

## 2.1 Survey design

### 2.1.1 Stratification: London and Birmingham

In view of the small overall sample size, it was decided to limit geographical variation within Britain to two locations. London and Birmingham were selected to include large populations with distinctively different experiences of the major trends in postwar Irish settlement. A sample size of 30 is thought the minimum size about which any statistical generalisation can be made (Dixon, Bouma and Atkinson, 1987: 149), so that Birmingham is slightly over-represented in the total sample (Birmingham 33, London 55). However, the importance of the 1950s generation justifies this balance.

These two cities account for over a third (35.2%) of the total Irish-born population in Britain (London 256,470; Birmingham 38,290). Since nearly two-thirds of the Irish-born population is clustered in large conurbations, a sample drawn from these cities represents a large section of the group.

The age structures of the Irish-born populations in the two cities contrast strongly, reflecting the different periods of immigration. The table below shows proportions of population in the two cities arriving in the two major waves of the 1980s and the 1950s. Whereas London received well above the average proportion of young migrants in the 1980s, in their twenties in 1991, Birmingham had only a small representation. However, the proportion of Birmingham's Irish-born population who arrived in the 1950s is much higher than the national average and comprises over two-thirds of the total in the city. Taken together the proportions in the two cities are close to the national average.

**Age groups in the main waves of migration, 1991**

| Age Group | Total in GB % | London % | Birmingham % |
|-----------|------------|----------|--------------|
| 20-29 | 12.7 | 19.6 | 5.5 |
| 40-69 | 58.0 | 50.2 | 67.8 |

Source: Crown copyright, 1991 Census

### 2.1.2 Sampling areas within the cities

Stratified sampling methods were used in each city. At the first level, areas were chosen which provided a representative range of the total Irish-born population. The selection was made on the basis of the 1991 Census characteristics of wards, such that the profile of the combined samples matched the city average for the Irish-born population according to distributions of age, in employment/ unemployed, housing tenure and car ownership.

A sample size per ward of approximately 15 was chosen, leading to the identification of two wards in Birmingham and three in London. In Birmingham two wards with high proportions of Irish-born population (Figure 2.5) but contrasting socio-economic background were selected. Erdington had the highest percentage Irish-born population (6.9%), and was an area of owner-occupied housing and relatively low unemployment. Sparkbrook (5.4%), also a strongly Irish area, had much higher rates of unemployment as well as private rented accommodation and local authority housing. This was the 'twilight' area studied by Rex and Moore (1967) in their classic study of immigrant settlement in Birmingham in the 1960s.

In order to identify a matched sample of Irish-born people in the much larger conurbation of Greater London, a preliminary stratification by borough was made. The three boroughs selected were Islington, an inner London borough with one of the highest percentages of Irish-born population (7.1%) and a varied socio-economic composition: Harrow, an outer London borough with an increasing, young Irish-born population (4.9%) and with a higher overall socio-economic profile, and Lewisham (3.4%): an Inner London borough well outside the traditional cluster of Irish population in the northwest of the city (Figure 2.4).

Islington and Harrow have large Irish communities and were chosen to include clusters of Irish settlement within large conurbations which are the typical experience of life in Britain for a large proportion of the Irish-born population (see Part One, Section 3.2.6). These areas are served by Irish community groups and welfare agencies so that the extent to which evidence reported in Part Two reflects wider experience within these communities can be assessed.

Lewisham was included as a contrast to these two boroughs as result of experience from interviews in Birmingham, which suggested that the presence of Irish neighbours may provide a cushion against hostile attitudes. Moreover, access to specifically Irish services was restricted, although there was an Irish Centre. Interviewing was much more difficult in Lewisham, partly because of the small number of Irish households which could be identified in the electoral register.

Wards within these boroughs were then selected on the basis of their Irish-born population proportions and socio-economic characteristics. At a further level of stratification, clusters of three adjacent census enumeration districts within each ward were identified to maximise numbers of Irish-born people for ease of contact. Street names and house numbers lying within the boundaries of the enumeration districts were noted and checked on the ground.

### 2.1.3 Systematic matching sampling

Households containing Irish people within the enumeration districts were initially identified by names in the electoral register. Irish names are usually quite distinctive, especially when a combination of first and surnames are considered. This method omits those who are on the register, but do not have distinctively

Irish names, as well as those who have not registered. Snowballing methods amongst those contacted helped to add missing names. The method initially includes people with Irish names who were not born in Ireland and may have a distant, or no known, Irish connection so that an accurate assessment of the response rate would require much more extensive fieldwork.

In order to achieve a geographical spread throughout the area, households were sampled systematically (eg every fifth door), with replacement, to produce the target number per ward. One member of the household was interviewed, so that quotas by gender, age group, housing tenure and economic activity (employed, unemployed, retired) could be achieved. The response rate amongst those identified as Irish-born was 61%, a figure which was probably reduced by the aim to achieve immediate responses by 'cold calling' and by the uncomfortable nature of the material revealed by those who did participate. However, the strong common threads running through the completed interviews suggests that they successfully captured widely-shared experiences.

### 2.1.4 Interview schedule

A detailed individual interview schedule (Appendix B) was constructed to investigate:

**background**: gender; age group; area of origin; religion.

**migration history**: year left Ireland; reason for choosing Britain; migration within Britain; intention to remain.

**housing history**: tenure patterns; household structure; experience of homelessness, mortgage applications, temporary accommodation.

**employment**: qualifications; jobs in Britain; income.

**anti-Irish experiences**: at work; travel; self identification; treatment at times of IRA bombings in Britain; interactions with police; treatment while claiming benefits, healthcare; perception of attitudes towards Irish people in different countries.

**recognition of Irish specificity:** preference for Irish benefits staff; classification as an ethnic group.

Three interviewers, one Irish-born and two second-generation Irish women, carried out the majority of the interviews. The remainder were conducted by the research team. Training was given to all interviewers to ensure consistency. Interviews took place during March-April 1995 in Birmingham and July-August in London. The interviewers called at the selected addresses, explained the purpose of the interview and completed the schedule at the time or at a later appointment. Interviews took between 45 minutes and one and a quarter hours to complete.

164

## 3. Description of the sample

Bearing in mind that two cities with specific characteristics were selected for the pilot study, the characteristics of the sample represented the national range of demographic and socio-economic characteristics well (Appendix B). Clearly, the larger the number of subdivisions in each category, the lower the likelihood of a very close match, especially when such a wide variety of dimensions is being considered.

The gender division of interviewees exactly mirrored that of the Irish-born population in Britain (53.0% women, 47.0% men). Differences between the two cities were also reflected, Birmingham having a lower than average proportion of Irish-born women (49.5%) and London having a slightly higher proportion (54.5%). This balance is important in the light of different experiences of women and men, for example in employment and dealings with service providers.

Age groupings of the interviewees was fairly close to the national spread, differing in ways which reflected the immigration experience of the two cities. Younger informants (20-39) were slightly over-represented overall (35.2% compared with 27.7%), as result of larger numbers in London, and the middle-aged group (40-59) under-represented (31.8% compared with 39.9%), especially in London. The older age group (60-79) was close to the average proportion (31.8% compared with 29.0%). Since this group was largely missing from the findings reported in Part Two, this was an important outcome.

Grouping of migrants by year of arrival brought out clear differences between the two cities. By far the most important decade for the Birmingham sample was the 1950s, 14/33 (42%) arriving between 1951-60. Migration to London, by contrast, was much more evenly spread between 1940 and 1980, after which a very large upturn had taken place. A total of 20/55 (36%) had arrived in the latter period.

When the Irish origins of the sample are compared with national figures, it can be seen that the Northern Irish-born are somewhat under-represented. They form 27.3% of the total in Britain, but only 14.8% of the sample. In large measure this reflects the different settlement patterns of the two groups. The Northern Irish-born population is much more evenly spread within the country (Figures 2.7 and 2.9) and is significantly less concentrated in conurbations (Table 2.7). A much larger sample size would therefore be necessary to take these geographical variations into account. However, when the 1991 Census totals for the two cities are compared with the sample distribution, a much closer fit is found. In Birmingham, 18.2% of the interviewees originated in Northern Ireland (1991 Census: 20.1%) and in London the total was 12.7% (1991 Census: 16.5%).

Housing tenure was used as an indicator of socio-economic position, despite its known shortcomings. Again the distribution accorded quite closely to national Census figures, with differences reflecting the city characteristics of Birmingham and London. Thus, although there were lower than average rates of owner-occupation amongst the Irish-born populations (47.7% compared with a national average of 55.4%) and higher rates of local authority renting (30.7% compared with 26.6%), the proportions in the sample reflected actual figures in London and Birmingham more closely. In Birmingham, 60.6% of the sample were owner occupiers compared with 52.35% of the Irish-born population in the city, and in London the figures were 40.0% and 44.0% respectively. Similarly, local authority renting was very close to the city average in each case (Birmingham 30.3%, average 33.0% and London 30.9%, average 28.9%).

Finally, the economic activity profile of the sample was widely spread. Overall the proportion of paid employees was somewhat lower than the national average (36.5% compared with 45.2%), though the Birmingham sample matched the city proportion closely. This was accompanied by higher proportions of self-employed workers in both cities (Birmingham 9.1%, average 4.0% and London 12.7%, average 7.4%). Proportions unemployed were somewhat higher than in the Census totals (12.5%, compared with 6.8%), especially in Birmingham. In view of the high representation of unemployed people in the Irish groups' clientele described in Part Two, this provides useful insights.

The background of the sample therefore suggested that it provided a good representation of the spread of characteristics of the Irish-born population outlined in Part One, especially those of the two geographical locations where the survey was conducted. This is important since the experiences recounted by respondents also relate to these places. It is not yet possible to generalise statistically to the whole population in Britain, but the findings give a good indication of the broader picture.

# 4. Context of labour migration to Britain

Migration from Ireland has already been shown to be highly responsive to demand for labour in Britain. Answers to the question: 'When you left Ireland, why did you choose to come to Britain?' confirmed that the sample constituted a labour migrant force, which made its own transfer arrangements to the British labour market, thereby saving the British economy costs of recruitment and provision of accommodation. One of the major ways in which these arrangements were made was through reliance on relatives and friends already settled in Britain.

Reasons for choosing Britain as a migration destination thus fell into two main categories. One was the search for employment, illustrating the flexibility of this source of labour. In all 39% of women (18) and 38% of men (17) gave job-related reasons for their choice. Overwhelmingly this was speculative movement, in response to generalised demand for labour, rather than prearranged entry into a specific job.

Young Irish people were able to respond to these demands because of the existence of familial and social networks in Britain. Thus, the second category was presence of relatives, and to a lesser extent, friends. Of the total sample, 33% of men (14) and 39% of women (18) gave this as the reason for their choice. This was also part of a movement to Britain for work, but, in this case, relatives and friends were the source of information and provided a base from which to start the search process.

Almost all respondents had travelled independently as young adults, only a small minority accompanying a spouse or parent (9%).

## 4.1. Housing

A range of questions was asked about access to housing in Britain. The aim was to assess the extent to which difficulties were experienced as the result both of migration and of discrimination in the housing market.

It was clear that as migrants the respondents had experienced considerable initial difficulty in establishing themselves in independent accommodation. Very commonly the first few weeks or months were spent living with relatives or friends in cramped conditions and in danger of eviction by landlords. This hidden form of homelessness was particularly prevalent in London where 35/55 (64%) reported initial arrangements of this kind. Proportions were higher amongst those arriving in the 1980s and '90s.

> *I stayed with these people I didn't know at all, for two weeks. I came over with a friend and he didn't know these people either. He knew the guy who was living with them. He rang him the day before we came over because our accommodation was messed up. He wasn't there, but the girls said to stay anyway. Then he came back and they let us stay for two weeks. Then I stayed*

*with another friend of mine, on the floor in the sitting room, for another week.*
(Man, IR, Lewisham, arrived 1995)

More permanent solutions were also found most readily within the migrant community. Word of mouth was more common than advertisements as a way in which the repondents found housing.

*When I first came over I got digs - my sister arranged it. When I got married, because no-one wanted you if you were married, expecting a baby, especially at that time. If you had a dog, you'd get a room, but not with a baby. We stayed with a friend for a while... and I got a flat through a friend at work. He was a Kerryman also, and he got me flat with this estate* .
(Man, IR, Islington, arrived 1949)

*Through the Irish in Islington Centre - the Roger Casement Centre. A girl from the South, she was squatting in a flat and I bought the keys from her.*
(Woman, IR, Islington, arrived 1988)

When moving outside the migrant community to dealings with the state, respondents reported difficulties. Half (45/88) of the respondents had applied for local authority housing. Of these 36 (80%) were eventually successful. Those who were not gave long waiting lists as the reason, and a number believed that they had been discriminated against because of their Irish origins.

*We were on the list and people from Lancashire - they were British - got priority over me. They were on the list well after me. We were not well looked after in that respect.*
(Woman, IR, Erdington, arrived 1951)

*They said I wasn't here long enough and that I had left a house in Ireland. But it was my husband s house and not mine. They kept asking me why I left Ireland. I told them I left a violent marriage. They wouldn't give me anything because I was Irish. They weren't sympathetic at all.... I had to stay with my brother in a two-bedroom house. He's got two kids, I've got seven. They never gave me any help, no lists or anything. It's because I was Irish.*
(Woman, IR, Lewisham, arrived 1991)

Another woman, herself born in Britain, but taken back to Ireland as a child by her parents, returned to London in 1989:

*When we arrived, we were staying with my husband's brother, his wife and child, and my brother's sister. When they went back to Ireland three or four months later, we found out they had been squatting, although we had been paying them rent. We were evicted.*

*We were put into a B and B in Kilburn. It was terrible, four in one room. People were hitting my daughter. The council said 'Why not go back where you came from?' I felt it was holding us back, being Irish. We were on the list for five years. They told us to forget it. They said 'You're the wrong colour'. We need 450 points but we've only got 53. We're now renting for this two-bedroomed flat for £125 a week - a three-bedroomed council house would be £60.*

*People can't understand why they're not doing anything for us. My husband has given up. They said 'Why did you come over here in the beginning?' My husband says 'Play on the fact that you're born here', but they say 'Where was your husband born?' When I say 'Ireland', they say 'Well that's it then'. It isn't right. The couple round the corner, she's from Dublin, he's from Jamaica. When he went to the council it was easy. Another girl, Irish mother, black father, she's got a place by getting involved with an Englishman. You shouldn't have to.*
(Woman, IR, Lewisham, arrived 1989)

This is a graphic example of how migration constitutes making yourself intentionally homeless. It is also interesting for the ways in which people have to manipulate both nationality and 'colour' in order to get access to decent, affordable housing.

Even where people were eventually housed by the council, one third reported difficulties. Several commented on the difference between their treatment as Irish people and that of other groups. A woman in Islington, who had arrived in 1986, was allocated unsuitable housing:

*It took a long time, an awful lot of hassle. It was on the seventh floor, with three kids under eight. They said 'Either take it or leave it'. Before I was in temporary accommodation. I feel myself that if I'd been a coloured or an English person, I'd have been treated better. I couldn't use the lift because I'm claustrophobic - I had a medical certificate to prove it.*
*I got this place through mutual exchange. If it was left to the council, I'd still be there.*
(Woman, IR, Islington, arrived 1986)

Another woman, long established in Birmingham, said:

*New housing was getting built and I asked for a new house because of my disability. But the agent said they were only for Asian families. I went to the housing department to get what the others get.*
(Woman, IR, Sparkbrook, arrived 1940)

In addition to their own problems, nearly half the respondents (41/88) reported that they knew of other Irish people who had experienced difficulties in gaining satisfactory accommodation. The proportion was higher in London (55%) than in Birmingham (33%), reflecting housing shortage, higher prices and the later period of arrival of London migrants.

By contrast, those who applied for mortgages (50/88) were successful, with only one application being turned down. A higher proportion of mortgage applications were in Birmingham, where 27/33 had applied, reflecting the longer-established community and greater availability of affordable housing.

One solution to the problem of finding affordable housing, especially for single people, was to take a job with live-in accommodation. This helps to account for the popularity of hotel and bar work, as well as nursing.

169

*I've always had accommodation through my employment. I changed from nursing to what I'm doing now [Metropolitan police].*
(Man, NI, London, arrived 1990)

As migrants, therefore, Irish-born people have particular problems in gaining access to satisfactory accommodation. In the first instance, solutions are sought within the community, through reliance on relatives and friends for initial housing and information about subsequent opportunities.

The costs of supporting a labour migrant group are thus borne by the group itself to a considerable extent. Where state support is sought on the same grounds as the indigenous workforce or other labour migrant groups whose disadvantage is acknowledged, the Irish may fare worse. Again, they meet the situation where they are not seen as being entitled to the same rights as the national population, but are also not represented as sufficiently 'different' to have their particular needs recognised.

## 4.2 Employment

Labour migrants have been recruited in post-war European countries, including Britain, both as additional labour in growth industries and as replacement labour for white, native-born workers who have moved to better paid, pleasanter areas of work (Castles with Booth and Wallace, 1984). The vast majority have therefore been recruited into the secondary sector, construction and manufacturing, rather than the tertiary sector of commerce, banking and administration.

There have been fewer opportunities for labour migrants to move out of their original circumstances and become upwardly mobile like the white native-born population since the need for their labour in lowest level jobs has continued.

The quantity of such jobs has declined, however, especially after the recession of 1974-75, when restructuring of production took place on a worldwide scale, known as the New International Division of Labour. Migrant labour, and in Britain the racialised subsequent generations who remain associated with it, were hardest hit by these changes and have subsequently experienced much higher levels of unemployment.

In part, higher unemployment levels reflected the declining sectors into which they had been recruited and retained, but discrimination in hiring, promotion and firing was also a factor.

Castles et al. (1984: 157) point out that the special vulnerability of these groups to exclusion from skilled areas of work

> *can be used to partially cushion other workers from the effects of the crisis. This reduces the social and political strains of the process of restructuring for capital and the state.*

The Irish labour migrant workforce in Britain has shared many of these characteristics. The vast majority of migrants have been recruited to unskilled areas of work. The unusually high concentration of Irish-born women and men in Social Classes IV and V, noted in Part One, contrasts with the experience of British-born internal migrants from Scotland and Wales. Strong similarities were apparent between the occupation profiles of Irish-born women and those in the Black Caribbean Census ethnic group.

During the 1980s, however, the Irish also responded to labour shortages in the tertiary sector of the British economy. In the age group 18-29, the Irish-born were more strongly clustered in the occupation categories demanding higher education qualifications and have therefore constituted a significant 'brain drain' from Ireland. There was no evidence from the Census figures that overall highly educated Irish-born people were being employed below the level of their qualifications. Moreover, well-qualified Irish women have been in great demand as nurses for decades, again filling a labour migrant niche alongside African Caribbean women.

The Irish, therefore, share with other labour migrant groups the benefit they provide to the recruiting country of saving the costs of education and support during childhood. In the case of the highly educated, this is an even greater contribution to the British economy. Because of the proximity of Ireland and its special status as 'not a foreign country' (Ireland Act 1949), this labour supply remains extremely flexible, responding closely to upturns and downturns in demand in different sectors of the economy. In the case of young, single people, unemployment can also be exported and a trained workforce recalled when needed. No other source of labour provides such large quantities of flexible workers, including a significant proportion with high educational qualifications, able to support themselves outside the state welfare system to such a marked degree.

### 4.2.1 Range of occupations of sample

The sample illustrated clearly the distribution of migrant labour outlined above. Amongst men in full-time paid employment there was a clustering of occupations in the secondary sector, mainly construction (6/20) and lower skilled services, such as security, portering, pub/hotel management (6/20). Of those in administrative/professional tertiary sector occupations (6/20), only two were in the higher income range (dentist, actuary). Two remaining respondents were in semi-skilled or skilled trades. The one part-time worker was a musician.

A high proportion of the economically active was unemployed (10/31) including a marked concentration in the construction industry (7/10). The self-employed (10/31) were in a very wide range of occupations including the hotel trade, construction and clerical work.

Amongst women, full-time paid workers were clustered in the professional/ health area (6/14) and clerical work (6/14). A much higher proportion of women than men were in part-time work (9/23), the majority domestic workers (6/9). The part-time workers were older women, all but one having arrived before 1980.

Only one woman was classified as unemployed, reflecting greater demand for women's labour, especially in unskilled categories, as well as low rates of qualification for benefit as result of part time conditions of employment.

### 4.2.2 Classification of employment

When the occupations of the sample are classified by social class, it can be seen that the sample mirrors in important respects the national patterns of employment of Irish-born women and men identified in Part One from the 1991 Census.

**Registrar General's Social Class**

| Women | Employed | | Unemployed | | Census 1991 |
|---|---|---|---|---|---|
| Social class | No. | % | No. | % | % |
| I | 1 | 4 | 0 | 0 | 3 |
| II | 8 | 35 | 0 | 0 | 35 |
| IIIN | 5 | 22 | 0 | 0 | 26 |
| IIIM | 3 | 13 | 0 | 0 | 6 |
| IV | 5 | 22 | 0 | 0 | 17 |
| V | 1 | 4 | 1 | 100 | 11 |
| Total | 23 | 100 | 1 | 100 | 100 |
| **Men** | | | | | |
| I | 2 | 11 | 1 | 11 | 8 |
| II | 4 | 22 | 0 | 0 | 25 |
| IIIN | 1 | 6 | 0 | 0 | 8 |
| IIIM | 6 | 33 | 3 | 33 | 32 |
| IV | 2 | 11 | 1 | 11 | 16 |
| V | 3 | 17 | 4 | 44 | 9 |
| Total | 18 | 100 | 9 | 100 | 100 |

An alternative measure of social class is the Cambridge Occupational Scale which places jobs in a hierarchy based on similarity of lifestyle and therefore of generalised advantage/disadvantage (Prandy, 1990). This avoids the known weaknesses of the Registrar General's Social Class scale which allocates all members of an occupational group to the same class, regardless of actual work done.

Using this scale, it can be seen even more clearly that women in the sample were clustered at intermediate occupational levels. This was equally true of full- and part-time workers. It is important to modify the apparent clustering of women from the Irish Republic in higher social classes, which the Registrar General's groupings imply. Only one woman classified herself as unemployed, and fell into the lowest grouping.

By contrast, men in the sample were clustered at the lower end of the scale, unemployed men being even more strongly clustered in the lowest occupational categories. Those in the lowest paid jobs are, therefore, most vulnerable to unemployment, mainly because they meet employers' demands for a flexible workforce which can be taken on and laid off as market conditions change. Migrant workers are regarded as most suitable for these jobs for a number of reasons. They may return home when they become unemployed, their expectations of permanent work may be lower and there is less opposition from the indigenous workforce when migrant workers are put out of work.

**Cambridge Occupational Scale scores**

| **Women** | Full-time | | Part-time | |
|---|---|---|---|---|
| Camscore | No. | % | No. | % |
| 0-20.00 | 2 | 14 | 1 | 11 |
| 20.01-40.00 | 10 | 71 | 7 | 78 |
| 40.00-96.00 | 2 | 14 | 1 | 11 |
| Total | 14 | 100 | 9 | 100 |
| **Men** | | | | |
| 0-20.00 | 7 | 35 | 7 | 78 |
| 20.00-40.00 | 8 | 40 | 1 | 11 |
| 40.01-96.00 | 5 | 25 | 1 | 11 |
| Total | 20 | 100 | 9 | 100 |

Source: Survey; Crown copyright OPCS (1993) 1991 Census Ethnic Group and Country of Birth Tables Part 2; HMSO CASOC package.

### 4.2.3 Level of employment

It has been argued that migrant labour is frequently employed below the level of qualifications and experience it has achieved. Castles et al (1984) argue that this is because it is recruited to fill the least desirable jobs and continues to be needed in those areas. A recent study shows that whilst highly qualified Republic Irish-born people in Britain are matched to appropriate occupations, there are significant levels of occupational under-achievement amongst the less qualified (NESC, 1991). Overall, the Republic Irish-born are more likely to be found in working-class occupations than would be predicted from their educational qualifications. Possible reasons advanced include the pursuit of Irish occupational niches, such as construction, perhaps arising from the short-term view that high pay is the priority, failure of British employers to accept unfamiliar Irish qualifications and ethnic discrimination.

The most relatively disadvantaged group are those with higher school-leaving qualifications (Leaving Certificate, equivalent to A-level), who are less likely to achieve intermediate non-manual positions than the white British-born population. The NESC report identifies four sources of this under-achievement, relating it both to the migrant labour experience of the Irish-born in Britain and to discrimination in the British labour market. These include:

(i) Inadequate knowledge of procedures for securing non-manual/white collar jobs, where the search time is longer than for manual jobs and needs considerable financial support.

(ii) A different style of interpersonal interaction may make young Irish people appear less confident at interview.

(iii) Ethnic stereotypes about Irish stupidity reinforce an unwillingness to accept the equivalence of the Leaving Certificate with A-levels.

(iv) Lack of access, as a migrant group, to informal networks in Britain which contribute to recruitment in  many manual and service jobs, so that it is necessary to  fall back  on occupational niches like construction.

Responses of the sample to Question 30a 'Do you feel that you are being employed at an appropriate level for your experience and qualifications?' supported the view of Irish occupational under-achievement. In all, 18/43 (42%) said 'No', but the answers were evenly spread across qualification levels at Leaving Certificate and below. In some cases this reflected contentment with lower responsibilities which manual work may entail. An Irish man with the Leaving Certificate, who was employed as a porter, believed his qualifications were not recognised but expressed his ambivalence:

> I feel demeaned by being a cleaner. Lots of Irish don't use their qualifications -
> I'd say the majority. They choose an easy life. There's bigger money in manual
> work. They get less in an office job for which they are qualified.
> (Male porter, IR, Sparkbrook, aged 60-69)

Others felt that they had been the victims of deskilling or had considered the possibility of discrimination.

> I'd rather do my trade [toolsetter trainer], but those jobs aren't there now. They
> can buy in the finished product cheaper than the raw material in England.
> (Male building worker, Sparkbrook, 50-59)

> I feel I've gone as far as I can, although I feel I could be a grade higher. I failed
> four promotion boards but I threatened them with the CRE and I passed the next
> one!
> (Female civil service clerical worker, NI, London, aged 30-39)

On the whole, however, respondents saw their reluctance to achieve jobs commensurate with their qualifications as a personal decision. Again, this reflects a short term view of migrants' stay in Britain.


### 4.2.4 Discrimination in employment

Evidence of discrimination in access to employment and in gaining promotion or further training opportunities were also investigated. Respondents were asked

Q25a 'Have you experienced any difficulties in getting employment at any point since you came to Britain?' A total of 68 of the 83 respondents who had applied for work while in Britain (82%) answered 'No' . This illustrates clearly the strong demand for Irish people's labour, especially in the past.

*Never been out of work. Never got a week's dole. I don't believe in the dole.*
(Woman, IR, Erdington, arrived 1932)

*Any job I went for I got.*
(Woman, IR, Harrow, arrived 1961)

*No trouble. I think because Irish people have come over here as nurses. Areas where traditionally Irish people are very acceptable.*
(Woman, IR, Islington, 30-39, arrived 1988)

*In the 1970s it wasn't too difficult getting any kind of work. During the '80s it became tougher.*     .
(Man, IR, Islington, arrived 1970)

However, many qualified this by stressing that it was only easy to find work if they were prepared to accept anything, that is low-paid work with poor conditions.

*I don't think there is a problem. Some are choosy. The work is there if you look for it.*
(Woman, IR, Erdington, arrived 1959)

*Money was always a problem - four kids near together, so I was always trying to get any job. No trouble getting a job, though there was getting a job that paid me well and I was happy in.*
(Woman, NI, Harrow, arrived 1948)

Amongst those experiencing difficulties, decline in job opportunities was the main reason given (6), followed by lack of experience (3). Only four felt that Irish origins might have been a factor, two stressing the lack of a reference as a serious problem.

*My ethnic background. People have a fixed response to an Irish background and to a West Indian background. I don't want to know anything about this country. I am totally biased about this country. People make you feel a certain way because of being Irish .*
(Woman, IR, Islington, arrived 1986)

*In Brighton, yes. That's why I went back to Ireland. Perhaps my age was against me, rather than being Irish.*
(Man, NI, Islington, arrived 1986)

*I tried to get a job in a hospital, but, because I didn't have a reference they didn't take me. I had a reference from a parish priest but they didn't pay any heed to it.*
(Woman, IR, Erdington, arrived 1932)

*I've been to thirty interviews, rang hundreds of people. References, you need references, they're terribly important. I tried a couple of Irish employment*

*agencies, like the Shamrock and Cara. They don't help you unless you have references for what you want, unless you want building work, which is hard enough to get. Unless you have a place to live, near where you're working. It's immediate start for labouring but you need a place to live.*
(Man, IR, Lewisham, arrived 1995)

The very small minority who believed that they may have been discriminated against when they applied for jobs is not surprising given the nature of the labour migration flow from Ireland. Irish people were seen as suitable candidates for the jobs in which there were shortages, namely low-paid manual work and a few niche areas such as nursing. That there is only a small minority who think they have been discriminated against also reflects the absence of anti-Irish discrimination from discourses about equal opportunities. Because no legitimacy is accorded to discrimination as an explanation for their experiences, no language exists in which Irish people can construct meanings for their experiences.

More important is evidence of an inability to enter higher levels of work or to achieve promotion. Respondents were asked whether their Irish qualifications had always been acceptable (Q 26a). Answers showed that 35/85 (41%) felt that they had been, while a further 45 (53%) had not needed to specify what they were. This reflects the unskilled nature of the jobs they were seeking. Only five (6%) had experienced any difficulty, especially with the Leaving Certificate (equivalent to A-level, though more like the Baccalaureate).

*They don't understand it. They assumed it was below O-level to have the Leaving Certificate.*
(Woman, IR, Islington, aged 30-39)

*Not at Camden, I had to explain what the Leaving Certificate was and was not given due regard. So it could potentially affect my grade and pay.*
(Woman, Islington, IR, aged 20-29)

*They don't recognise them at all. They don't understand the level so they can't compare [Intermediate Certificate].*
(Woman, IR, Harrow, aged 20-29)

It seems most likely that discrimination against Irish people would operate within the occupational hierarchy rather than at point of entry. As labour migrants, Irish people are needed in areas where there are shortages, mainly those considered undesirable by the British-born population. However, mechanisms may well operate to exclude labour migrants in the competition for better paid jobs. These practices are hard to detect. The mechanisms are likely to be subtle and defensible by perpetrators on other grounds. Irish people may also be deterred form seeking promotion by the wish to avoid trouble.

Four respondents gave instances of being blocked from promotion.

*To better myself. I think it was being Irish that stopped me. Being Irish, I didn't get promotion in the library when I think I should have. I went to race relations but they said I wasn't discriminated against. It might have been my attitude - I'm*

*outspoken and I believe in fairness. They [race relations] said it was personality.*
(Man, NI, Erdington, aged 40-49)

*I may have been overlooked for promotion because I was Irish. They didn't want Irish people over English people. I just accepted it. It was so in the airforce.*
(Man, IR, Erdington, aged 50-59)

*On the buses no Irish were offered promotion. It was made clear to us that we were there to do the work - even in the union we were not expected to speak, just expected to do what they decided. Neither were there any opportunities in the Metropolitan Police - it's very male-oriented and being an Irish woman there was no chance. The aim was to hang on to what you had, not look for more.*
(Woman, NI, Harrow, 60-69)

*It's hard to tell. Being in the Civil Service since 1980 a lot has occurred - in 1981 the Hunger Strikes, the Brighton bomb. Generally, English people ask me what religion I was brought up in to see what side of the fence I am. I am agnostic/atheist. Also being a woman goes against me, but being Irish definitely does not help.*
(Woman, NI, Islington, aged 30-39)

*No, I didn't put in for it. As a home help I loved the job I was doing. And to be honest with you I don't think the Irish stood a chance for it. There were girls I know who applied and never got it. This was another reason.*
(Woman, IR, Islington, aged 60-69)

The low rate of reported discrimination also reflects Irish encapsulation within an Irish world of work, especially in the construction industry.

> *No, because I've always worked with a lot of Irish fellas, a lot of Irish gangs. I got promotion as such because I was a ganger man.*
> (Man, Islington, IR, aged 30-39)

> *No, but then I've worked for Irish people, for the nuns. I've never had any problems I have to say. Nothing serious, but you do get people talking under their breath. I don't find it particularly tolerant [practice nurse].*
> (Woman, IR, Islington, aged 30-39)

The great difficulty in pinpointing discrimination against Irish people within the workforce underlines important differences in appropriate research procedures to assess the extent to which it occurs. Moreover, the self-restrictions imposed by Irish people to avoid such experiences make the magnitude of the issue extremely hard to judge. Discrimination testing based on use of Irish actors to make telephone enquiries about jobs, for example, is unlikely to yield meaningful evidence. Nevertheless the evidence reported here suggests that discrimination is experienced in a variety of situations where Irish people compete for promotion with the white British-born.

## 4.3 Claiming benefits

As labour migrants, Irish people are disproportionately employed in low paid occupations, where risks of unemployment are higher and housing subsidy may be necessary. A significant number are thus likely to need state support at some time in their lives. People from both parts of Ireland are entitled to claim benefits on the same grounds as the British-born. Those from Northern Ireland are United Kingdom citizens, of course, while those from the Republic have been given identical status under the provisions of the Ireland Act (1949). Restrictions on the benefits rights of other EU citizens have not been applied to the Irish, so that legally there are no grounds for different treatment and thus there should be no discrimination.

Respondents were asked a range of questions about their experience of claiming benefits in Britain to assess: treatment at benefit offices: extent of non-claiming; use of advice agencies; use of Irish staff as service providers

### 4.3.1 Treatment at benefit offices

### 4.3.1.1 Social Security claims

About half (42/88, 48%) of the respondents had claimed Social Security benefits at some time. The proportion of men (58%) was higher than that of women (41%) reflecting higher levels of unemployment amongst men and lower entitlement to benefits among married women.

Those who had claimed were asked to describe their treatment by the staff, including specific mention of their Irish background and general attitudes towards them as claimants (Q52b).

Ten (24%) gave examples of particularly unhelpful treatment, usually related directly to their Irish origins. In most cases this involved questioning their rights to receive benefit, including accusations of fraud.

*Only once. They had this form to fill in, to say what part of Ireland I am from and why I came over. They asked me loads of questions about what I'm doing here, how long I'm staying. I resented their questions. I find a lot of Irish people over here suffer from stress. You have to socialise to deal with it. It's a transformation, coming over here.*
(Man, IR, London, aged 30-39)

*Lots of hassle. If your money doesn't come out, you have to go up there all day. Lots of hassle when I first came over, waited a long time to get money. They asked 'Why did you leave, why come here?' They wanted to know everything. The attitude wasn't good for you.*
(Woman, IR, London, aged 30-39)

*It was like trying to get blood out of a turnip. They told me it was the system. They brought everything Irish up - why are you here etc. I was offended because I felt we were grilled. If they did it to any other nationality, they'd be up for racism right away. The majority of Irish people I know had the same problem.*
(Woman, IR, London, aged 30-39)

*I was once accused of fraud and given a hard time. I should have complained as I wasn't guilty, but I never got around to it. I didn't think it was because I'm Irish. But I never thought about it much.*
(Man, NI, London, aged 30-39)

*Very unhelpful in Brighton. Interviewed by five fraud squad officers and accused of fraud. Took about five hours in the office - it was a frightening experience. You don't know what you are going to be charged with. There was a delay of a month before I got any money. Luckily I had people I could depend on.*
(Man, NI, London, aged 20-29)

The responses illustrate the agencies' comments in Part Two about reception of Irish people in benefit offices, and underline the need for the support they provide, especially for those with no alternative resources. Such experiences are likely to confirm anxieties about an Irish identity and contribute to the adoption of a low profile in Britain. They may also deter Irish people from claiming benefits to which they are entitled. Negative attitudes arise from, and reinforce, stereotypes of the Irish as fraudsters who come to Britain specifically to claim benefits.

### 4.3.1.2 Other benefits claims

A smaller number of respondents had also claimed other benefits. Housing (14/85, 16%) was the most important, followed by health-related benefits (sickness: 4, invalidity: 3, attendants': 3).

The main problems encountered in claiming housing benefit were long waiting times, both for claims to be admitted and for money to be received, and reluctance to admit eligibility on the part of officials.

> It took a long time to realise that I was not intentionally homeless.
> (Woman, IR, London, aged 30-39)

> I put in for a loan and I had to wait, but everybody has to. One day, in Archway, I waited from nine till five and I still wasn't seen. But I know they were biased against Irish people.
> (Man, IR, London, aged 30-39)

> They did give a payment, but we had to wait four to five weeks. They thought we should have stayed in Ireland. 'Why did you leave, why come here, why not stay?'
> (Woman, IR London, aged 50-59)

> They didn't want to give them because they thought you were holding something back. You were made to feel that you were lazy. [Because you were Irish?] I don't really know, but it could be like that in general. But the Irish do have a bad time.
> (Woman, IR, aged 30-39)

> If there's an Irish person working there, it's OK. But others there don't want to know. At the start they asked me why I came over. They gave me a loan of £160 for eight of us to furnish my place from top to bottom! Another woman who was black got £400. It's a crooked system. I'm not treated fairly. I'm not meant to be here. Very cold. They don't care.
> (Woman, IR, aged 30-39)

### 4.3.1.3 Demands for identification

Evidence of difficulties experienced in having their identification accepted and the need for multiple types was provided by the respondents. Many people had to provide at least three. Even a man from Northern Ireland was asked for a passport.

> You name it, everything. Birth certificate, National Insurance number, PRSI number, where I was living. Passport, yeah, everything like like that, even though you had shown your birth certificate.
> (Woman, IR, Islington, aged 30-39)

> Birth certificate etc. They asked for a passport, which I didn't have. But I could refer them to a previous claim, I knew what I was talking about.
> (Man, NI, Islington, aged 20-29)

*My passport used to cause uneasiness - they would look at it and look at you. I had great trouble getting a National Insurance number - I was put on a list, but only got it last year. I have an English birthplace.*
(Woman, IR, Lewisham, aged 30-39)

*The kids' and my birth certificate. They asked me for a passport and a driver's licence, but I don't have those. They wanted those most but I fought it. If it does for everyone else, it'll do for me. I got my bank account at the end, at the NatWest - I showed my National Insurance card, provisional licence (I got this as I thought it would help).*
(Woman, IR, Lewisham, aged 30-39)

Again these findings confirm reports from Irish agencies documented in Part Two. They illustrate the uncertainty about Irish status in Britain by front line staff in benefits offices, and lack of training received. The fact that a small random sample produced evidence of these additional demands for identification from Irish people underlines the frequency with which it occurs.

### 4.3.2 Extent of non-claiming

A number of people are deterred from claiming benefits to which they are entitled by the attitudes of benefits staff. Respondents were asked whether they had ever decided not to claim benefit or had stopped claiming for this reason (Q55a,b).

Six answered this question positively, and a further three said that they would have stopped but had no alternative means of support.

*When I was out of work, I did without.*
(Man, IR Erdington, aged 50-59)

*It would have been a factor in not bothering to claim emergency payments, travel vouchers etc. You want as least contact with the DSS as possible.*
(Man, NI, Islington, aged 20-30)

*They made me feel guilty and you shouldn't be there asking them for money.*
(Woman, IR, Islington, aged 40-49)

*In the end I stopped pursuing it because of the rigmarole I had to go through.*
(Woman, IR, Islington, aged 20-29)

*Couldn't do, no other way of living, but I would if I could.*
(Woman, IR, Islington, aged 50-59)

*Well I couldn't afford to. I'd like to. It'd be nice to be independent. Because of the attitude of the staff. I was made to feel like dirt on their shoes.*
(Woman, IR, Islington, aged 30-39)

Another group of respondents did not claim benefits to which they were entitled out of pride, and a feeling of stigma attached to this form of income. Most of these were older people who placed a high value on independence and saw welfare payments as a sign of failure rather than a form of insurance to which they had contributed.

> *I'd go to Oxfam first, before the benefits. That's my pride.*
> (Woman, IR, Erdington, aged 40-49)

> *In 1967 - when my husband got pneumonia - they sent me 18 shillings, but I sent it back. I was insulted and I borrowed from a neighbour and paid back at a pound a week.*
> (Woman, IR, Sparkbrook, aged 40-49)

> *We are independent people. We had our health and aren't afraid of hard work.*
> (Woman, IR, Harrow, 50-59)

> *Never apply for benefits because it wasn't the done thing. A disgrace, none of my friends have.*
> (Woman, IR, Harrow, aged 60-69)

> *It's pride. I'd prefer to scrub the streets than ask a penny from anyone. I've told my children to do the same.*
> (Woman, IR, Islington, aged 60-69)

> *But I don't like claiming anyway. It feels like begging.*
> (Man, IR, Islington, aged 30-39)

> *I have a pension so I'm OK. I don't want to go. You earn your money, not go looking for it.*
> (IR woman, Harrow, 70-79)

Stereotyping the Irish as 'benefit scroungers' is thus strongly at odds with this strand of Irish cultural values. But the stereotype is widespread and operates to discourage legitimate claims and to reinforce Irish people's feelings of inferiority in English eyes.


### 4.3.3 Help in making claims from Irish and other agencies

Respondents were asked whether they had turned to Irish advice centres for help in making claims, in order to assess the extent of their use by the Irish population as a whole. Only three people, all in London, had sought help from Irish agencies, suggesting that need is much more widespread than measured simply by the agencies' statistics. The finding that only 3% (3/88) had resorted to Irish welfare centres strongly corroborates the view that issues raised by Irish groups in Part Two have much wider application to the Irish population in Britain.

Reasons for not using these sources include lack of knowledge about them and the wish to retain independence. Many felt that there was no need to use these services because they knew their entitlements. Others tapped informal sources of information within the Irish community. Problems uncovered in this survey, therefore, represent additional layers of difficulty experienced by Irish people which do not reach existing monitoring systems.

A larger number had consulted non-Irish agencies (13), most mentions being made of the Citizens Advice Bureaux in both London and Birmingham. One respondent in London commented that most of the other clients she met there were Irish.

There remains, however, a large unmet need for advice. Several respondents had only discovered their rights by chance.

*My father died. I could have had the ticket bought. You don't realise.*
(Woman, IR, Islington, aged 20-29)

*I don't think I'm entitled unless someone tells me. I heard about the bus pass and I have it now.*
(Man, IR, Islington, aged 60-69)

### 4.3.4 Use of Irish staff as service providers

Ethnic monitoring procedures have brought out the need for ethnically sensitive service provision (Butt, 1994). However there has been very limited recognition of Irish needs of this kind. Respondents were asked whether they felt it would be desirable if more Irish people were employed as staff dealing with benefit claims, This question was also intended to reveal further experiences of Irish people in benefit offices.

More than half of the respondents (49/88, 56%) felt that it would be better to have more Irish staff, 14/88 (16%) did not think this was necessary and 24/88 (27%) were undecided or could not say. The proportion of positive responses was slightly higher amongst those actually using the offices (26/42, 62%).

The reasons given for preferring Irish staff fell into two main categories. These were: fairness (better treatment by officers; receive benefits entitled to, accept identification; avoid stereotyping; adequate representation; equality of job opportunities) and understanding of Irish clients (knowledge of background; no language difficulties; cultural empathy, behave in the same way)

(i) Fairness

There was a strong feeling that Irish people do not get fair treatment at present and that other ethnic groups, who are represented in staffing, are advantaged.

*A lot of Irish people who come over get bother. [It should be] just the same way black and Asian people are employed.*
(Woman, NI, Erdington, aged 20-29)

*I'm sure it would be beneficial to have a representative for the community. Any ethnic group should have their own representative.*
(Man, IR, Islington, aged 60-69)

*They could look at the situation properly. They wouldn't just throw money away and give it to those who needed it. The Asian people in this country get what they like.*
(Woman, IR, Erdington, aged 60-69)

*When I went in first, a coloured person said 'No'. The next time, an Irish girl was there and I got my money. If there's one of your own there, they'll help you out. You'll get a better deal. That's how it works. More Irish people are needed to help out.*
(Woman, IR, Lewisham, aged 30-39)

It is notable that the comments about Asians in the quotes above came from interviewees in Birmingham. They were not representative of the majority of respondents but undoubtedly reflected some aspects of the social construction of ethnic minority groups in the city and the invisibility of the Irish by comparison. The main point being made by Irish people is their own lack of recognition as an ethnic group.

Respondents thought that Irish officers would recognise identification without difficulty and not question entitlement through ignorance of Irish people's rights.

*Because they know what a birth certificate is for a start.*
(Man, IR, Islington, aged 30-39)

*There are no set guidelines. I know people that had their qualifications questioned and subsequently turned down in their applications.*
(Woman, NI, Islington, aged 30-39)

*Because of stereotypes of 'feckless Irish' - it would be useful to have people who understood the conditions of Irish people. For example, we don't have to have a passport.*
(Woman, IR, Lewisham, aged 40-49)

*The number of people I know of in Birmingham who aren't getting anything from the services that I think they're entitled to. This comes from my work with homeless centres.*
(Man, NI, Erdington, aged 40-49)

Employment of Irish officers would remove the problem of stereotyping by British people.

*Well, I suppose Irish people should be employed in proportion to their numbers. Staff should be made aware, not relying on stereotypes.*
(Man, IR, Islington, aged 40-49)

*A lot of Irish people get turned back if there's someone English behind the counter.*
(Man, IR, Harrow, aged 30-39)

Problems with British people in official positions generally, as well as the need for Irish people to take on positions of responsibility and respect, were illustrated by the respondent who said:

*It would be nice to come across the Irish in an official capacity.*
(Woman, IR, Islington, aged 40-49)

(ii) Understanding of Irish clients

Respondents felt that Irish benefits officers would understand the specificity of Irish people's situation which might reduce levels of stress experienced at present.

*Would have more awareness of position people are in as newly arrived. They need to be directed to Irish agencies.*
(Woman, IR, Islington, aged 20-29)

*Most definitely. It would help Irish people to relax and they wouldn't feel so bad explaining their problems. I think they'd get more help. More Irish people should work for the council. Because the Irish won't stand up for themselves, they won't claim.*
(Man, IR, Islington, aged 30-39)

There was a particular emphasis on language barriers experienced by many Irish people when they talk to benefits staff.

*Better knowledge of people's backgrounds - would understand them better, especially how they speak. I've heard of difficulties people have had. Benefit staff describing someone they don't understand as 'having a shamrock growing out of his mouth'.*
(Man, IR, Harrow, aged 60-69)

*Because they understand you better and you can explain better. Some say 'Oh, you talk too fast'. I'd say they are putting on an act.*
(Woman, IR, Islington, aged 50-59)

Some made the point that Irish officials would operate in culturally understood ways, emphasising the real but rarely acknowledged differences between British and Irish ways of behaving.

*Because there'd be more understanding of an Irish person's needs and how they communicate, understand people. Irish people prefer a conversation to questions and answers.*
(Man, IR, Islington, aged 30-39)

*Irish people would understand each other better and they are more helpful to one another. In the banks, the Irish help and fill out forms for others - the English banks won't do that.*
(Man, IR, Harrow, aged 60-69)

### 4.3.5 Conclusions

Reports of experiences of claiming benefits bring together a number of important issues.

- Stereotyping of the Irish as feckless and untrustworthy leads to their rights being questioned. This can mean delays in delivering the benefits to which they are entitled, which is particularly problematic for migrants who do not have an established base to fall back on.

- The stereotype is actually at variance with the cultural values of many Irish people who prefer to be self reliant and feel uncomfortable depending on welfare benefits.

- Whereas cultural difference is acknowledged for black and Asian minorities, the assumption in Britain is that Irish people share a common British culture. In fact, different ways of interacting can lead to misunderstanding of Irish people's behaviour.

- Language differences are not treated seriously. Accents are seen as inferior and used to stereotype the Irish as stupid.

The cumulative effects of these encounters with British state policies in essential areas of Irish people's lives, where their daily income and housing is involved, is to reinforce for both the British majority society and for the Irish themselves, doubts about the entitlement of Irish people to equal rights. Thus

- Irish difference is not recognised, so that cultural factors, including language, are seen as inferior versions of the British standard.

- At the same time the Irish are seen as having fewer rights and to be 'foreign' to the extent that they should carry passports and go home - leave the country or return to Northern Ireland - if they become unemployed or homeless.

- Irish people have no channels by which to challenge unequal treatment, or perhaps even ways of recognising it as such.

# 5. Racial harassment

## 5.1 Police

People come into contact with the police and judicial system for a very wide variety of reasons, ranging from trivial encounters to serious criminal involvement. In any situation there is potential for a reaction to an Irish accent or any other indication of an Irish origin. Respondents were asked a very broad question (Q47a) 'Have you ever had any contact with the police or appeared in court?' Altogether 51/88 (58%) reported some form of contact.

These respondents were asked (Q47b) 'What was your experience?' Negative reactions to their Irish origins were reported by a quarter (13/51, 25%). The seriousness of the racial harassment varied from a hostile manner to assault resulting in hospitalisation. It must be remembered that these incidents were uncovered in a sample of Irish-born people and so indicate a substantial level of anti-Irish racism in the British justice system which is never catalogued.

The following categories could be identified:

(i) Serious assault and injury

This case was recounted to us by an Irish woman in London. It has never been reported in the press.

> *The neighbours next door were having an argument. The son was beating the husband. The mother came round to ask my husband to help. My husband calmed the son down, but after he left it started again. The mother came running round again, this time with two policemen. My husband put his hand across the door as they were going to come straight into our house. The policemen dragged him out front, arrested him and took him to the police van. They kicked him under the seat, bruising his head and leg. He had to go to hospital.*
>
> *The case is in court now. There's a photo of him [pointing]. In the van they called him 'Irish cop basher'. They handcuffed him and threw him out headfirst. 'You Irish this and you Irish that'. He was kicked in the groin and they made another comment. He definitely got the worst of it because he was Irish.*
>
> *He appeared in court. The charges were thrown out, but he was bound over for one year. He took it to save arguments.*
> (Woman, IR, Lewisham, aged 30-39)

(ii) Racial harassment on the street

A man in London reported frequent abuse by police on the street.

> *The police (from Kentish Town) were abusive, calling us 'Paddy bastard' etc. I wasn't charged with anything. They just abused us on the street. They used to stop Irish people coming out of pubs and abuse them - not so much now. I didn't think so much about it .*
> (Man, NI, Islington, aged 30-39)

One respondent was himself a police officer and confirmed the prevalence of such behaviour amongst the police.

> *Undoubtedly there are cases where people have been stopped because of their ethnic background and that will include the Irish. Young Irish men walking home drunk, may start a fight. I hope they are treated fairly in my presence. I would say my presence makes a difference though.*
> (Man, NI, London, aged 40-49)

(iii) Arrest/search under the PTA

A man (aged 20-29) interviewed in London reported the arrest of his family.

> *I was lifted in Brighton by the police. One of my brothers was also in custody at the time. Our whole family was arrested. They had been watching us and following us for quite some time. It was very frightening. No charges were ever brought.*
> (Man, NI, London, 20-29)

Another couple in London were stopped and searched.

> *They stopped me and my husband one night coming home from a dance up in Cricklewood. They searched the boot. But that was when the Troubles were on, I'm going back twenty years now.*
> (Woman, IR, London, aged 60-69)

(iv) Stereotyping: drunkenness, IRA

In two cases the police made the incorrect assumption that situations of public order involving Irish people were related to drunkenness. A single Irish man living in lodgings in Birmingham, who had suffered an industrial injury which affected his memory, was assumed to be drunk.

> *I was sitting in the park because I had lost my key. It was early in the morning and they arrested me and charged me with being drunk and I had to pay a fine. I suppose I wasn't supposed to be in the park. I think the policemen wanted a day off in court. I wasn't drunk. They don't do it now. They won't come out of the station now. Things have really changed.*
> (Man, NI, Sparkbrook, aged 50-59)

An Irish woman in London said that a complaint about assault was ignored when the police heard Irish accents. It was dismissed because of assumptions of the Irish complainants' drunkenness.

> *I had gone out for the evening with workmates, one of whom was Irish. During the course of the meal, in a Greek restaurant, one of the waiters urinated on our table. When we complained to the duty manager a fight was started. The police were called and treated it as a case of the usual drunken Irish. There were no arrests.*
> (Woman, IR, Islington, aged 40-49)

One respondent, who had been harassed by her neighbour, felt more angry about the police reaction to her complaint.

*When a neighbour tried to touch my daughter I called the police. The policeman asked me 'What do I think about the IRA?' It was totally irrelevant. It was because I was Irish. I said to him that he shouldn't have asked that. The police didn't do much about it at all. I got my male relative to have a word with the neighbour. There was a lot of pressure on the Irish here. My brother knows people who have had similar treatment, related to their Irishness. The system does it. Ordinary English people are OK. The policeman was English.*
(Woman, IR, Lewisham, aged 30-39)

(v) Hostile police attitudes

A number of respondents reported police hostility towards them which they could only interpret as anti-Irish.

*I had an argument with the girlfriend. She locked herself in. I broke the door down, she threw a mirror out of the window. She rang the police. They said 'You're Irish'. I couldn't understand why they were so hostile towards me in my own home.*
(Man, IR, Islington, aged 30-39)

*I don't want to go into it. Maybe some of the comments weren't overtly anti-Irish but they could be construed as anti-Irish. Maybe just cold, off handish manner, maybe difficult to explain.*
(Man, IR, Islington, aged 30-39)

*I was in court for squatting and busking. Non-payment of poll tax. Felt in-built hostility. Can't remember anything direct being said. I was made to feel an outsider.*
(Man, IR, Islington, aged 40-49)

(vi) Moved from job

One respondent in London was working in a civilian job for the Metropolitan Police. Her boyfriend was Irish. She was told that unless she gave him up she would be moved from her job in a top security building. She gave up her job.

(vii) Court experiences

Two incidents of Irish accents carrying undue attention were reported. In one instance this was thought to have resulted in losing the case.

*Traffic offence. The barrister apologised for losing the case but said it was difficult for him because of all the Irish accents and that a 'well-spoken' opponent might have won on that.*
(Woman, IR, Islington, aged 20-29)

*I was stopped by the police, no MOT, no insurance, an Irish licence. The judge was totally baffled by my accent. I was trying to explain and he couldn't get out of his mind asking me where I was from. He looked at me and said 'Irish, are you sure? With that accent you ought to be West Indian'. He was totally taken away*

*from the idea of the case. All the court laughed. So did the police - they were amazed. It's like I have to explain myself every time.*
(Man, IR, Islington, aged 30-39)

The lack of acknowledgement of the black Irish community is vividly illustrated here. It confirms the difficulty in arguing that the Irish are not simply a subcategory of 'white'.

It appears that anti-Irish attitudes are strongly ingrained in the police force and justice system. Irish accents trigger reactions out of all relation to the context in which they are heard. This is particularly serious because the police are in a position of authority, and have the power to enforce their prejudices, including the apparently legimate use of violence. Recently cases against the police have been successfully prosecuted, but these are rarely reported outside the Irish press (eg *Irish Post,* 1996).

## 5.2 Neighbours

Harassment by neighbours was an issue raised with Irish welfare agencies. In order to assess the extent to which this was experienced in a wider sample of Irish people, respondents were asked Q48a 'Has your Irishness ever been a factor in your relations with your neighbours, now or in the past?'

Responses to this question, however, were influenced by the sampling method. Since more strongly Irish enumeration districts within representative wards had been selected, many respondents had mainly Irish neighbours. This was particularly true in Birmingham. In all 20/88 (24%) specifically said that their neighbours were all or mainly Irish. For this reason Lewisham was included in the London sample, since Irish settlement is much less clustered there and Irish people are more exposed to English, and other, neighbours.

Nevertheless neighbour harassment was reported by 17/88 respondents (19%) and a further four said that they kept a low profile: 'We keep ourselves to ourselves'. Interestingly Lewisham was over-represented amongst positive responses, from respondents who had experienced anti-Irish comments or stronger abuse.

*Little comments, joking. I sometimes say 'Pack it in', brush it off. It does get annoying. I do Avon in this street. I hear people saying 'It's just the Irish Avon lady' - no name, no face, just 'Irish', that's it. I do introduce myself.*
(Woman, IR, Lewisham, aged 30-39)

*One neighbour. Called me 'Irish washerwoman'. It's a joke. Better than being 'bastard'.*
(Woman, IR, Lewisham, aged 50-59)

*We were getting Irish abuse from our neighbours. My wife was called an 'Irish cow', 'fucking Irish bastards' etc. They threw glass in the baby's swimming pool. The council sent officers out and the abuse has since stopped.*
(Man, IR, Lewisham, aged 60-69)

190

*My previous neighbours didn't like me. I think it was because I was Irish. They didn't like my kids playing out in the garden. They complained about the noise. They expected me to muzzle my kids.*
(Woman, IR, Lewisham, aged 30-39)

Another Lewisham respondent felt a sense of shared identity with other migrants in her neighbourhood.

*A positive factor with current neighbours. For example, one is German, another Nigerian, and there is a sense of exiles together.*
(Woman, IR, Lewisham, 40-49)

Nearly a quarter of the sample 20/88 (23%) specifically mentioned that all, or most, of their neighbours were Irish so abuse was not an issue. However, different forms of harassment by neighbours were also recorded, including: generalised resentment, especially by the English; more open hostility in the past; and abuse related to IRA activity.

(i) Generalised resentment

Among those not living in Irish neighbourhoods, strong feelings of being resented and excluded were reported. These undercurrents of anti-Irish feeling call into question the 'myth of homogeneity' binding the 'white' community together. It suggests an endemic anti-Irishness in British society, which is clearly conveyed in verbal and non-verbal ways.

*There's a guy downstairs here and I reckon he's pure anti-Irish. Who you are friendly with is the Irish.*
(Man, IR, Islington, aged 20-29)

*Only where the English are concerned. Not a lot of people like the Irish. They're [English people] hard to talk to. So I just didn't bother.*
(Man, IR, Islington, aged 30-39)

*You're never ready for these things. I think the way the English people deal with it, they're uncomfortable with it. This Jamaican girl I know has had the same kind of experience. People not acknowledging you on another occasion, maybe it's a cultural difference. The resentment is more common here, but it could be any race. [Had trouble with her neighbours, but the council would not reallocate her]*
(Woman, IR, Islington, aged 30-39)

*It always has been a factor. Simply because of my easy-goingness, and not conforming to the English way. I like to live a free and open life. I don't like to be restricted. I do get a lot of stick for being Irish. I hate the restrictions of this country. Over here everybody knows your business and wants to destroy you - it's mostly the English people. They've caused me troubles, but not to my face. If I went out, just keep myself quiet. They tolerated me, but they didn't want me to converse in any way. They didn't know how to socialise.*
(Man, IR, Islington, aged 30-39)

*In digs, might be six or eight of us. Family next door were English and wouldn't be happy that there would be a crowd of Paddies next to them. At different times, in different digs.*
(Man, IR, Islington, aged 30-39)

*My brother has a lot of trouble with his neighbours. Always shouting anti-Irish comments across the fence. And the children. The old lady next door thinks she can say anything. They share the drive.*
(Man, IR, Islington, aged 30-39)

(ii) More open hostility in the past

It is often forgotten by British people that until the 1950s and 1960s it was much more acceptable to voice anti-Irish attitudes. Many respondents in both Birmingham and London gave instances of overtly discriminatory expressions, including 'No Irish' signs in advertisements for housing and employment. This clearly indicates the existence of hostile attitudes in the period before IRA activity resurfaced in Britain in the 1970s.

*We were never allowed visitors. When we first came, they didn't want children, animals or Irish. Usually a notice in the window, 'No Irish'. This was mostly in Handsworth, not Erdington. At that stage there were very few Irish around. In general they didn't seem to like Irish people, although they gave us rooms.*
(Woman, IR, Erdington, aged 60-69)

*I was in Park Road. The landlord thought I wasn't good enough for him, in his lodging house. He wanted to overcharge me. I met him in the Bear and gave he a punch.*
(Man, IR, Sparkbrook, aged 70-79)

*Years ago you'd keep yourself to yourself. I was a bit afraid. With the bombing you felt so ashamed. When we came to England first I know people would say 'No Irish' for accommodation and even jobs, 'No Irish' on the board. Years ago in the 50s and 60s.*
(Woman, IR, Islington, aged 60-69)

*In Friern Barnet. We were there seventeen years and we were made known that we were no fit people to be there. They thought we were renters and would be moving in - a very Jewish area. Because of our jobs we dressed differently and we had a very old car - we didn't have the standing. Here is much less hostile - a more mixed area.*
(Woman, IR, Harrow, aged 60-69)

## 5.3 Schools

Respondents were asked whether their children had told them about any anti-Irishness they or other children had experienced (Q50b). Nearly a quarter (11/50, 22%) reported some incidents, mainly at school, even though almost all had attended Catholic schools where most children had Irish backgrounds. Proportion were almost identical in Birmingham (20%) and London (23%).

Some harassment came from teachers.

*My little girl. Some bitch of a teacher kept going on about 'green'. It was the way she said it.*
(RC school, Lewisham)

*Son reported: The teachers picked on Irish kids and they played truant from school. They never said anything, they were all Irish anyway.*
(RC school, Erdington)

*You were treated better if you had money and I always felt I would've had a better response without the accent. My daughters should have been put into O-levels but were put into CSEs (and all got grade 1s). I don't know what the teachers were doing.*
(RC school, Harrow)

In most cases the incidents involved name-calling by other children

*They were afraid to say they were Irish at school because of anti-Irish comments - you're Mick or Paddy.*
(RC school, Harrow)

*They said they'd be calling them 'Paddies'.*
(State primary, RC secondary, Islington)

*In playgrounds. They are proud of being Irish. They got stick when they were kids.*
(RC school, Sparkbrook)

*My daughter was told she talked funny. It bothered her for a while. She doesn't want to change, she's proud of it. Though the majority of children at the school are of Irish descent. In the B and B, that bothered her. They picked on her, not others of her age.*
(RC school, Lewisham)

*They are well able to stand up for themselves. They know her Irish background. But she pulls them up. It goes on every day in every place you work.*
(RC school, Erdington)

Often, however, the Irish background of other children was given as a reason for shelter from abuse. Respondents pointed out that their children had usually chosen Irish friends.


### 5.4 At work

### 5.4.1. General atmosphere

In order to uncover any evidence of racial harassment in the workplace, respondents were asked Q 32. 'How would you describe the atmosphere where you currently work?'

An overwhelming majority of the respondents claimed that the atmosphere was good (33/41, 80%). Whilst this appears to be evidence of the acceptability of

Irish people in the labour force, it must be remembered that they are strongly clustered in particular areas of work. Thus workmates in these areas will also be Irish and there is less exposure to anti-Irish attitudes. A number of respondents qualified their answer in this way.

> *Sound - no problems - you don't have them on the buildings.*
> (Male construction worker)

> *There's a lot of Irish go in there, 90% Irish. Jovial atmosphere. Most of London isn't a community. But this is a wee community pub - everyone knows everyone's business. Because it's Irish.*
> (Female cook/cleaner)

> *It's good. I get on with all the teachers. They are all used to me.*
> (Female school helper, RC school)

When the positive answers are compared with numbers describing their co-workers as all or mainly Irish (Q 31b), it can be seen that nearly one third (10/33, 30%) fall into this category.

However a significant minority (6/41, 15%) qualified their answer to indicate that their experience was not totally positive.

> *It's more positive than in Northern Ireland because of the Catholic/Protestant divide in the workplace. That was oppressive because I was the only Irish Catholic woman in a senior position. Whereas here, to be accepted I have to go along with the joke/laugh. I can't say it offends me. Here everyone makes fun of me and I don't like it, but it's not the blocking of me behind the scenes. Everything is more open in England than in Northern Ireland - in meetings people are always saying 'We don't say that', 'It's those Irish people, we never know what they're going to say', 'We don't use that word like that'. Everyone, as soon as I open my mouth, gets laughing and says 'Let's be jolly'. People mimic my accent or sing snatches of Irish songs.*
> (Female lecturer)

> *If you keep your political views to yourself, it's better. You're better off going in, doing your day's work, basically.*
> (Male bookbinder)

> *All right. They can be petty about things and make snide remarks: 'Is that the Irish way of doing things?'*
> (Female accounts assistant)

It should be noted that the professional women who gave a more positive view of life in England was doing so from a low comparator: Northern Ireland. In her interview she described a work context of continual low intensity harassment and verbal abuse.

Occasionally (2/41) the atmosphere at work was described as 'bad'. Such experiences may have caused some Irish people to leave their jobs and look for work where they would not be harassed.

*It's a bit racist. The Asian workforce get comments and I get comments from English people.*
(Male baker)

*You look forward to 5.30 and hate 9.30 in the morning. The others are all right. I'd prefer another Irish person in there. It does help.*
(Female office worker)

In order to take this into account, as well as include a wider range of work situations, a further question was asked: Q33a: 'Has there been a good atmosphere at all the places you have worked in the past?' This question was answered by a much larger proportion of the total sample, that is all those who had ever been in paid work in Britain.

Again the great majority reported a good atmosphere (57/80, 71%). However, nearly a third of these had worked in mainly Irish workforces, sheltering them from anti-Irish abuse to a greater or lesser extent. But a much higher proportion of this larger sample reported anti-Irish racism in the workplace. Of the 22 reporting a bad atmosphere, 19 related this to racial harassment of various kinds. This represents 24% of the total sample interviewed. Birmingham and London were equally represented, as were women and men. There was a greater tendency for people from Northern Ireland to report harassment, (4/9) though the sample size is small. There was also slightly greater reporting of negative experiences by younger respondents (30% of those under 40,; 20% of those aged 40+).

Some harassment was related directly to IRA bombing campaigns, but much represented ongoing stereotyping.

*They made tea and threw it out rather than give it to me. They wouldn't talk to me. Some of them would.*
(Female factory worker, IR, aged 40 49, Sparkbrook)

*I've had hostility. Manor House, during the Hunger Strikes. But generally a lot of ignorance about Anglo-Irish politics. Images, negative images of the Irish. General hostility - as soon as they hear the accent they start taking the piss.*
(Male unskilled worker, construction/porter, IR, aged 40-49, Islington)

*Simply because they look at you differently being Irish. Once you're Irish, you're different. They don't say it to you: it's 'thick Paddy' or 'mad Paddy'. You'd hear them. They'd always ask you silly questions. Everyone that comes from Ireland gets a lot of stick about Northern Ireland. You have to be out there to see how Irish people are treated. Because I'm half West Indian I get a hundred and one questions. Black-listed. At Hawker and Siddeley, colour segregated. Turner and Ross was worse. Toffee-nosed English people. They were always unsure of how I was a welder, being Irish, you know?*
(Male welder, IR, aged 30-39, Islington)

*I've been called an 'Irish bastard' at times.*
(Male labourer, IR, aged 60-69, Lewisham)

*Great on a site - the Irish are kings on the site, everyone respects them. Three to four months in a garage - bad, definitely because I was Irish. And in several other places. But I think it's getting better. People are beginning to realise.*
(Male labourer, IR, aged 30-39, Islington)

*But I'm constantly reminded that I'm Irish. A day can't go by and I'm made to know it. I think the Brummies are the worst. One girl told me about an Irishman who rang up that she couldn't understand. She said 'I should have passed him on to you'. I said 'I'll pass all the English on to you then'. There's no reason why she can't understand and why should I understand any better?*
(Female office worker, IR, aged 40-49, Erdington)

*Most of the time, apart from when there's a crowd of Brummies who think Paddy is stupid.*
(Male carpenter, IR, aged 30-39, Sparkbrook)

*When I worked in non-Irish agencies, particularly in the homeless day centre, there would be comments after atrocities. After the Enniskillen bombings one co-worker said 'You can't justify that, don't even try'. In Brighton I used to get abuse because I was dealing with telephone bets and I would get called a 'thick Irish git'. You couldn't mess up, otherwise you got called a 'thick Irish git'. But employers were supportive. When I worked for an advice centre, we got abusive phone calls, intimidating calls.*
(Male community worker, NI, aged 20-29, Islington)

*Only one incident. You always felt you weren't liked, especially by the upper-middle classes. There was a feeling of coldness.*
(Female office worker, IR, aged 40-49, Islington)

*Because I was Irish. Just general abuse, shouting, roaring at you. Lot of bad language. 'Clear off home', that sort of thing. Generally around the time of bombing. 'Thick Paddy'. It happened in one of our groups - 'The Irish are dopey'. A student. Most people on the course are PC, couldn't express such views.*

*On the building site, most of us were together. English lads were at us. Furniture would be broken. My father had it when he came here in the 50s. There were signs. I thought in the 80s it would be changed, but it wasn't.*
(Male nurse, IR, aged 30-39, Islington)

Thus middle-class status, and white-collar occupations, did not protect Irish people from these forms of harassment though they often took subtler forms.

*In two places it was good, but not so much in another, especially in Lewisham. There was, however, a form of casual anti-Irishness among colleagues. A lot of assumed attitudes which mistook humour for what I would call racism - made it hard to challenge. Comments on how you're 'Irish' if you do something wrong. I think if I'd been black, this would not have occurred, or would have been dealt with.*
(Female welfare worker, IR, aged 40-49, London)

*When I worked in the Solicitor-General's department it was very middle-class white. I had remarks made and anti-Irish jokes about the Hunger Strikes. But also there were a small percentage of people who were very nice. But in the past few years there's been greater regard for the Irish.*
(Female clerical worker, NI, aged 30-39, London)

*[Said good] I was always very popular. I used to go out and drink with the English people. The point is you meet the educated people in the civil service, not the awkward English, you know? I find the English tolerant if you know how to pass yourself. You can't start getting drunk and throwing yourself around without getting into trouble.*
(Male civil servant, IR, aged 70-79, London)

The response of many people to bad experiences was to leave the job or to keep a low profile. There was widespread acceptance of a level of anti-Irish harassment as normal.

*Normally, in the majority there has been a good atmosphere. But others have had bad communications. It doesn't bother me because I keep my head down. It's always been an English-orientated.*
(Male engineering designer, IR, aged 40-49, Birmingham)

*[Said Good] On the whole, because of the mix of nationalities. They [the Irish] are hard workers and willing. There have been places where being Irish wasn't accepted. The feeling was about the overall population of Irish people, not only me.*
(Female catering/cleaning worker, aged 40-49, IR, Sparkbrook)

*It's hard to say. It's a hard life for everybody. If you are on a building site and there's a crowd of English people, they give you a hard time and you keep on working.*
(Male labourer, aged 30-39, IR, Sparkbrook)

*There were a few anti-Irish people but generally you can give it back. One boss was particularly anti-Irish.*
(Female clerical worker, aged 70-79, IR, Harrow)

*[Said good] The majority were Irish and we laughed the comments/jokes off.*
(Male construction worker, 60-69, IR, Erdington)

There is, clearly, a significant level of racial harassment of the Irish in the workplace. Recent cases brought to industrial tribunals with the support of the CRE represent the tip of the iceberg of abuse which is largely unrecognised and therefore cannot be challenged when it occurs.

The main points to emerge from this wider sample are:

• None of the sample had considered taking any legal redress for the abuse they had been subjected to, and only a very small minority had complained to the management. Incidence of racial harassment in the workplace is thus much more widespread than the few cases which have been brought so far. However, it is taken-for-granted, explaining why such a high proportion described the atmosphere at work as good, despite all the qualifications outlined here.

- Irish people suffered less abuse when they remained in workplaces which were predominantly Irish. Since these are often unskilled occupations, this may help to explain lower levels of social mobility within the Irish-born population. Irish people may be deterred from applying for jobs in English-dominated occupations.

- Some of the abuse was related to specific IRA bombing incidents, but in most cases these exacerbated an underlying stereotyping which could be continuous. The main stereotype drawn on in the workplace was that of stupidity.

- Abuse was directed against Irish people in general, rather than particular groups or individuals. Both women and men were targeted, those from Northern Ireland and the Republic were seen as equally connected with IRA incidents, and all age groups and generations reported similar experiences. Although openly abusive comments were more frequently made to unskilled workers, white collar workers were also subjected to demeaning remarks.

### 5.4.2 Anti-Irish comments and jokes at work

In order to examine a central aspect of harassment at work in greater detail, respondents were asked the additional question: Q34a 'Have you ever heard anti-Irish comments or jokes at work?' Cases of discrimination in the workplace successfully taken up with CRE support have involved verbal harassment which focused on stereotyping and jokes.

The great majority of respondents said that they had heard anti-Irish remarks expressed at work, A total of 65/82 (79%) answered 'Yes', very similar proportions in Birmingham (25/33, 76%) and London (40/50, 80%), a far greater proportion than had described the atmosphere as 'bad'. The minority who did not report hearing such remarks included 10/17 who worked with some other Irish people but only five who were in predominantly Irish workplaces. This group was distributed across age groups and social classes, but a distinctive feature was the high proportion of this total who were women (14/17, 82%). It may reflect the greater prevalence of 'joking' in male interaction.

A supplementary question asked for details of the content and context of the remarks. Accounts revealed a number of common features.

### (a) Content of anti-Irish remarks

(i) Prevalence of jokes

Half of those reporting anti-Irish remarks drew attention to jokes (33/65, 51%). Many claimed to accept them as 'only a bit of fun', but all jokes stereotyped the Irish as stupid, and some were clearly intended to be hostile and offensive rather than humorous.

*If English ones get into tempers, they get nasty and come out with jokes about the Irish. I've given as good as I get.*
(Male baker, Erdington)

*You know when they are in a joke, but then you would know when they want you to pick up from it. You got the feeling they didn't like the Irish very much.*
(Female school helper, Sparkbrook)

*People were OK. Couple of jokes were offensive. I pulled them up on it.*
(Female office worker, Islington)

*I've heard the 'silly Paddy-Irishman' jokes, portraying the Irish as thick. Bobby Sands jokes after he died were really sick. It was a very painful time. It always came from young men, never young women.*
(Female civil servant, Islington)

However, only one respondent classified these jokes and comments specifically as racist.

*It's a big thing about racism. No-one would dare tell a black joke to a black person. But no-one gives two shites about telling an Irish joke to an Irish person.*
(Male nurse, Islington)

(ii) General theme of stupidity

By far the most common theme of jokes and comments was Irish stupidity. This was specifically mentioned by 12/65 (19%) of the sample who reported hearing anti-Irish remarks.

*We definitely do [hear comments]. Paddy is thick, they always say that. We tell them he's not.*
(Male hospital porter, Erdington)

*Always about Paddies on the road. I'd say it needs brains to work on the road, not to walk upstairs with a piece of paper in your hand. Sometimes I wonder I wasn't sacked because I always stood up for the Irish.*
(Female clerical worker, Harrow)

*This thing that the Irish are thick, stupid. You get a lot of that from people who don't like the Irish, the older English generation.*
(Male unemployed building worker, Islington)

*They have all sorts of jokes. But they did have more Irish jokes. Always that the Irish were stupid. The 'three Paddy' jokes.*
(Female carer, Islington)

*One occasion in college, talking about different countries. When Ireland came up, one English person said 'Oh the Irish are thick'.*
(Female student nurse, Islington)

*Make the Irish out to be thick - as long as they think that, it's their downfall.*
(Male police officer, Islington)

*There was once when everyone was talking about medicine and someone said it was easier to qualify in Ireland, implying we weren't as intelligent. It's usually about intelligence.*
(Female practice nurse, Islington)

### (iii) Stereotyping by name

One way of reminding Irish people about their difference, and linking it by implication to stereotypes about stupidity, is by name-calling.

*One time a fella called me 'Pat'. I had to tell him it wasn't my name.*
(Male unemployed caretaker, Sparkbrook)

*Mostly joking. But it's not very nice from some people. They call you 'Pat' even when they know your name would persist.*
(Male retired fitter, Harrow)

*Everybody called me 'Paddy', so that didn't come as a surprise to me. When I first came over all the English called me 'Pat' which upset some, but it didn't upset me because that was my name you know?*
(Male retired steel fixer, Islington)

*At all the jobs - a constant feature. Each time I had to decide how to react. Always jokes about stupid Pat and Mick. I named my sons those names deliberately just to show Pat and Mick weren't.*
(Female house warden, Harrow)

*I objected to being called 'Paddy' by the supervisor. So when he called any of us 'Paddy' we all got up. So he learned our names next time. I went up against eight Englishmen for the supervisor job and I didn't expect to get it.*
(Male gravedigger, London)

### (iv) Stereotype of drinking

Again a strong link was made between Irish origin and alcoholism, and this was extended to all Irish people.

*About the Irish and drink - mostly said in jest, not being anti-Irish.*
(Female charity worker, Islington)

*Always give a comment back. Irish being 'thick', assumption that all Irish drink.*
(Female accounts manager, Islington)

*Ones that would reflect the reality of the situation. Sometimes IRA, Irish people drinking too much.*
(Male dentist, Islington)

### (v) Ridiculing accents

The key identifier of Irish people is accent. It is particularly significant therefore that Irish people are ridiculed about it. This harassment takes the form of expressing the opinion that Irish accents are a substandard form of English and taking for granted that mimicry is a legitimate source of amusement. Although some felt strong enough to defend themselves, others were silenced by this mockery. Some may have found it too personal to mention.

*I picked one up - a service engineer. He heard my voice and said 'Begorrah' and I told him off. He said OK. I don't give it and I don't expect it.*
(Female office worker, Erdington)

*One man I worked for said how long had I lived in this country and I told him. I said ten to fifteen years. And he said 'And you still talk like that'. It hurt me.*
(Female secretary, Erdington)

*When you say 'three' - a lot of ways you say things. Thick Paddy. They mimic and take the piss of the accent.*
(Female accounts assistant, Harrow)

*They take the piss out of the accent. It's not nasty, but it's ongoing. A mate from Leitrim has a strong accent and drops his 'th'. They say it back to him. Not nasty but still offensive.*
(Male nurse, London)

*Sometimes, when they hear the accent, 'I don't want to know anything more about her'. Unconventional people I find I get on with more. Those who are unsure of their place in society.*
(Female practice nurse, London)

*I heard comments when I did part-time building work. It is quite intimidating. The building sites were the worst. But you also overhear anti-Irish comments from the public. Jokes would be made of your accent. It gets infuriating after a while. We don't speak 'the Queen's English'. I got into rows about that.*
(Male housing manager, London)

*Some of them say 'Speak in English'. It's never been worse than in this job. He asks 'Where are you from and when are you going back?'*
(Female office worker, Erdington)

*When I went for the supervisor's job I was told that I might be wise to get elocution lessons.*
(Male gravedigger, London)

Significantly, all these respondents were in white collar/blouse or in skilled and supervisory jobs. These are areas where the English 'middle-class' accent is most highly valued and where the overt use of 'joking' may be less common. One woman professional worker felt that style of speaking was also seen as unacceptably different:

*At meetings for example, it's not just the accent that's the problem. It's more usual in Ireland to play with language, many more registers. Here it is seen as stepping out of line.*
(Female lecturer)

## (b) Context of anti-Irish remarks

The most striking feature of these remarks was their persistence and pervasiveness. Many respondents prefaced their replies with 'All the time'. Places given specific mention were building sites, factory shop floors and pubs.

*All the time. Typical Irish, just shrug it off.*
(Male unemployed labourer, London)

*You do, I think you do everywhere.*
(Female practice nurse, London)

*Millions of them - normally in the pub at lunchtime.*
(Male unemployed design engineer, Birmingham)

*At any time. If there's a group of English lads, they always make comments, especially if there's only one or two of us. They give us a hard time.*
(Male unemployed labourer, Birmingham)

*Before [I became involved in] the music situation. Hospitals, factories, building sites, shops. General anti-Irish atmosphere. Especially if you didn't agree with the establishment view. 'Fuck off back to Ireland'. 'If you don't like it over here, why don't you go back to your own country?' As if you should be grateful.*
(Male musician, London)

*There's always those little jokes. I'd never mix with the factory people. I never wore my shamrock at work - I wouldn't, but I wear it to mass.*
(Female teamaker, Sparkbrook)

*They have all sorts of jokes. But they did have more Irish jokes .... Just the shop floor.*
(Female former machinist, London)

*I was in a cleaning job and the English cleaner brought up issues. I got the impression she thought the Irish should be back in Ireland. I found myself defending my family. It ended in a heated verbal argument. It was St Patrick's Day. I was wearing a shamrock and went to my local pub and she came in with a Union Jack - but she looked a fool.*
(Female school helper, Birmingham)

Some mentioned that there had been a noticeable rise in anti-Irish comments at times of IRA bombings.

*Sometimes even from clients, especially after something happened in Northern Ireland. Comments about the Irish - they should be shot and things.*
(Female nurse, London)

*Definitely during the bombing period. There was a bomb in Oxford Street when I worked there and comments were made after that.*
(Male retired security officer, London)

The mismatch between numbers of respondents describing the atmosphere at work as bad (20%) and those reporting anti-Irish jokes and comments (79%) is a further evidence of the widespread acceptance of anti-Irish racism as normal in Britain. This helps to explain why only four respondents, all in London, had complained to the management about particular incidents. In two cases, these complaints were taken seriously and action followed.

*We reported our labourers to the council for racist abuse. The council sorted them out.*
(Male gravedigger, London)

*I made a complaint once. I found a page of Irish jokes on the photocopier at work, about 1986. I went up to the Chief Clerk (who was black) and an enquiry was launched. The perpetrators were never found. But we suspected the bailiffs as they were very racist.*
(Female clerical worker, civil service, London)

Another respondent reported that action was taken about an incident she had witnessed:

*Once I was working at a ward in another hospital where I was the only Irish/white person. There was an elderly Irish man on the ward and it was St Patrick's Day. A black nurse said, 'Oh Paddy thinks he's in the blight time'. I was very angry at that. Yes, the above incident was the only one. I felt really annoyed, but I had no back-up, so I couldn't say anything. If that'd happened today, I would've done something about it. The above incident was disgraceful. The senior staff nurse, who was also black, pulled the nurse up and had a word with her.*
(Female nurse, London)

In two other cases, however, the management had been unwilling to take up complaints, or to pursue them after an initial poor response.

*Once a user wrote a very offensive letter to me, hoping some Irish man would break my bones. I tried to take it up with the managers, but they wouldn't, saying the client was 'just like that'.*
(Female welfare worker, London)

*A colleague in Camden referred to being down the Kilburn High Road and there was a fight and she said 'Isn't that what you Irish do all the time, get drunk and fight all the time?' She's an African-Caribbean woman. Mary went to the line manager and complained and asked that the woman be spoken to as she worked in an equal opportunities context. The manager (an elite British man) spoke to her, she threw a wobbly and he backed off and came back and wanted to dismiss it.Mary asked that equal opportunities training be discussed with her but it never went further. One of the woman's African-Caribbean colleagues told her she was out of order but she took no notice.*
(Female charity worker, London)

Respondents did not associate their negative experiences directly with discrimination in employment, though some recognised that this was a possibility which was hard to prove.

*I did a business course here. I tried to set up my own business, but I was fobbed off. I could put it down to being Irish, but I really put it down to the ignorance of the English people.*
(Male welder, London)

### 5.4.3 Irish people's attitudes to comments/jokes

The mismatch noted above needs further explanation. Clearly, anti-Irish remarks at work are very widespread, and noticed by the great majority of respondents. Yet a large number chose to dismiss them as 'just a bit of fun' or attempt to ignore them, especially in some situations. Many reasons could be suggested for this situation:

- Preference not to attract even more attention by standing out against such harassment. This is particularly the case when the accent is being mocked and will be highlighted if more words are exchanged. Such an attitude represents the low profile adopted especially by the older generation of Irish migrants.

- Internalisation of guilt about IRA bombings. Irish people may share the view that they are in some way implicated through national origin.

Respondents were asked whether they found these remarks offensive or not. Their answers were classified into four groups

(a) Positive attitude to jokes, accepting them as just another kind of joke, inoffensive, humorous.

(b) Negative attitude, but hearers choose to ignore rather than challenge or acknowledge the comments/jokes as racist.

(c) Negative attitude, but rejection of the comments/jokes varies, depending on the situation. These are defined as contingent.

(d) Negative attitude, these remarks are strongly rejected and seen as racist.

### Q34d Did you find these jokes/comments offensive or not?

| Response type | Number | % |
| --- | --- | --- |
| Positive | 21 | 30 |
| Negative - ignore | 11 | 16 |
| Negative - contingent | 17 | 24 |
| Negative - reject | 21 | 30 |
| Total | 70 | 100 |

The table brings out much more clearly the negative impact of anti-Irish comments on the Irish population in Britain, and the variety of strategies adopted to deal with it. Altogether 70% (49/70) of respondents had a negative response to these comments and jokes, though only about a third had the confidence to reject and challenge racist remarks at all times. A much larger proportion had ambivalent feelings or feared to draw attention to themselves by speaking out.

(a) Positive

A substantial minority of the respondents (21/70, 30%) said that they had no objection to jokes and comments about the Irish. Men were much more likely than women to respond in this way (15 men, 6 women). These respondents made comments such as:

*Just in fun.*
(Male unemployed labourer, Birmingham)

*In some cases I was telling them myself.*
(Male engineer, Birmingham)

*Never. It's the way you'd say it. They'd be friends of mine.*
(Male clerical worker, civil service, London)

*I find them funny. I wouldn't take it as being horrible. Just somebody having a laugh at my expense.*
(Female cook/cleaner, London)

*We can laugh at ourselves.*
(Female school meals worker, Birmingham)

(c) Negative - contingent

A large group of respondents said that their response to anti-Irish comments depended on a range of factors including content, manner, and their own mood. This reflects ambivalence and a reluctance to see all situations as negative.

*It depends on what they say. If they talk and say 'He was one of the good Irish' (that is, most are not) that offends me. If they say that, I would pull them up on it. I'm offended if they say the Irish are a bit thick.*
(Female secretary, Birmingham)

*It depends on the context of the conversation. I feel hurt because they have that attitude. It's mostly the English. If I take part I talk about Irish comedians. It's only the Irish can laugh at ourselves.*
(Male baker, Birmingham)

*No, I've never found it that way. Because I think it's just a certain type of people. It depends on the way those jokes are told. Certain people might take offence or they might be told to create offence.*
(Female retired cleaner, London)

*Certain times. It depends how you feel on the particular day. Sometimes you pass them off as being ignorant.*
(Male unemployed welder, London)

*I'd feel hurt. And I just wanted the ground to open up and swallow me. If the question arose, I'd say it wasn't me, but they still feel the same. Two months ago, at a bus stop in Newington Green, a woman heard my accent: 'I was only saying to my friend, there's more Irish here than blacks'. I didn't pursue it.*
(Female home help, London)

## (d) Negative - reject

The final group of respondents overtly reported feelings of anger at remarks they heard. They felt entitled to reject demeaning comments. Some openly challenged those making anti-Irish comments, but others kept feelings of hurt and vulnerability to themselves.

> *Because they make me feel angry. They think the Irish are thick, stupid. I was made to feel I had come out of a mud hut with pigs and chickens. Derogatory remarks - I was made to feel lower than the rest.*
> (Female clerical worker, civil service, London)

> *I did find them offensive in both contexts. I felt vulnerable as I was given no support to deal with issues. Only one other Irish person was employed there.*
> (Female welfare worker, London)

> *Because I wouldn't say it about anybody else and I don't see why they should treat me like that. I'm just as good as anybody else.*
> (Male nurse, London)

> *Very insulting. Taking a race of people and insulting them.*
> (Female office worker, London)

> *I've lived here too long to listen to that. I saw the police looking at Bernard Manning telling racist jokes. It's terrible - it's not funny.*
> (Female office worker, Birmingham)

> *I was asked by somebody. I said it represented an offence to all my ancestors.*
> (Male plumber, Birmingham)

> *Jokes I wouldn't, but the comments I find extremely offensive. Because they are condemning a whole race. Very ignorant of Irish history. When I talk to them they would change their tune. But I still find it offensive.*
> (Male police officer, London)

> *There was a comment once at work, an Indian girl actually: 'My mother said that the Irish women were normally scrubbers'. I took her to task.*
> (Female credit controller, London)

This was one of a number of comments made by other ethnic minorities based on stereotyped views of the Irish.

A high proportion of the respondents in this group were in white-collar occupations, suggesting that this category may feel more confident in asserting the positive sides of their Irish identity and their right to equal treatment. There were approximately equal numbers of women and men.

Generalised anti-Irish attitudes took on greater significance at times of IRA bombings.

> *These made me feel very conscious of the political situation and made you feel very vulnerable. They made you feel England was a hostile place. I watch Irish*

*football games at home rather then go to the pub because I expect hostility.*
(Male housing manager, London)

*When they're intended - you are better off in your own country. I find myself politely putting the person in their place and say it's not my fault. I'm just trying to live my life the best way I can. I find it offensive when they make it clear they don't want you - you are only something on the end of their shoe.*
(Female school helper, Birmingham)

*It can hurt you especially if there is a bomb or anything has happened in Northern Ireland. It isn't nice - we haven't done it, it's nothing to do with us. 'It's the fucking Irish'. We seem to get the cold shoulder against it. That upsets me a lot.*
(Male hospital porter, Birmingham)

*It often felt like a feeling of hostility, always a feeling that it was there and could always get to be more in certain circumstances. Especially the time on the buses.*
(Female house warden, London)

Jokes are a powerful and pervasive way in which Irish people are subjected to hostility and stereotyping in forms which are hard to combat, since there is no recognition of their racist basis. It is particularly difficult for individuals to challenge this racism when they lack support or are in a vulnerable position. Moreover, the jibe that they 'lack a sense of humour' if they stand out against this harassment is a powerful silencer.

# 6. Impact of Northern Ireland on Irish experiences in Britain

## 6.1 Stoppages at ports and airports

All Irish people are potentially subject to the operation of the Prevention of Terrorism (Temporary Provisions) Act (PTA) which was introduced following the Birmingham pub bombings in November 1974. Many encounter its effects at ports and airports, where examining officers have the power to stop and examine anyone entering or leaving the country. There is no requirement that the officer must have a reasonable suspicion of involvement in terrorism, simply that individuals

> *shall be in a category or there should be special circumstances which in his view make it reasonable that he should find out and that he should ask questions.*
> Lord Donaldson, 1980. (Cited in Hillyard, 1993: 18).

As Hillyard (1993) points out, 'In other words, it is lawful for examining officers to stop and examine someone simply because they are Irish'.

In all 51/85 (60%) of the sample had been stopped at least once, 11 (13%) for over an hour. This illustrates that numbers of people affected by stoppages under the PTA are far greater than official statistics show. Only stoppages lasting over an hour are recorded officially. However the majority are shorter than this. When asked whether anything else had occurred, half (24) said that they had been searched, and a quarter (13) had been questioned about the origin and destination of their journey. Many had been asked for proof of identity (8) and to complete a form (8). Two had been detained and then released.

The main purpose of the stoppages appeared to be intelligence-gathering. Whilst the Northern Irish-born were most likely to be stopped, people from the Republic were also frequently checked.

> *Numerous very personal questions about work, lifestyle, colour of clothes, residence, who I was visiting and seeing - in the first year I was stopped every time I went via Birmingham/Belfast.*
> (NI Catholic women aged 50-59).

> *My ID cards from college were taken away to be photographed and my address book was looked through. Regularly I am asked to fill out a card.*
> (NI Catholic man aged 20-29)

> *By security for ten minutes. They wanted an address of where I was travelling to. There was no follow-on.*
> (IR woman aged 40-49)

> *Normal routine checks - just ask destination and purpose of visits.*
> (IR woman aged 50-59)

Many respondents saw these abnormal checks, which are contrary to provisions of freedom of movement within the EU agreed at the Treaty of Rome, as 'usual' and 'routine'. However, feelings of intimidation and anxiety about the consequences were common.

> *Once they had to hold the ferry - we didn't miss the ferry any time. Usually there is just a check. They searched my bag. They gave me no reason or apologies either. It's frightening though.*
> (IR woman aged 60-69)

> *I used to feel, in Heathrow, isolated, sort of put aside. It made me feel self conscious. Not at Stansted or Luton though. Briefly, but nothing very big. Just a few minutes.*
> (IR woman aged 30-39)

> *For one hour. By the Special Branch in 1981. I was wearing a Bobby Sands badge going through Heathrow to Belfast. I had to fill in an Alien Form. They made no comment about the badge I was wearing. I showed my pass for the Lord Chancellor's Office. I don't know if there was any follow-up after. I often regretted filling in the form and telling the truth about where I worked etc. because it's now on file. Maybe it has stopped my chance for promotion, who knows?*
> (NI woman - Catholic origin - aged 30-39)

In order to assess the extent of these experiences, respondents were asked if they knew of other people who had been stopped. Many (34/85, 40%) reported that other members of their family and friends had been stopped for surveillance purposes, or simply that they knew of 'lots'. One pointed out that the true figure was probably higher as people kept it quiet.

> *Most people don't say about it. You learn not to say in case there was someone around who couldn't be trusted. You'd never know who people are connected to.*
> (NI Catholic woman 60-69)

The apparently indiscriminate application of examining officers powers were frequently noted.

> *Mainly young men. Some cousins, Kath's brother, about as harmless as you can get. They were touring Ireland in a car north to south. Two were of Irish descent and one was a doctor, about as inoffensive as you can get.*
> (RI woman 60-69)

> *My mother - she would have her baggage searched. A little old lady on her own - she just used to give them her bags. Every place she went, they pulled her in.*
> (IR woman aged 40-49)

> *My wife's aunt was strip searched in Christmas 1990 - six were taken off a coach and asked for identity and strip searched. The Irish are penalised.*
> (IR man aged 20-29)

*The worst case was a friend of mine (from a Nationalist background) who was stopped going to Paris, and as a result missed her flight. She was stopped again, held for five hours and her fiance, who was travelling with her, was advised not to get involved with such a troublesome family.*
(NI Catholic man 20-29)

*My brother was stopped every time. He was a hurler and whenever he passed to and from London and Belfast he was stopped because he was carrying a hurling stick. He was stopped by the Special Branch for 40 minutes to one hour. No follow-up. It's just accepted that you get stopped. Men always get stopped.*
(NI woman -from Catholic community - aged 30-39)

A major effect on the Irish population in Britain of these experiences is thus strong pressure to keep a low profile. Irish people curtailed their activity and reduced their travel. Problems of raising issues of anti-Irish discrimination were increased.

*It discouraged people from going back home, being stopped and questioned. The vast majority have nothing on them. It's their [port authorities ] hostility - they're not impartial.*
(IR man aged 60-69)

The findings from the sample reinforce those detailed in Part Two. The great majority of these stoppages were not recorded and appear in no official statistics. But they remind the Irish community in Britain that they are all  suspect  and should feel guilty about their Irish origins.


## 6.2 Responses to IRA bombings in Britain

Anti-Irish hostility was dramatically increased by IRA bombing campaigns in Britain. Attitudes which had been expressed openly in the 1950s and 60s in the advertisements in newsagents  windows as 'No Blacks, No Irish'  and 'No Irish need apply', became raised to a new level of intensity. Kirkaldy (1979) traces the revival after 1968 of nineteenth-century Punch cartoon images in the British press, depicting the Irish as apes and subhumans. The main changes in the British attitudes arising directly from the bombings were:

- Intensification of pre-existing stereoypes portraying all Irish people, from North and South, as violent, mindless terrorists. Very little attempt was made to understand the political situation out of which the bombings came.

- Easier justification of anti-Irish discrimination and racism. It now appeared self-evident that the Irish should be treated with dislike and contempt.

Irish responses to this hostility invariably took the form of avoidance of contact with British people and attempts to remain invisible by staying silent. Irish people were easily identifiable, especially at the local level. In their own neighbourhoods Irish origins were already known, and to strangers, accents were the main identifiers. Self-protection in both cases took the form of 'keeping their heads down'. These responses illustrate very clearly the ambivalence of Irish people in

Britain about their exclusion from consideration as a separate ethnic specific rights and needs. It explains:

- Reluctance to make claims for resources to which they are entitled.

- Lack of a concerted protest at racist treatment, partly as result of fear of being identified, but also shame arising from a partial acceptance of 'guilt by association'. Attacks and intimidation were not reported to the police, who were perceived as sharing negative stereotypes of the Irish.

### 6.2.1 Birmingham bombings

The Birmingham pub bombings in November, 1974 were a landmark in the heightening of British hostility towards the Irish after the renewal of open conflict in Northern Ireland in 1968. Twenty one people were killed, including nine Irish people, and others were seriously injured. This was one of the first major bombings in Britain.

Birmingham experienced a very large increase in numbers of migrants from Ireland during the 1950s as result of labour shortages in manufacturing industries. This immigration was associated with strong expressions of anti-Irish feeling. In their study of Sparkbrook, Rex and Moore (1967) found that animosity against the Irish was at least as great as that against 'coloured' groups and sometimes higher. For example

> Mr C saw the Irish as the main problem-group among newcomers. Riddled with North-South animosities, they 'got boozed up to the eyeballs', became fighting mad, and punched and kicked one another in the street.
> (Rex and Moore, 1967: 70)

Although there were slightly more unfavourable mentions of the 'coloureds' than for the Irish and 'tinkers' together, unlike all other groups except the Pakistanis, there were no favourable mentions for the Irish (pp 82-83). For their part the Irish felt themselves to be heavily discriminated against in Birmingham, especially in housing (p 88).

Against this background of low-level and latent anti-Irish attitudes in Birmingham, the bombings intensified hostility dramatically. Irish people suffered a backlash in many other parts of Britain, but the aftermath of the bombings was experienced most intensely in Birmingham itself. The British reaction was an outpouring of hatred against Irish people as a whole, which ranged from physical attack to shunning. The Irish response was the adoption of a low profile to avoid recognition.

In response to the question: 'Were you living in Birmingham in 1974, when the Birmingham bombings occurred? If yes, what was your experience and reaction at the time?', respondents described graphically the backlash experienced in different arenas.

## (i) Workplaces

Workplaces were important sites of physical threats and intimidation. As labour migrants most Irish people were in paid employment, often in large groups, and were clearly identifiable. In order to avoid clashes between workers, some managers sent Irish workers home.

*My son was sent home to stay at home for a few days. There must have been nastiness going on. He's a bricklayer. But he didn't tell us at the time.*
(Woman, IR, Erdington, aged 60-69)

*My husband was thrown off the bus. It's not like we did it. It wasn't our fault. In the car factory they were working with spanners and hammers. He was frightened. The police sent coaches to bring them home. He had his mouth busted - stitches.*
(Woman, IR, Sparkbrook, aged 60-69)

*There was a lot of hostility. I worked in Typhoo then. The management and unions met to discuss it. We were told to keep our heads down and not get excited.*
(Man, IR, Sparkbrook, aged 50-59)

*I was working at Rover and the director rang to enquire if I was being harassed, that I should be allowed to go home. I was the only Irish person and they couldn't have been nicer. The Rover workers in the factories marched out to campaign to send the Irish back home.*
(Woman, IR, Erdington, aged 50-59)

Others who stayed at work were ostracised and made to feel invisible.

*People at work stopped speaking to my aunt in Southalls.*
(Man, NI, Erdington, aged 40-49)

*Dead silence when I went to work - the silence spoke enough.*
(Woman, IR, Erdington, 80+)

*I felt dreadful - there weren't any Irish at work in the hospital. I was the only one not called in - although I only lived up the road from the hospital - to do the emergency packs, but I went in to volunteer. I got the cold shoulder and abuse.*
(Woman, IR, Erdington, aged 80+)

*My husband was away - I didn't know about it. I went into work and asked a gentleman who I always bathed first. He said 'I don't want you to do it now or later'. I saw the sister and told her about his funny mood. She said 'Are you surprised? You obviously haven't heard about the bombings. Just carry on'. His wife came in and said her husband wasn't bathed. I stayed on to do it and he apologised - we were both crying. He never said any more about it. I didn't realise about the trouble until I came here.*
(Woman, IR, Erdington, aged 60-69)

(ii) Neighbourhood

Irish people were also subjected to physical and verbal attack in their neighbourhoods. Intimidation by anonymous threats were also commonplace.

*People called out 'Molly Malone' as I walked down the street because I was Irish. I was hurt and mad for weeks.*
(Woman, IR, Erdington, aged 60-69)

*They treated us horribly and treated us like dirt. Our children could just as likely to be in the bomb. They were bad to us in the shops. Englishmen did not treat us the same as the day before. You could not blame them for that.*
(Man, IR, Erdington, aged 60-69)

*We didn't get a good reaction from the neighbours. If there is trouble, you are all tarred with the one brush. Mr H asked if I would like a brick through my window. We kept our head down and carried on.*
(Woman, NI, Erdington, aged 70-79)

*This was a terrible time. All the Irish community was in shock and people reacted to them. I took my children to school and an English woman gave us verbal abuse. She said 'Why don't you fucking go back?' I asked her to think that people in the bomb were Irish. The doctors and nurses trying to save them were Irish.*
(Woman, IR, Sparkbrook, aged 40-49)

*I got nasty phone calls saying they'd get the children and burn them and to go back to where I'd come from. I'll always remember that. She was oldish and didn't live in our street. She knew where we lived. I got the police in and I had to change my number.*
(Woman, Erdington, aged 60-69)

(iii) Public areas

Irish people were shunned in shops and pubs. Again many chose to avoid such ostracism and the risk of abuse.

*There was a lot of ill-feeling then. People were not served in shops. I had no reaction where I worked. I didn't agree with it.*
(Man, IR, Sparkbrook, aged 50-59)

*Oh, very bad. I didn't like it. There wasn't a lot thought of us in 74. Nothing was said to me, but you could see the grudge was there. You wouldn't be made welcome in the pub. There wasn't much time for us after that. There's no welcome. We kept quiet.*
(Man, IR, Sparkbrook, aged 50-59)

*It was dreadful - I never opened my mouth for a week. We were all glad when they picked someone up to blame for it - it was awful. Thank God I wasn't at work. My sister said it was being discussed all the time. I had a pain in my shoulder from being humped.*
(Woman, IR, Erdington, aged 40-49)

*I stayed inside - I thought I'd be shot. I kept out of the way.*
(Man, IR, Sparkbrook, aged 70-79)

*It was a bit bad. I went to one shop and they wouldn't sell me any sugar. It's not as if we'd done it.*
(Woman, IR, Sparkbrook, aged 40-49)

Anti-Irish hostility was indiscriminately applied to anyone identified as Irish.

*Friends with Irish names received nasty letters and phone calls.*
(Woman, IR, Erdington, aged 50-59)

The impact of the event continued to be felt long afterwards:

*The local community singing and dancing finished after that bomb. It wasn't a nice thing for the Irish. Police came to other people knocking them up in the night and everything.*
(Man, IR, Erdington, aged 70-79)

*Even so, many years after...I feel that feelings run high about Irish people - they still don't want us here. The black people said that they got a rest at that time as the Irish got the brunt of it.*
(Woman, IR, Sparkbrook, aged 40-49)

However this backlash did not take into account either the inclusion of the Irish amongst the dead and injured or the shame felt by many Irish people.

*When I got to work - it was awful. I felt ashamed. The atmosphere was awful. You got comments. The Irish were more upset than anyone else really.*
(Woman, IR, Erdington, aged 50-59)

### 6.2.2 Experience after other bombings

Both samples were asked about their experiences after other bombings. Although many in Birmingham felt that by comparison, reactions were less severe than in 1974, Irish people in London reported high levels of hostility.

The main features of this hostility were: its virulence; lack of connection with any understanding of the political background; blanket application to all Irish people; triggered solely by hearing Irish accents.

Respondents in London reported:

*It was insulting. In the early 1970s the Birmingham bombs - the wave of anti-Irishness was horrific. I was refused service in a shop. I was made to feel that being Irish was a bad thing. I tried to hide my accent. That was the beginning of it. Up till 1974/5 there was a whimsical thing. Then the violence thing was revived. We were feared rather than patronised. People would just ignore you. I've been made to feel that you just don't belong.*
(Man, IR, Islington, aged 40-49)

*The neighbours said 'Your crowd's at it again'. I ignore a lot of it.*
(Woman, IR, Lewisham, aged 30-39)

*The Birmingham bomb made me sick. I was verbally attacked. 'Fuck off, Paddy'
etc. It was people who didn't know me.*
(Man, IR, Lewisham, aged 60-69)

*A general intolerance. My neighbour asked me if I was a 'sleeper'. This really
angered me. It makes you keep your head down.*
(Man, NI, Islington, aged 20-29)

*It's dreadful really. I've been put out of shops, down the West End, Great
Portland Street - had a lady panic, send for her husband. He came downstairs,
threw me out of the shop. I could have done something about it, but what's the
point? Just one or two incidents. Even mates that I've worked with for years.
Eddie from Wales, I've seen him blank me. Mates in the pub they come out with
comments like 'Bloody Irish murderers, they should all be shot'. Even governors,
some of them can be well bad culprits.*
(Man, IR, Islington, aged 30-39)

*The last few years hasn't been so bad. Mountbatten, Hunger Strikes and
Brighton, I could feel the anti-Irish hostility. Someone said 'They should go to
Ireland and 'blow the lot up'. I have had someone labeling me an IRA supporter
because I am a Catholic. Because of the drunken stereotype, I make a conscious
effort not to drink on certain occasions.*
(Woman, NI, Islington, aged 30-39)

*There's been anti-Irish comments, especially at times of IRA trouble, they they
would apologise for present company. 'Take Ireland out in the Atlantic and sink
it', 'Nuke the bastards', 'Shoot the whole fucking lot of them'.*
(Man, NI, Islington, aged 40-49)

*They destroyed it for all the Irish. I would avoid going into shops, couldn't.
You'd have to go out [as a carer] and you'd hear them saying 'Fucking so-and-
sos' and 'They've no business bombing our country'. I'd just get the shopping and
be gone. Clients were hostile, but they were lovely old people. They'd say: 'Send
all the Irish back'.*
(Woman, IR, Islington, aged 60-69)

The main Irish responses to these outpourings included: keeping a low profile,
particularly keeping silent in public places, and restricting social contact to the
Irish community to reduce contact with British people.

Respondents reported:

*Well, you get a certain amount of anti-Irish feeling about, stirred up by gutter
rags like the Sun. Wonder how Irish people can read the Sun. I've always been in
the Irish community, so nothing is directed at me. You just know there is a
general atmosphere of hatred towards Irish people because of the IRA/INLA etc.*
(Man, IR, Islington, aged 30-39)

*When there was bombing here, I always kept quiet on buses and trains. I was
careful - I knew they would recognise my accent.*
(Woman, IR, Lewisham, aged 50-59)

*No, except in general terms, nothing insulting. I don't mix with those kinds of people. I have very firm friends.*
(Woman, IR, Harrow, aged 70-79)

### 6.3 Adoption of a low profile

### 6.3.1 Restriction on activities in Britain

Ways in which fear of identification as Irish had restricted people's lives in Britain were investigated. Respondents were asked whether they had refrained from participating in formal community organisations, or political and cultural activities because their Irish associations might draw unwelcome attention (Q39, 40, 41).

The great majority of respondents said that they had not been deterred. Not all are interested in such activities or have easy access to them. However, a small number acknowledged that they had been afraid to identify themselves as Irish in this way.

(a) Community organisations

Seven respondents (8%) said that they had avoided joining community organisations for fear of repercussions.

*You couldn't join anything because I know the Irish here were under surveillance. And it is as well not to be getting nationalistic.*
(Woman, IR, Harrow, aged 60-69)

*No, well I think one would be worried about anything being predominantly Irish over here. Because I think English people would be worried about you then. Because of Northern Ireland, I think. My husband is a member of an Irish professional association. I don't think it is necessarily a good thing here. I think in America it's a good thing. I suppose I'd be worried to join anything here, worried about nationalist extremists.*
(Woman, IR, Islington, aged 30-39)

*I think it'd be a bad idea. I don't know why. [Are you wary of it? Nods].*
(Woman, IR, Islington, aged 50-59)

*Very true. That's ambiguity, my dilemma. Fear of being labelled.*
(Woman, NI, Erdington, aged 50-59)

b) Political activity

Another small section of the sample (8, 9%), only half overlapping with the previous group, had decided not to join political organisations to avoid unwelcome attention.

*I've always been conscious of Special Branch and police surveillance and you are just attracting attention. Just to be Irish is to be accused anyway. I knew a police inspector and was in a pub at the time of the bombings. He pointed me out*

*saying 'He's one of them'. I had done nothing.*
(Man, IR, Erdington, aged 50-59)

*I just don't want any trouble. I can imagine going up to court and renewing my [publican's] licence. I know for a fact it would harm me.*
(Man, IR, London, aged 30-39)

*I never deliberately stopped myself, but I never considered it because of that. Because you could be labelled.*
(Woman, IR, Islington, aged 30-39)

(c) Cultural activity

Very few (3) went so far as to avoid participation in cultural activity for fear of identification. A respondent in Birmingham, however, pointed out that Irish cultural activity, which had been organised in Catholic parishes, virtually ceased after the pub bombings in 1974.

*They stopped after the pub bombings. Dancing, plays, singing. It went from eleven priests to three.*
(Man, IR, Erdington, aged 70-79)

However the vast majority of the sample said that they had not been deterred, but were not interested in belonging to organisations. Common responses were:

*Never joined anything like that.*
(Woman, IR, Sparkbrook, aged 70-79)

*Never bother.*
(Man, IR, Sparkbrook, aged 50-59)

*Don't join associations, full stop.*
(Woman, IR, Harrow, aged 20-29)

*I don't join in political things, I'm not politically-minded.*
(Woman, IR, Erdington, aged 40-49)

*I never join anything.*
(Man, IR, Erdington, aged 70-79)

This illustrates the important difference between the sample of Irish people interviewed in Birmingham and London and those who have contacted Irish community organisations and whose experiences were recorded in Part Two. Most of the sample had never contacted any community organisation.


### 6.3.2 Playing down an Irish identity

Respondents were asked Q42a. 'Have you ever felt the need to play down your Irish identity?' A substantial minority replied positively (17/88, 19%). The single most important source of identification was accent and way of speaking, so that playing down an Irish identity meant altering this accent or keeping quiet. Interestingly women were far more likely than men to admit to hiding their accents, comprising 12/17, (71% of those giving this response).

A few had reacted to perceptions of general unacceptability, especially on first arrival, but many were protecting themselves from the backlash against IRA bombings.

> At the beginning because of people's reaction to my accent, taking the mickey out of the way you say words and you don't want to be seen as stupid. So I changed how I spoke, but not now.
> (Woman, Islington, aged 20-29)

> I think so, initially when I came. I was very conscious of myself. Now I don't care what they say any more. I think I'm not very confident anyway, I'm a bit shy. I think, yes, when I first came here there were a lot of terrorist bombings and it did bother me. Now the Troubles are over it doesn't bother me as much. But it is very different living here. At the end of the day, I think everybody's feeling better about being Irish.
> (Woman, IR, Islington, aged 20-29)

> When I came over at seventeen, I think you did because there was a lot of trouble. Didn't talk out loud, in case it triggered off. But then, I decided I didn't care.
> (Woman, IR, Islington, 30-39)

> Often it would be better not to have my accent.
> (Woman, NI, Harrow, aged 60-69)

> Afterwards I have thought, why didn't I bring in an Irish dimension [to a debate]? But I am put off by the fact that people might groan. If it's safe I will raise it... All part of wanting to be included and not excluded.
> (Woman, NI, Erdington, aged 50-59)

> When I rang up for car insurance, I rang and got a different quote with an Irish and an English name. There was £100 in the difference.
> (Woman, IR, Harrow, aged 20-29)

Others described going to considerable lengths to avoid drawing attention to their Irish background.

> In Brighton I wouldn't go to political meetings because I was scared of being lifted. You think about the Birmingham Six or the Guildford Four and wonder if it could happen to you. When I am stopped at the airport I never reveal that I work for an Irish association. I would say the council etc. In pubs, I order a drink saying as little as possible. Also I would never approach the police to ask directions etc.
> (Man, NI, London, aged 20-29)

> I felt in the wrong place at the wrong time. At the height of the Troubles I know people who have had trouble so it meant I didn't advertise I was Irish.
> (Man, IR, Erdington, aged 40-49)

> The police would be one anyway. When you get stopped by the police you put on a cockney accent.
> (Man, IR, Islington, aged 20-29)

A particular problem was faced by a Northern Irish Catholic man who joined the police force.

> *Initially in police circles, in Hendon. After the first five months there were a lot of bombs. Some were quite nearby. They thought there was one in Hendon and it had to be evacuated. At a party in Hendon, me and other Irish blokes, with quite a lot of people who worked in the City, felt awkward. Entering a discussion, people see you're Irish and you try to play it down. Since then it doesn't bother me. While living in a section house, I used to go out and be Jack the Lad. I came back and people would ask where I'd been, and if I'd been out planting a bomb. Sometimes you just reacted.*
> (Man, NI, London, aged 20-29)

But the majority said that they did not attempt to conceal their Irish identity. A considerable number made a point of stressing their pride in their Irish origins (27/88, 31%), whilst others said that they could not avoid identification because of their accents (7).

# 7. British attitudes to the Irish

It is clear from the evidence presented by the respondents that varying levels of anti-Irishness are widespread in British society. There is a climate of acceptance of anti-Irish racism and racial harassment as 'normal' so that the possibility of discrimination is not recognised. This deters Irish people from speaking out against racist treatment, in the belief that they will not be taken seriously. Moreover, because discrimination is unrecognised, racist treatment may also be interpreted as personal rather than a systematic attack on the group as a whole.

Respondents were asked two more general questions about their experience of being Irish in Britain:

Q38a 'Have you ever seen or heard anything directed against the Irish in Britain which you objected to?'

Q11 'How do you think Irish people are viewed in the USA, Britain, the rest of Europe, Australia and other countries?'

These questions were asked specifically because people may organise their lives so as to avoid direct experience of racist treatment and thus appear to have few problems. They may work largely with Irish people and socialise in Irish circles, as a number of respondents have indicated. However, they may be well aware that anti-Irish attitudes exist.

## 7.1 Anti-Irish experiences in Britain

The majority of respondents (57/88, 65%) stated clearly that they had seen and heard things directed against the Irish in Britain which they had rejected, either openly or privately. This finding contrasts sharply with the 79% reporting a 'good atmosphere' at work, reinforcing the idea that varying levels of anti-Irishness exist and that different coping strategies are adopted.

Although the remainder of the sample said that they had not encountered anything they objected to, it was clear that this was partly the result of avoiding or ignoring painful situations. Women were predominant in this group (20/31).

> *I keep away from trouble.*
> (Woman, NI, Erdington, 60-69)

> *I can't think of anything. I just mixed in and took no notice. If you are looking for trouble you'll find it.*
> (Woman, IR, Erdington, 80+)

> *It's great if you are working. I wouldn't rear kids here. One Irish can get a bad name and they brand the rest of us. We go to an Irish pub - well, there is an English bar, but we never mix with them - it's totally separate. The staff are Irish too. We know most of our friends from the pub.*
> (Woman, IR, Harrow, 20-29)

*A lot of how you are treated is down to your own attitude. If you join with an attitude that he's a copper and he's going to be anti-Irish, then it's likely to happen. I think my experience has been quite positive - partly because I've gone into a caring profession and nurses are well thought of in Ireland and here.*
(Woman, IR, Harrow, 30-39)

*The only incident I had was a guy calling out to me and calling me an 'Irish bastard'. He was probably on drugs. You get comments, but you'd get that with every nationality going. I think older people might be more anti-Irish. I don't know. You do get comments but you just ignore it. England has offered me training I couldn't get in Ireland.*
(Woman, IR, Harrow, aged 20-29)

Amongst those who did object to what they had witnessed or experienced, four main situations were mentioned, though there was considerable overlap between them. It must be remembered that respondents were asked this question without prior warning and little time to call up memories. Their responses represent immediate impressions rather than a carefully considered catalogue of events which might have been forthcoming if more time had been allowed. These were thus spontaneous reactions which understate, rather than exaggerate, the full range of anti-Irish experiences in the sample population.

(i) Media representations

A large number of respondents said that they objected strongly to the way Irish people and issues were represented in the British media. This was the single largest category specifically identified, mentioned by 21/57 respondents (37%).

*Press, television, the whole media. Their whole attitude to the Irish. They still see the Irish as someone to make a joke out of. They refuse to take them seriously.*
(Man, NI, Islington, aged 30-39)

*In the media I have. Irish people are viewed as peasants, pixies and priests. Well, it's probably true in many ways. I don't think it bothers people as much now, as Irish people are becoming more educated. That we are religious freaks. People have asked me what being a Catholic means for us. Sometimes you're an Irish Catholic rather than just Irish. Usually it's the peasant thing. Like about the Kennedys being Irish and corrupters, and it's not surprising. In America and Australia you hear about the success stories. It boils down to a class orientation.*
(Man, IR, Islington, aged 30-39)

Many referred to entertainment programmes as particular instances where derogatory images and comments were freely expressed. A high proportion of older Irish people was included in this sample.

*I don't enjoy anti-Irish jokes at work or on TV. In a show at Christmas, Russ Abbott told anti-Irish jokes at the Hippodrome and I didn't like it.*
(Woman, NI, Erdington, aged 50-59)

*On TV, the so-called comedians.*
(Man, IR, Erdington, aged 50-59)

*TV mostly - the comedians.*
(Man, IR, Erdington, aged 60-69)

*I don't like the anti-Irish jokes on TV, but on the radio I only hear people standing up for the Irish.*
(Woman, IR, Harrow, aged 70-79)

*Some episodes in drama on TV. They kind of look down on the Irish.*
(Man, IR, Harrow, aged 60-69)

*I don't look at plays and films because they don't depict us very well.*
(Woman, NI, Erdington, aged 70-79)

*Well, apart from the TV programmes that take the piss out of us. And Terry Wogan, especially his latest programme. When the Grand National had a false start and the Irish National had no problem: 'Look, a backward country like Ireland can show us how to start the National!' Des Lynam laid into him - that was unusual.*
(Man, IR, Islington, aged 30-39)

*On the television, people making remarks about Irish people. I don't take too much notice because that's part of life.*
(Man, IR, Islington, aged 60-69)

*I'm sure there has been. I can't think of an example. They are very general and on TV.*
(Woman, IR, Harrow, aged 70-79)

One respondent pointed out the lack of specific programming for the Irish in Britain.

*The only Irish programme we get over here is* The Late, Late Show, *Gay Byrne. We don't receive enough news from home. I'm in the dark really. I'd like to see more Irish programmes. The others get their news and programmes.*
(Woman, IR, Sparkbrook, aged 40-49)

The other major area of concern was newspapers, many of which were also felt to be biased against the Irish.

*Regular comments in the press about Irish people and benefit fraud and cartoons which are racist. Also the general attitude of the British press to Ireland. If Northern Irish people do well they're 'British' and if they don't they're 'Irish'.*
(Man, NI, Islington, aged 20-29)

*The tabloids and the* Evening Mail *were anti-Irish for a time. Even the local throwaway newspaper - they had a crack at the Irish.*
(Man, IR, Erdington, aged 50-59)

*Norman Tebbit in the* Sun *- he writes every Thursday. The worst is the* Daily
Mail *for jokes and comments.*
(Man, IR, Erdington, aged 60-69)

*Remarks in the paper. A few remarks on TV and in the papers that I don't like. In
the* Express *John Junor said the Irish were pigs and rolling in muck. There are
others. I can't think of their names. It's very degrading and I don't agree with it.*
(Woman, IR, Harrow, aged 50-59)

*If you read the papers there's a slight little looking down. But in England the
journalists look down on everybody . But it's not so much now as it was twenty
years ago..... For years, everybody seemed to be leaving Ireland, so people here
rightly thought there was nothing in Ireland. But now music, media - the profile
has changed a lot.*
(Man, IR, Islington, aged 60-69)

Some drew attention to what they saw as misleading coverage of the Northern
Ireland conflict.

*Papers were biased during the Troubles. You never heard what Unionists did -
they caused far more deaths.*
(Woman, IR, Islington, aged 60-69)

*When the Troubles were on - the media coverage. There have been things -
nothing that really upset me.*
(Woman, IR, Erdington, aged 40-49)

*After the Brighton bombing, in the press. I know there are things in the press, the
tabloid papers - not exactly a correct image of Irish people.*
(Man, NI, Islington, aged 20-29)

(ii) Anti-Irish experiences connected with Northern Ireland

The majority of experiences recounted were not simply connected to recent IRA
activity, although this was often an added element to the hostility. However, a
few respondents reported specific incidents they had objected to, which must be
seen in the context of the Northern Ireland conflict and PTA.

*A friend was strip-searched on Seven Sisters. Late at night the police stopped
him and went further when they heard his accent. They told him they didn't have
to have a reason to take them in. In Holloway Road, the police have been in after
the World Cup and ordered everyone out of the pub at the end of the match. If
you asked 'Why?' as the police herded you up Holloway Road, you were just
immediately picked up.*
(Woman, IR, Islington, 20-29)

*On marches - Bloody Sunday marches - the BNP hurled missiles.*
(Man, NI, Islington, aged 20-29)

Others reported an intensification of negative comments.

*I heard them say 'The Irish should be sent back home'. They didn't know I was Irish.*
(Woman, IR, Islington, aged 60-69)

*You get it all the time, especially going on about what goes on in the Six Counties - it being part of the UK, about the Irish always fighting among themselves.*
(Man, IR, Lewisham, aged 40-49)

An important consequence of this climate of anti-Irish feeling in Britain was to turn Irish people in on themselves and reinforce socialisation within the Irish community.

*I never went to English men's working clubs. You don't go to places to be insulted.*
(Man, IR, Sparkbrook, aged 60-69)

*The talk in pubs. They'd say 'Look at those Irish bastards'. A couple of English said it. I go to an Irish pub now.*
(Woman, IR, Sparkbrook, aged 40-49)

(iii) Hostility and abuse

Hostile remarks, often accompanied by abuse, were reported by a large number of respondents. They occurred in a wide variety of arenas in addition to those previously examined in some detail. These remarks were frequent and apparently unrelated to the context in which they are made. The first comment was made by a man who had described the atmosphere in his workplace as 'good' - because it was an Irish environment - illustrating the care with which that finding should be interpreted.

*A few comments like 'bloody Irish' or 'Irish bastards' in jobs, factories, shops, like that. I can't think of any specific instance.*
(Man, IR, Islington, aged 40-49)

*'Paddies' or whatever. Just about the IRA, 'Irish bastards'.*
(Man, IR, Islington, aged 30-39)

*I've been called an 'Irish bastard' when I intervened in a racist attack on a young Chinese woman.*
(Man, NI, Islington, aged 20-29)

Two respondents mentioned that the issue of Irish neutrality was a specific trigger to anti-Irish expression.

*There has been prejudice. For example on VE Day. They were going on about Irish neutrality without recognising the Irish input in the army and Irish nurses, like my sisters in Manchester. It is the same about the First World War. There's no recognition of our contribution, there never is.*
(Man, IR, Harrow, aged 60-69)

*The Falklands War sent the English completely patriotic. They gave out about the Irish nor supporting England. There were three people in work who wanted*

*to join up, but didn't. But it was just banter, mostly from men.*
(Woman, NI, Islington, aged 30-39)

Often, however, comments were part of a more insidious atmosphere of exclusion, recognised by Irish people but so commonplace as to be hardly noticeable in the majority population. The respondents seemed to be resigned to them and adopted a survival strategy of ignoring them as far as possible.

*Little comments. You could expect it. We ignore them and don't get involved.*
(Man, IR, Erdington, aged 60-69)

*You hear it all the time. Little remarks, comments. But what can I do about it?*
(Man, IR, Islington, aged 30-39)

*I've had comments about being a Catholic - that was really about being Irish.*
(Woman, IR, Harrow, aged 70-79)

A striking feature of the comments is the continuous repetition of expressions of anti-Irishness, particularly for those in the lowest paid jobs.

*I wish I'd never had to leave Ireland in the first place. At home, at least you don't find yourself defending yourself. You have to prove yourself all the time, to show you are worth something. Life might have been easier back home. What have I achieved? Everything is a struggle. We never had any breaks. I've always had to be working. I've been exploited - the minimum wage. If you are desperate you'll do it and I did. I was desperate. All I have is this house, an ex-council house. I'm proud of it but it's so little really and I've worked hard to get it. It's been a struggle.*
(Woman, IR, Sparkbrook, aged 40-49)

*Only that workmen who come over here are treated badly. One incident which I remember was a man came in a pub with a bag of tools and a suitcase and said 'This is all I have to show for ten years in England'.*
(Woman, IR, Islington, aged 40-49)

These case studies throw light on the low social mobility levels identified in Part One of the report.

iv) Stereotyping

A more specific form of anti-Irish hostility drew directly on negative stereotypes of the Irish. These were employed in a wide range of social interactions, including many outside the workplace.

*In Tesco's I was standing at the checkout with my little one. I heard shouting, commotion, but I wasn't taking any notice. An office by the door opened and a lad came out. When he opened his mouth he was Irish. He had his daughter, he was very annoyed. He'd been accused of shoplifting. He kept saying 'You've upset the little girl'. Security guards were pushing him. There were comments from people around and the cashier, 'Wouldn't you know it, they have to be Irish. They come over here and cause trouble'. I could feel the tears, the hairs at the back of my neck. I said to the cashier 'You won't want me to pay'. Everyone round went*

*quiet. It was well out of line, the way they were treating this man. They should not make an example of him in front of everyone, pushing him.*
(Woman, IR, Lewisham, aged 30-39)

*There are loads of incidents of a small nature, a constant drip of anti-Irishness in, for example, the media, the police. In the local butcher's a few weeks ago, his comment on hearing I'd just returned from Ireland was 'Like the rest of them, just come back to claim your benefits?'*
(Woman, IR, Lewisham, aged 40-49)

*We were in Scotland, coach touring, and they were telling stupid Irish jokes. I went up and objected and he didn't put them on again. I wrote to Shearings and they defended them, saying most people like them. I said they were stupid, insulting and I discouraged my friend from going on the coaches.*
(Man, IR, Sparkbrook, aged 60-69)

*The GAA [Gaelic Athletic Association] bought land by the airport and we were not allowed to play football on it. They didn't want us because we were Irish and it's a posh area. Since the Race Act came into force they had to give us permission. We had the ground thirty years and we've only been given permission coming into our eighth year. We were turned down every time we applied.*
(Man, IR, Erdington, aged 60-69)

The comments of others reinforced the picture of a background of negative stereotypes against which they lived their lives. They were strongly rejected as untrue. But often they went unchallenged, because Irish people were afraid to stand out or felt there was no point.

*There has been occasions where you'd find that. I don't know how you'd put it, I suppose you would be a bit intimidated by the remarks. 'Paddy' was only capable of digging the roads, that kind of thing. That would upset me more than anything because there's good Irish as well.*
(Man, IR, Islington, aged 60-69)

*The only thing I hear is when they put them down. 'You must be stupid, you're Irish'. And because you're Irish you have to drink. Everybody does, but the Irish stand out more for them. When you think of the hooligans, they're English. The match [in Dublin] - England started it.*
(Woman, IR, Islington, aged 20-29)

*For myself, personally, it's not that I turn a blind eye to it, but I'm weatherbeaten to it. They say the Irish are rowdy, go out and get drunk and wreck the place.*
(Man, IR, Islington, aged 30-39)

Many people reported hearing stereotyped remarks about the Irish in Britain which reflected resentments arising from their migrant status.

*Reference has been made about coming over and getting council houses and the*

*English couldn't get them. In the hospital, comments made about Irish people having lots of children.*
(Man, IR, Erdington, aged 40-49)

*Some of my friends think that everyone from Ireland came to England to claim social security. I've had arguments over that.*
(Man, IR, Erdington, aged 40-49)

*Several times. Things to do with work. 'The Irish coming over and taking all the jobs'.*
(Woman, NI, Islington, aged 30-39)

*You hear it. 'How many more is there here?' You take no notice.*
(Woman, IR, Sparkbrook, aged 60-69)

*Well, I've heard 'Irish Paddy' and 'Get back to where you came from'. Things like that. It's upsetting. It is hurtful. I never say anything back. What's the point?*
(Woman, IR, Islington, aged 60-69)

*Couple of friends who work on the sites have been stopped as they leave their accommodation carrying their tools. They always had to explain where they were going so early in the morning. The police say things like 'Oh yeah, that's what you came over from Ireland for, to work all hours'.*
(Woman, IR, Islington, aged 20-29)

The stereotypes matched most closely characteristics attributed to working-class Irish people. Middle-class respondents described the consequences for them.

*There is a way in which the Irish are all viewed as navvies and associated with male pub culture. This causes me to hold back a bit.*
(Woman, NI, Erdington, aged 50-59)

*I think the English are surprised when they see it [success]. They have this tendency to think they know more - colonial superiority! So caught up in class.... I do think it's not the most successful place for Irish people. It's all very subtle. I suppose there's people who wouldn't employ [Irish people].*
(Woman, IR, Islington, aged 30-39)

The main findings about anti-Irish attitudes in Britain include

- Its widespread character. The majority of the sample could immediately identify instances of behaviour which they had found insulting, hurtful and intimidating. Evidence was drawn from a spectrum of social situations, including pubs, the street, shops and a coach trip, as well as the workplace.

- Although some described these as isolated incidents, a number of respondents said that they experienced them in some form 'all the time'.

- Many Irish people did not openly challenge hostile or demeaning attitudes, but chose avoidance mechanisms including:
  ignoring comments;
  remaining in an Irish environment as far as possible.
  The hidden nature of these experiences, discussed only within the safety of

Irish situations, means that Irish welfare agencies which attempt to raise these issues have very little systematic evidence on which to draw. Their assertions can easily be ignored.

- Negative stereotypes of the Irish were constantly reinforced on television and in the press. There appeared to be no sanctions against the repetition of anti-Irish jokes as a legitimate form of entertainment.

- The intensity of anti-Irish comments and imagery, and its acceptability in the British population, increased at times of IRA activity, but this was not the main form mentioned by the sample.

## 7.2 Specificity of anti-Irish attitudes in Britain

In order to investigate the extent to which anti-Irish attitudes draw on longstanding problematic relationships between Britain and Ireland, respondents were asked to compare the reception of Irish people in different national situations.

### Q11. 'How do you think the Irish are viewed in Britain, United States, Europe and Australia?'

|  | Britain | | US | | Europe | | Australia | |
|---|---|---|---|---|---|---|---|---|
|  | N. | % | N. | % | N. | % | N. | % |
| Positive | 27 | 31 | 69 | 78 | 47 | 53 | 60 | 68 |
| Negative | 19 | 22 | 1 | 1 | 3 | 3 | 1 | 1 |
| Neither/ Mixed | 41 | 47 | 5 | 6 | 11 | 13 | 3 | 3 |
| Don t know | 1 | 1 | 13 | 15 | 27 | 31 | 24 | 27 |
| Total | 88 | 101 | 88 | 100 | 88 | 100 | 88 | 99 |

A striking finding is the contrast in attitudes towards the Irish perceived between Britain and other parts of the world. Only a third of respondents felt that the Irish are viewed positively in Britain, compared with 78% who gave this answer for the United States and 68% who thought that Irish people had a positive reception in Australia.

However, since many people were unable to give an opinion about other parts of the world, the proportions perceiving a negative response are even more revealing. Nearly a quarter (22%) felt that Irish people were viewed negatively in Britain, compared with negligible figures for other destinations. The Irish do not appear to feel they have a problem relating to all others, but that the specific relationship with Britain creates difficulties.

But the majority of respondents (47%) gave an ambivalent answer, saying that Irish people had a mixed response in Britain. Overall, therefore, nearly 70% had some reservations about Britain, but the issue was a complex one.

# 8. Demand for recognition as an ethnic group

The final question asked whether respondents thought that the Irish should be recognised as an ethnic minority group in Britain. This had been a very strong recommendation from the Irish agencies and groups interviewed in Stage Two of the research, who were, of course, particularly concerned with the welfare of disadvantaged sections of the population. In Stage Three the extent to which these views were echoed in the wider Irish population was assessed. This question also provided a summary of views of the experiences of Irish people in Britain and further insight into their attitude to the place of the Irish in British society.

Overall, a majority of those questioned gave a strong positive answer (50/85, 59%). A minority gave a firm No (24/85, 28%) and the remaining 11 (13%) were ambivalent. No significant differences by gender or age were identified. Proportions saying 'Yes' were almost identical in Birmingham and London, though a higher proportion in London were negative rather than ambivalent in their opinion.

**Q 62a 'Do you think the Irish should be recognised as an ethnic group in Britain?'**

|  | Yes | | No | | Don t know | | Total | |
|---|---|---|---|---|---|---|---|---|
|  | No. | % | No. | % | No. | % | No. | % |
| Birmingham | 19 | 58 | 6 | 21 | 8 | 24 | 33 | 100 |
| London | 31 | 60 | 18 | 35 | 3 | 6 | 52 | 101 |

## 8.1 Positive responses

Four main reasons were given:

- Similarities in Irish position and experience to that of other, that is black and Asian, labour migrant groups and their descendants, including specifically racist treatment.

- Entitlement to similar benefits as these other groups.

- Recognition of Irish contribution to the British economy, that is of the benefits of labour migration.

- Recognition of Irish cultural difference in Britain

| Reason | No. | % mentioning |
|---|---|---|
| Like other ethnic groups | 25 | 50 |
| Recognise anti-Irish racism | 5 | 10 |
| Should receive benefits | 16 | 32 |
| Contribution recognised | 12 | 24 |
| Cultural difference recognised | 9 | 18 |
| Identification/representation | 3 | 6 |

(i) Should be treated like other ethnic groups

Many respondents (50% of those favouring an 'ethnic' label) made the point that the Irish are treated like outsiders, but not given the recognition which can now be claimed by other groups.

> They have segregated everyone else - if everyone else is, we should be. We are not ashamed of what we are. They treat us differently when they want to. We should be heard for a change.
> (Woman, IR, Lewisham, aged 30-39)

> We are classed as foreigners - people remind you and we are not well thought of. That comes from the Troubles - it does not matter if you are from the North or the South. They don't really recognise it as a country.
> (Woman, IR, Erdington, aged 40-49)

> Because there's an awful lot of comments, racist remarks, discrimination. With the black person, it's 'You're racist', and why not for the Irish? Had to put up with an awful lot of abuse and racism. Should be like any other nationality, any other culture.
> (Woman, IR, Islington, aged 30-39)

> Well, we're not British, so I suppose we have to be really. I think we are, well they have made us feel that way, anyway.
> (Woman, IR, Islingtom, aged 30-39)

> Because of past years' discrimination - and there still is. The Irish would be recognised and it would make things fairer for people. A lot don't recognise what Irish people's experience is because they are white.
> (Woman, IR, Islington, Aged 20-29)

The overwhelming impression is a feeling of injustice about the treatment of Irish people. The respondents were not demanding a recognition of their 'white' superiority, but equality of treatment, especially when there are parallels in their experience of racism.

(ii) Benefit entitlement

A specific consequence of non-recognition of Irish ethnicity is lack of entitlement to benefits which can be claimed by recognised groups. This was mentioned by 32% of those favouring recognition as an ethnic group.

> There's an awful lot of benefits given to ethnic groups that the Irish don't come into. There are those missing out on benefits. In comparison to other groups the needy Irish miss out.
> (Woman, IR, Erdington, aged 50-59)

> They are definitely different. It's hard to explain. They don't think or act the same. They'd have more protection. I think more Irish are deprived, or down

230

*and outs, because they are not recognised. They are thrown in with the locals and get a raw deal.*
(Man, IR, Sparkbrook, aged 60-69)

*One of the main reasons is that it would allow for ethnic monitoring - and then we would see if there was discrimination. Due to cultural differences and cultural needs we should be recognised as an ethnic minority and can argue for specific services for specific needs.*
(Man, NI, Islington, aged 20-29)

*I see all the Pakistanis getting everything they ask for. They are afraid to say 'No' to them. They would appreciate us more - we never stood up for ourselves, so they don't appreciate us.*
(Man, IR, Erdington, aged 60-69)

*I think they should be - it's a touchy subject. They would get more funds. Unfortunately some elderly men are in a bad way because of work on buildings etc. and their own drinking.*
(Man, IR, Harrow, 60-69)

Most of these comments are about what is perceived as the better hearing for claims afforded to those who have achieved recognised status as ethnic groups. It represents a response to the racialisation of issues in Britain simply in black/white terms, and the problematic position of the Irish because of the 'myth of homogeneity' of whiteness. Again respondents are registering their bitterness at being 'left out' and unrecognised. Demands for ethnic monitoring arise directly out of these strong feelings about the invisibility of anti-Irish discrimination in British society.

Responses also reveal ambivalence. One respondent, who answered positively, recognised the problematic trade-off which existed between the benefits and disadvantages of being recognised as an outsider. For those who had no status to lose, the benefits might outweigh the disadvantages. But for those in higher status positions, claiming an Irish identity linked a middle-class Irish person with the overarching stereotype of inferiority.

*I feel very ambiguous - because of the outsider/insider thing. You can get concessions through it but it means being classed an outsider. All Irish people I've met are unemployed or in low status jobs and I'm upset about it. Others I don't meet, probably because they're keeping a low profile. It is threatening for people that I assume a leadership role as an Irish person - a teachers' group I have to do long term work with are confrontational to me, don't want me speaking on their behalf, make anti-Irish remarks. Whereas a group of nursery teachers, who see themselves as marginalised, identified with me and let me speak for them.*
(Woman, NI, Birmingham, aged 50-59)

(iii) Contribution recognised

A sizeable group of respondents favouring recognition (24%) felt strongly that the economic contribution of Irish people in Britain was undervalued, because their presence was not acknowledged. The work they had done as labour migrants was not attributed to them. These comments reflected the lack of understanding by British people of the role of the Irish as labour migrants in the British economy. Because the reasons for Irish settlement in Britain are little understood, Irish people are often seen as 'scroungers' who simply leave bad conditions in Ireland to benefit at the expense of British taxpayers. The respondents on the other hand had a much clearer picture of their own value.

> *Why not? They built the hospitals and the roads, so they should get something. I said it to somebody. They are naming roads after Asian people, I said 'Why not Irish people - they built the roads. McAlpine Way !'*
> (Woman, IR, Erdington, aged 60-69)

> *They built all the country and Birmingham. It would be a quare country without the Irish.*
> (Man, IR, Sparkbrook, aged 70-79)

> *It's difficult. We should be acknowledged. Irish people have played a good part rebuilding this country - 90% of the lads on the roads are Irish. We should be given more credit but we are not, I feel.*
> (Woman, IR, Sparkbrook, aged 40-49)

> *Would feel more wanted - youngsters feel unwanted. They are more educated now, get very good jobs. They don't get housing and different things*    .
> (Woman, IR, Islington, aged 60-69)

(iv) Cultural difference recognised

Other respondents (18%) believed that Irish cultural difference was not understood by the British. This adds weight to the earlier comments about the need for Irish employees in benefits offices.

> *There is a lot of hidden discrimination against Irish people and I think it would be a way of focusing on it and recognising it - and in terms of culture and language the Irish are a separate ethnic group anyway.*
> (Woman, IR, Lewisham, aged 40-49)

> *We have huge cultural differences from the English. We are a totally different race and should be recognised. More councils should recognise this. It's not a hate thing of the English - I have grown to like the English.*
> (Woman, NI, Islington, aged 30-39)


## 8.2 Ambivalent responses

Those who felt unable to give an unequivocal answer to this question (13%) were mainly reluctant to separate out the Irish from the British on grounds of numbers and length of residence. They were also unwilling to be given this label. Finally, some were doubtful of any benefits.

*There's so many Irish people here. I don't think there's much difference. It's probably people who haven't lived here for long.*
(Woman, IR, Erdington, aged 60-69)

*There's too many of them. Almost every house is related to some Irish.*
(Man, IR, Erdington, aged 40-49)

*It's a tangled web of relations between English and Irish - a lot of intermarriage. I feel a sort of solidarity with other ordinary workers.* (Woman, IR, Harrow, aged 40-49)

*I don't like the word. They should be treated the same as the British. I think the Irish have done more for Britain than the British have - so they should be treated well.*
(Woman, IR, Harrow, aged 50-59)

*I don't think they should be really. I think they have a right. Because the majority are here to make a living, make a few bob and enjoy themselves in the meantime. I mean, what benefits would they get from being classified? I can't see it anyhow.*
(Man, IR, Islington, aged 60-69)

## 8.3 Negative responses

Just over a quarter of the sample (28%) would prefer that the Irish were not given a specifically ethnic status in Britain. The reasons expressed included anxiety about identification and a belief that there was or should be no difference between the Irish and the British. However, there was overlap in these positions - the desire to be accepted as culturally similar to the British included a desire to be distanced from black and Asian minorities in Britain. A small number of people stated that there was no need for an ethnic designation because they perceived no problems.

Reasons therefore could be classified as:

• Desire not to cause difficulties, fear about labelling and of identification;

• Denial of ethnic or cultural difference;

• No problems perceived, or self reliance preferred.

| Reason | No. | % mentioning |
| --- | --- | --- |
| Not want to cause difficulties | 11 | 46 |
| Not an ethnic group | 7 | 29 |
| Same culture | 2 | 8 |
| No problems | 5 | 21 |
| Self reliance | 2 | 8 |

(i) Desire not to cause difficulties

The largest single reason given was anxiety about the consequences of separate designation. Several issues were involved, including the desire to keep a low profile and the belief that integration was a desirable goal.

*I don't think we should get into a huddle. If you live in another country - when in Rome, do as Romans do... The Irish society and its federation was good in a way, but it could be too narrow. Sometimes it is that that could cause trouble with people.*
(Woman, IR, Harrow, aged 70-79)

*Political correctness - it wouldn't do any good and would result in a lot of petty bureaucrats shouting about what they don't know about. It generates resentment - a place like London is bound to have all sorts.*
(Man, IR, Lewisham, aged 40-49)

(ii) No ethnic difference

Another group of people expressed the view that the Irish should not be viewed as a separate ethnic group. In part, this was based on the close relationship between Ireland and Britain, an expression of the 'myth of homogeneity'. It also represented a wish to avoid conflict and the recognition that all working class people face difficulty in having their needs recognised.

*We're all part of the British Isles. We should get on without the word ethnic. While we are here we get on well together. It's like putting a split between us. Nothing has happened to make me be described as ethnic.*
(Man, NI, Erdington, aged 40-49)

*Because when people are recognised as such it causes problems and other things come up. The English are discriminated against and have a lot of problems getting benefits and it's their country.*
(Woman, RI, Islington, aged 30-39)

## 8.4 Conclusion

Although there was a wide range of responses to the question, the overwhelming impression from the responses was of a group who felt unrecognised for their positive contribution. There was difference of view about the appropriate strategy to adopt in order to achieve an acknowledgement of this position. The majority felt that campaigns by African-Caribbean and Indian, Pakistani and Bangladeshi minorities had brought them more benefits than disadvantages, including recognition of their experience of racism and access to a fairer distribution of material resources such as housing. Clear parallels in the position of the Irish within British society were seen.

# 9. Conclusion

The most striking finding from the pilot survey of individuals was the high levels of anti-Irish hostility routinely encountered by Irish people in Britain. The interviewees gave spontaneous answers to a wide range of questions, making it likely that they recalled only part of their experience. Yet they revealed a catalogue of demeaning treatment which built into a cumulative picture of 'normal' levels of harassment, punctuated by a number of more frightening and aggressive acts.

This evidence strongly corroborates the points made by Irish welfare agencies and community groups in Part Two of the report. It is very important to remember that very few (3) of the interviewees had contacted such groups, so that this pilot study confirms the view that cases documented by the groups are not the experiences of what is only a small number of disadvantaged Irish people but represent the tip of an iceberg. The 'battle' faced by Irish groups to have Irish issues acknowledged is not a fight for the rights of a small minority but the most visible part of a much larger, hidden, problem.

Experiences during the past fifty years recounted by interviewees reinforce the idea that anti-Irish racism is endemic in British society. Although levels and types of expression vary over time, an underlying acceptance of anti-Irish attitudes in British society means that this racism can surface in different forms. In the 1950s and 1960s, discrimination was overt and Irish people were exposed to signs reading 'No Irish' in London and Birmingham, now often forgotten outside the Irish community. The outbreak of IRA bombings in Britain in the 1970s sharply increased hostility, as interviewees' accounts of the backlash in Birmingham in 1974 graphically illustrate. Pre-existing prejudices were applied with renewed intensity to all Irish people, the vast majority of whom had no connection or sympathy with the violent incidents.

All aspects of Irish people's lives are affected by racism, which carries the potential for discrimination. Particularly serious consequences may arise when state institutions are involved. For example, 25% of those interviewed reported negative responses from the police, ranging from one case of serious assault to more commonplace verbal harassment. None of these cases had been investigated, suggesting a much higher level of unreported abuse than has been identified before. Discriminatory treatment at benefit offices was also described by 24% of the sample, despite the fact that they had equal entitlement with, or were, British citizens. This reflects both the ingrained attitudes of front line staff and lack of importance given to training by management.

In their everyday lives an even larger proportion could immediately identify instances of behaviour they found insulting and intimidating. The workplace is one area where the discriminatory effects of anti-Irish 'jokes' and comments are beginning to be recognised, and have been successfully taken up with CRE support, but evidence from the sample showed that these experiences are far more widespread in the Irish-born population.

Although only 20% specifically reported a 'bad atmosphere' at work, 79% had been subjected to anti-Irish 'jokes' and comments. Four people had made formal complaints. Harassment by neighbours on the other hand, although described by 25% of those living outside strongly Irish neighbourhoods, has received no official acknowledgement, although it has been reported to Irish agencies. From the survey it appears to be highest in areas with few other Irish people, so that those living outside London and Birmingham may be more at risk. This illustrates the need for this survey to be extended more widely within Britain. Harassment of 'second-generation' Irish children in schools was reported by 22% of the sample, showing the importance of including a wider definition of the Irish community.

The widespread acceptability of anti-Irish attitudes in Britain is reinforced and legitimised by the media. Interviewees specifically mentioned television shows and newspaper coverage as sources of unchecked negative stereotyping which they found offensive and hurtful. The blanket application of stereotypes, including stupidity, drunkenness, dishonesty and proneness to mindless violence, was applied to all Irish people, overriding class and gender divisions. A striking finding of the survey was the inclusion of professional and white-collar workers in the hostility. Although male manual workers appeared to experience the full strength of 'jokes', negative comments and ridiculing of accents were also used to belittle those in non-manual occupations. This group was more likely to challenge the perpetrators on the grounds of racism.

However, avoidance of situations in which they might be exposed to anti-Irish hostility was the principal response of many interviewees. They chose to adopt a low profile or 'heads down' approach. It is extremely important to bear this in mind when interpreting the findings of the survey. Relatively low proportions mentioning experiences of harassment and discrimination may reflect the construction of enclosed 'Irish worlds' in Britain - living in Irish neighbourhoods, socializing in Irish venues, working with Irish work-mates. These people were intimidated by the climate of hostility and preferred not to draw attention to themselves. Thus, although 70% said that they found anti-Irish jokes offensive, only 30% felt able to reject them outright. A substantial minority admitted that they had played down their Irish identity at times, especially by altering their accent or keeping quiet. Women were more likely than men to react in this way.

Paradoxically, while the difference of Irish people is highlighted by negative stereotyping, the specificity of their situation as labour migrants is overlooked. Thus, their distinctive roles and needs are not acknowledged and instead they are seen as 'scroungers' at benefit offices and on housing lists. Yet the interviewees' labour histories vividly illustrate their flexibility as a labour force responsive to the demands of the British labour market. Many pointed out that there was plenty of work in the past 'if you were not choosy'; in other words they filled jobs turned down by the indigenous population. Although more were now out of work, rates of unemployment amongst women were still low. Amongst men, they were greatest in the lowest socio-economic group.

The nature of the low paid, seasonal and cyclical work Irish migrants were required to do meant that they had needed support from the welfare system, 50% of the sample having applied for social security benefits at some time. But many of the costs of migration and settlement in Britain had been borne by the Irish community itself. For example, housing for new arrivals was usually provided by friends and relatives, so that they did not therefore appear as homeless or in need of housing on council lists. Unemployed single people often returned to Ireland, though those with families, captured in our sample, were more likely to remain.

Acceptance of the desirability of formal recognition of an 'ethnic' label for the Irish in Britain was thus an extremely complex issue. The disadvantages arising from non-recognition of their needs and contribution had to be weighed against a desire to retain a low profile to avoid hostility. However, the balance amongst the interviewees was in favour of formal recognition (59%). The major reason given was the similarity of the position of the Irish to that of black and Asian ethnic minority groups. Interviewees described bitterly their feelings of the unfairness of their exclusion from the benefits available to recognised ethnic groups and the overwhelming ignorance of British people about the positive contributions Irish people had made. A clear majority would thus favour ethnic monitoring.

The survey revealed a significant degree of anti-Irish racism in all areas of British life, which may lead to discrimination. This is manifested in many ways, ranging from physical attacks by police and neighbours to hostile and derogatory comments in workplaces, benefit and housing offices, on the streets and in the media. Irish people are constantly reminded that they are not entitled to an equal place in British society. On the other hand, they are not seen as sufficiently different for this racism to be acknowledged and to be afforded some measure of protection.

This pilot survey was able to highlight key areas of experience in two major conurbations in England. In the case of Birmingham, it showed that the predictions of Rex and Moore (1967), which were seen as 'signing off' the Irish as unlikely to be of future interest because of their opportunities for assimilation, were wide of the mark. Very little attention has been given to that fact until now. Although there are many similarities in the findings from Birmingham and London, there are also important differences. Irish people are scattered throughout Britain and a much more comprehensive survey of conditions in other cities, smaller towns and in a greater variety of regions, as well as Scotland and Wales is needed to provide a fuller picture.

# Conclusion and Recommendations

# Conclusion

The main findings of this research are that there is an extremely strong resistance to recognition of the distinctiveness of Irish experience in Britain which results in a lack of acknowledgement of Irish needs and rights, but that at the same time there is a widespread, and almost completely unquestioned, acceptance of anti-Irish racism in British society. We found that the evidence produced by Irish welfare and community groups was overwhelmingly endorsed by the sample of Irish people interviewed in Birmingham and London, even though most were not users of these services.

The spontaneous responses of a majority of the sample, none of whom was expecting to be interviewed, reveal a powerful sense of hurt and unjustified exclusion from an equal place in British society. There is clear evidence that events connected with Northern Ireland have heightened expressions of anti-Irishness at particular times. However, what also emerges is the extent to which deep-seated anti-Irish stereotypes form part of a more general response to Irish people. This affected many areas of interviewees' lives, including workplaces, access to housing, treatment at benefits offices and interactions with neighbours and the police.

In our view, the substantial body of evidence presented here strongly suggests that discrimination, as defined in the 1976 Race Relations Act, does play a significant role in generating these experiences, although in individual cases it might be hard to establish the exact causal circumstances. This is a serious cause for concern for the CRE and all agencies responsible for public policy decisions.

240

# Recommendations

Broad policy recommendations which arise from these findings include the need to make Irish issues more visible so that their existence and legitimacy is acknowledged. Fundamental to this is the collection of accurate data so that the nature and scale of problems faced can be measured and change can be monitored. Awareness of the racialised character of anti-Irish hostility also needs to be sharply increased, so that challenges can be made by Irish people who should be able to expect authoritative support.

We recommend to the CRE that they include an Irish dimension in all its future investigations of discrimination in public institutions or private companies.

**Specific Policy Recommendations:**

We recommend that the CRE actively encourages all government agencies, statutory bodies, voluntary sector organisations and agencies and private companies to consider and implement the following recommendations as appropriate:

♦ An Irish category should be included in all forms of ethnic monitoring, including Census ethnic categories, which have a major influence on the practice of other bodies. Our findings strongly reinforce the CRE's recommendations of 1994 to this effect.

♦ All service provision by local authorities, the DSS, Health Authorities, other statutory bodies and voluntary organisations:

- should process, collate and publish as a distinct category all Irish data collected as part of ethnic monitoring

- should include an Irish dimension in all equal opportunities policies.

- should recognise the specificity of Irish migrant experience, for instance in housing applications, claiming benefits, care of elderly people, health, the welfare of children.

- should include an Irish dimension in any resource allocation which specifically targets ethnic minority groups.

- should include an Irish dimension in any training of staff who are concerned with identifying ethnic differentiation or racial discrimination in access to, and receipt of, services and in employment.

- should include an Irish dimension in all plans for contracted service provision and community care

♦ The Housing Corporation should review its plans for future procedures for assessing need in order to ensure that the Irish are not disadvantaged.

♦ Health Authorities should include an Irish dimension to their provision, given the Census findings about the poorer health status of Irish people and the large numbers of older Irish-born people in Britain.

♦ There needs to be recognition of anti-Irish hostility as a form of racial harassment in a wide variety of situations, including workplaces, neighbourhood relations, schools and policing.

♦ The Irish should be included as a category in media standards relating to representation of minority groups, particularly in television entertainment programmes.

## Recommendations for Future Research

It is essential that the pilot survey carried out for this project, and reported in Part Three, is followed up by more extensive research which will explore further these policy recommendations and provide more broadly based evidence about the issues of discrimination identified in this report.

We recommend that the CRE urge the Economic and Social Research Council, Leverhulme, the Joseph Rowntree Trust and other appropriate research grant bodies that the need for this fuller picture about the Irish in Britain should be an element in their decisions about the deployment of research resources.

Additional research is urgently needed to include:

♦ Larger samples so that conclusions can be more firmly substantiated using statistical means, as was the case with the PEP/PSI studies. It would then be possible to provide substantive evidence about differences within the Irish population which have been suggested by the present survey. For example, a much larger sample would include greater numbers of people from Northern Ireland, who were underrepresented here, and also make it possible to distinguish the views of people from Catholic and Protestant traditions. Experiences by gender and social class have been shown to be different in certain respects and the implications of this should be explored further.

♦ Increasing the types of location for interviews to take account of a much wider range of experiences amongst Irish people.

♦ Similarities, but also important differences, were found in reports of Irish people's experiences in Scotland. This needs to be followed up by interviews with Irish people, particularly in the Strathclyde region where religious differences seem to be particularly salient, but also in areas such as south west Scotland where there is quite a substantial settlement of migrants from Northern Ireland. One issue that would be clarified by further research about Scotland is whether consideration should be given to extending the 1976 Race Relations Act to include religion.

♦ Different experiences in regions of England outside Birmingham and London were suggested by, for example, reports of harassment in Sheffield. Further investigation is needed of Irish experiences in areas of low Irish population.

Findings that hostility was greater in Lewisham than other parts of London support the idea that Irish neighbourhoods provide a cushion against harassment and prejudice evident in the wider community. Local conditions in other cities, such as continuing anti-Irish hostility in Liverpool, also need further investigation.

◆ Research into the practices towards the Irish followed by a variety of public institutions, statutory bodies and other agencies is also necessary if discrimination is to be identified and challenged.

◆ Extension of research to include the experiences of second-generation Irish people in Britain, especially in the light of recent findings about their significantly poorer health. To date assumptions that the second-generation Irish have assimilated into the 'white' English-, Scottish-, or Welsh- accented populations have been paramount. There are sufficient indications in this and other research to challenge these assumptions and warrant further exploration of their experiences.

# Appendix A

# Tables, figures and maps

**Table 1.1  Second generation Republic Irish-born Irish community in UK: 1971**

| Mother's country of birth | Father's country of birth | | | | |
| | UK | IR | NC | Eur | Els/NS |
|---|---|---|---|---|---|
| UK | 46,282,355 | 493,090 | 171,470 | 327,665 | 460,030 |
| IR | 400,105 | 361,800 | 9,545 | 8,220 | 13,720 |
| NC | 110,895 | 3,300 | 326,375 | 2,560 | 9,255 |
| Eur | 201,765 | 4,715 | 10,025 | 151,080 | 18,700 |
| Els/NS | 453,335 | 8,965 | 9,485 | 11,040 | 910,660 |

| | |
|---|---|
| 2 Irish Republic born parents | 361,800 |
| 1 Irish Republic born parent (father) | 510,070 |
| 1 Irish Republic born parent (mother) | 431,590 |
| Total | 1,303,460 |

Source: Crown Copyright, Census 1971, Country of Birth tables, Table 7.

**Table 1.2  Origins of non-Irish born parents, where father or mother was Irish-born, 1971: UK**

| IR born fathers married to mothers | | | IR born mothers married to fathers | | |
|---|---|---|---|---|---|
| from | Number | % | from | Number | % |
| UK | 493,090 | 56.6 | UK | 400,105 | 50.4 |
| IR | 361,800 | 41.5 | IR | 361,800 | 45.6 |
| NC | 3,300 | 0.4 | NC | 9,545 | 1.2 |
| Eur | 4,715 | 0.5 | Europe | 8,220 | 1.0 |
| Els | 4,590 | 0.5 | Els | 13,720 | 1.7 |
| Total | 871,860 | 99.5 | Total | 793,390 | 99.9 |

Source: Crown Copyright: Census 1971, Country of Birth Tables, Table 7.

**Table 1.3 Relative size of the Irish community in London, 1991**

| Group | Size | % |
|---|---|---|
| White non-Irish-born | 5,077,110 | 76.0% |
| Irish-born | 256,470 | 3.5 |
|   **a:** Ist and $2^{nd}$ generation | 641,175 | 9.6 |
|   **b:** Ist and $2^{nd}$ generation | 769,410 | 11.5 |
| Indian | 347,091 | 5.2 |
| Black Caribbean | 290,968 | 4.4 |
| Black African | 163,635 | 2.4 |
| Pakistani | 87,816 | 1.3 |
| Bangladeshi | 85,738 | 1.3 |
| Black other | 80,613 | 1.2 |
| Chinese | 56,579 | 0.8 |
| Asian other | 112,807 | 1.7 |
| Other other | 120,872 | 1.8 |
| Total | 6,679,699 | 100.0 |

a: correction factor 2.5;  b: correction factor 3.0

Source: Crown Copyright: Census 1991, Local Base Statistics, AGIY 1995.

**Table 1.4  Population living in England by birthplace in Britain and Ireland and Census-defined ethnic group, 1991.**

| Birthplace | Number | % | Ethnic Group | Number | % |
|---|---|---|---|---|---|
| England | 42,532,714 | 90.3 | White | 44,144,339 | 93.8 |
| Scotland | 743,856 | 1.6 | Black Caribbean | 495,682 | 1.1 |
| Wales | 545,381 | 1.2 | Indian | 823,821 | 1.8 |
| N Ireland | 211,133 | 0.4 | Pakistani | 449,646 | 1.0 |
| Irish Republic | 556,306 | 1.2 | Black African | 206,918 | 0.4 |
| **Total** | 44,589,390 | 94.7 | Bangladeshi | 157,881 | 0.3 |
| | | | Black other | 172,282 | 0.4 |
| | | | Chinese | 141,661 | 0.3 |
| | | | Asian other | 189,253 | 0.4 |
| | | | Other other | 273,721 | 0.6 |
| | | | **Total** | 47,055,204 | 100.1 |

Source: Crown Copyright, Census 1991, Ethnic Group and Country of Birth Tables 1, 6

**Table 2.1  Regional distribution of Irish-born population in Britain, 1991**

| Region | Total | % total Irish-born | % change 1981-91 |
|---|---|---|---|
| North | 16,301 | 1.9 | -0.4 |
| Yorkshire/Humberside | 40,690 | 4.9 | -9.5 |
| North West | 98,011 | 11.7 | -13.9 |
| East Midlands | 42,489 | 5.1 | -5.6 |
| West Midlands | 91,377 | 10.9 | -11.0 |
| East Anglia | 18,442 | 2.2 | +12.5 |
| South East | 412,863 | 49.3 | +7.0 |
| South West | 47,275 | 5.6 | +7.6 |
| Wales | 20,844 | 2.5 | +3.0 |
| Scotland | 49,184 | 5.9 | -19.3 |
| Total | 837,464 | 100.0 | -1.5 |

Source:  Crown Copyright, Census 1991, Ethnic Group and Country of Birth tables, Table 2.


**Table 2. 3 Regional destinations of one-year migrants (1990-91) from Ireland, compared with total Irish-born population**

| Region | Total Irish-born Total % | Total Irish-born 1-year migrants % | Irish Republic-born Total % | Irish Republic-born 1-year migrants % | Northern Irish-born Total % | Northern Irish-born 1-year migrants % |
|---|---|---|---|---|---|---|
| North | 1.9 | 1.2 | 1.3 | 1.0 | 3.6 | 1.8 |
| Yorkshire and Humberside | 4.9 | 3.7 | 4.3 | 2.7 | 6.3 | 8.3 |
| East Midlands | 5.1 | 3.3 | 4.7 | 3.0 | 6.0 | 4.6 |
| East Anglia | 2.2 | 1.8 | 1.8 | 1.6 | 3.2 | 3.0 |
| South East | 49.3 | 66.1 | 54.5 | 70.9 | 36.6 | 43.4 |
| South West | 5.6 | 6.8 | 4.8 | 4.4 | 7.7 | 18.0 |
| West Midlands | 10.9 | 4.5 | 11.3 | 4.7 | 9.9 | 4.0 |
| North West | 11.7 | 6.2 | 11.1 | 6.1 | 13.1 | 6.7 |
| Wales | 2.5 | 2.1 | 2.3 | 2.0 | 3.0 | 2.4 |
| Scotland | 5.9 | 4.4 | 3.8 | 3.7 | 10.8 | 7.8 |
| **Total** | 100.0 | 100.1 | 99.9 | 100.1 | 100.2 | 100.0 |

Source: Crown Copyright, Census 1991, Ethnic Group and Country of Birth Tables 1 and 9.

**Table 2.2 Largest local concentrations of people born in Ireland within Great Britain, 1991**

| All born in Ireland | | Born in Northern Ireland | | Born in the Irish Republic | |
|---|---|---|---|---|---|
| Area | % | Area | % | Area | % |
| | | Local Authority Districts (all ages) | | | |
| Brent | 9.0 | Corby | 1.6 | Brent | 8.2 |
| Islington | 7.1 | Wigtown | 1.5 | Islington | 6.2 |
| Hammersmith & Fulham | 6.8 | City of London | 1.5 | Hammersmith & Fulham | 1.1 |
| Camden | 6.5 | Richmondshire | 1.3 | Camden | 5.4 |
| Ealing | 6.0 | Hammersmith & Fulham | 1.1 | Ealing | 5.1 |
| Luton | 5.4 | Camden | 1.0 | Luton | 4.6 |
| Westminster, City of | 5.3 | Coventry | 1.0 | Westminster, City of | 4.5 |
| Haringey | 5.2 | Islington | 1.0 | Haringey | 4.4 |
| Harrow | 4.9 | Manchester | 1.0 | Harrow | 4.4 |
| Lambeth | 4.8 | Stewartry | 1.0 | Lambeth | 3.9 |
| Coventry | 4.6 | Westminster, City of | 0.9 | Southwark | 3.8 |
| Manchester | 4.6 | Rushmoor | 0.9 | Manchester | 3.6 |
| Southwark | 4.5 | West Wiltshire | 0.9 | Coventry | 3.6 |
| Wandsworth | 4.2 | Hyndburn | 0.9 | Wandsworth | 3.4 |
| Kensington & Chelsea | 4.0 | Kyle & Carrick | 0.9 | Hackney | 3.3 |
| | | Parliamentary Constituencies | | | |
| Brent East | 12.3 | Manchester, Gorton | 1.2 | Brent East | 11.2 |
| Hammersmith | 8.5 | Hammersmith | 1.2 | Brent South | 7.5 |
| Brent South | 8.2 | Coventry South East | 1.2 | Hammersmith | 7.3 |
| Islington North | 8.2 | Manchester, Withington | 1.1 | Islington North | 7.1 |
| Ealing, Acton | 6.8 | Birmingham, Erdington | 1.1 | Brent North | 5.9 |
| Holborn and St. Pancras | 6.7 | Corby | 1.1 | Ealing, Acton | 5.8 |
| Brent North | 6.5 | Roxburgh & Berwick | 1.1 | Holborn and St. Pancras | 5.6 |
| Manchester, Gorton | 6.3 | Brent East | 1.1 | Ealing North | 5.3 |
| Hampstead and Highgate | 6.2 | Holborn and St. Pancras | 1.1 | Hampstead and Highgate | 5.3 |
| Ealing North | 6.2 | Edinburgh East | 1.1 | Manchester, Gorton | 5.1 |
| Islington South | 5.9 | Ealing, Acton | 1.1 | Islington South | 5.1 |
| Birmingham, Erdington | 5.8 | Coventry North East | 1.1 | Westminster North | 5.0 |
| Westminster North | 5.8 | Islington North | 1.1 | Harrow East | 4.9 |
| Birmingham, Sparkbrook | 5.7 | Coventry North West | 1.1 | Birmingham, Sparkbrook | 4.7 |
| Harrow East | 5.5 | Manchester, Central | 1.0 | Birmingham, Erdington | 4.7 |

Source: Crown Copyright, Census 1991, (Owen, 1995)

**Table 2.4.  One year Irish-born migrants (1990-1991) to Britain by gender and region**

| Region | Total Irish born | | | | Women | | | | Men | | | |
|---|---|---|---|---|---|---|---|---|---|---|---|---|
| | RI born | % | NI born | % | IR born | % | NI born | % | IR born | % | NI born | % |
| North | 125 | 1.0 | 49 | 1.8 | 56 | 0.8 | 25 | 1.9 | 69 | 1.2 | 24 | 1.8 |
| Yorkshire/ Humberside | 331 | 2.7 | 221 | 8.3 | 184 | 2.8 | 136 | 10.1 | 147 | 2.6 | 85 | 6.4 |
| East Midlands | 371 | 3.0 | 124 | 4.6 | 172 | 2.6 | 62 | 4.6 | 199 | 3.4 | 62 | 4.7 |
| East Anglia | 194 | 1.6 | 79 | 3.0 | 95 | 1.4 | 43 | 3.2 | 99 | 1.7 | 36 | 2.7 |
| South East | 8,815 | 70.9 | 1,158 | 43.4 | 4,857 | 73.0 | 604 | 45.1 | 3,958 | 68.5 | 554 | 41.7 |
| South West | 546 | 4.4 | 480 | 18.0 | 254 | 3.8 | 174 | 13.0 | 292 | 5.1 | 306 | 23.0 |
| West Midlands | 578 | 4.6 | 107 | 4.0 | 284 | 4.3 | 54 | 4.0 | 294 | 5.1 | 53 | 4.0 |
| North West | 756 | 6.1 | 180 | 6.7 | 369 | 5.5 | 100 | 7.5 | 387 | 6.7 | 80 | 6.0 |
| Wales | 251 | 2.0 | 63 | 2.4 | 123 | 1.9 | 29 | 2.2 | 128 | 2.2 | 34 | 2.5 |
| Scotland | 462 | 3.7 | 208 | 7.8 | 258 | 3.9 | 112 | 8.4 | 204 | 3.5 | 96 | 7.2 |
| GB | 12,429 | 100.0 | 2,669 | 100.0 | 6,652 | 100.0 | 1,339 | 100.0 | 5,777 | 100.0 | 1,330 | 100.0 |

Source:  Crown Copyright, Census 1991, Ethnic Group and Country of Birth Tables, Table 9.

**Table 2.5: Interregional migration of Irish-born population in Britain, 1990-91 (2% Individual SARS)**

| To: | Base | N | Th | EM | EA | IL | OL | Rest SE | SW | WM | NW | WA | Sc | over GB |
|---|---|---|---|---|---|---|---|---|---|---|---|---|---|---|
| N | - | 24 | - | - | - | - | 1 | 3 | - | 1 | 1 | - | 2 | 10 |
| YH | - | - | 42 | 2 | - | 3 | - | 5 | 1 | 1 | 3 | 1 | 1 | 21 |
| EM | - | 1 | 2 | 47 | - | 2 | 4 | 5 | 4 | 1 | 3 | 1 | - | 17 |
| EA | - | - | - | 1 | 34 | 1 | 2 | 5 | 1 | - | - | - | 2 | 7 |
| IL | - | 1 | - | - | 1 | 152 | 38 | 6 | - | 1 | 3 | 1 | - | 58 |
| OL | - | 1 | 1 | 1 | - | 51 | 224 | 16 | 3 | 4 | 2 | 1 | 2 | 119 |
| Rest SE | - | - | 4 | 6 | 3 | 19 | 26 | 208 | 8 | 5 | 5 | 4 | 3 | 103 |
| SW | - | - | 2 | - | - | 2 | 3 | 13 | 73 | 1 | 1 | 3 | - | 26 |
| WM | - | - | 1 | 1 | - | - | 1 | 5 | 1 | 97 | 2 | - | 1 | 23 |
| NW | - | 3 | - | - | - | 1 | 4 | 2 | 1 | 4 | 128 | 3 | 1 | 40 |
| Wa | - | - | - | - | 1 | 2 | 1 | 1 | 2 | 1 | 2 | 28 | - | 14 |
| Sc | - | - | - | - | 2 | 3 | 2 | 5 | - | 4 | - | 2 | 55 | 27 |

Key: see Figure 2.1. IL: Inner London, OL: Outer London.
Source: Crown Copyright. ONS, Samples of Anonymised Records

## Table 2.6 Total and Irish-born populations living in conurbations, 1981, 1991

| Conurbation | 1981 | | | 1991 | | |
|---|---|---|---|---|---|---|
| | Total pop. | Ir-born pop. | Ir-born as % of total | Total pop. | Ir-born pop. | Ir-born as % of total |
| Tyne & Wear Met Co | 1,135,492 | 5,206 | 0.5 | 1,095,152 | 5,153 | 0.5 |
| South Yorks Met Co | 1,292,029 | 8,334 | 0.6 | 1,262,630 | 7,836 | 0.6 |
| W.Yorks Met Co | 2,021,707 | 25,857 | 1.3 | 2,013,693 | 22,193 | 1.1 |
| Greater London | 6,608,598 | 235,782 | 3.6 | 6,679,699 | 256,470 | 3.8 |
| West Midlands Met Co | 2,628,419 | 77,558 | 3.0 | 2,551,671 | 65,429 | 2.6 |
| Greater Manch.Met Co | 2,575,407 | 59,893 | 2.3 | 2,499,441 | 51,044 | 2.0 |
| Merseyside | 1,503,120 | 21,732 | 1.4 | 1,403,642 | 17,263 | 1.2 |
| Total in Br. | 53,556,911 | 850,391 | 1.6 | 54,888,844 | 837,464 | 1.5 |
| % pop. in conurbations | 33.2 | 51.1 | | 31.9 | 50.8 | |

Source:  Crown Copyright, Census 1981, Country of Birth tables, Table 2; Census 1991, Ethnic Group and Country of Birth tables, Table 2.


## Table 2.7 Total and Irish-born populations living in conurbations by gender, 1991

| Conurbation | Women | | | | | | Men | | | | | |
|---|---|---|---|---|---|---|---|---|---|---|---|---|
| | Total N | % | RI-born N | % total | NI-born N | % total | Total N | % | RI-born N | % total | NI-born N | % total |
| Tyne and Wear | 569,914 | 2.0 | 1,278 | 0.4 | 1,325 | 1.1 | 525,238 | 2.0 | 1,273 | 0.5 | 1,277 | 1.1 |
| S.Yorks | 648,499 | 2.3 | 2,391 | 0.8 | 1,356 | 1.1 | 614,131 | 2.3 | 2,699 | 1.0 | 1,390 | 1.2 |
| W.Yorks | 1,040,501 | 3.7 | 7,726 | 2.4 | 3,724 | 3.0 | 973,192 | 3.7 | 7,164 | 2.6 | 3,579 | 3.0 |
| Gr.London | 3,474,103 | 12.3 | 115,865 | 36.4 | 21,022 | 16.7 | 3,205,596 | 12.1 | 98,362 | 35.9 | 21,221 | 17.8 |
| W.Midlands | 1,309,521 | 4.6 | 25,510 | 8.0 | 5,066 | 4.0 | 1,242,150 | 4.7 | 25,416 | 9.2 | 7,353 | 6.2 |
| Gr.Manch | 1,291,040 | 4.6 | 19,714 | 6.2 | 6,694 | 5.3 | 1,208,401 | 4.5 | 18,125 | 6.6 | 7,150 | 6.0 |
| Merseyside | 737,276 | 2.6 | 6,663 | 2.0 | 3,209 | 2.6 | 666,36 | 2.5 | 4,785 | 1.7 | 2,606 | 2.2 |
| GB total | 28,313,890 | 32.1 | 318,212 | 56.2 | 125,718 | 33.9 | 26,574,954 | 31.8 | 274,338 | 57.5 | 119,196 | 37.4 |

Source: Crown Copyright, Census 1991, Ethnic Group and Country of Birth Tables, Table 2

**Table 3.1 Household family type, total and Irish-headed households, 1991 (10% sample)**

|  | Total households | | Irish-headed households | |
| --- | --- | --- | --- | --- |
|  | Number | % | Number | % |
| **Household with no families** | **634,444** | **29.6** | **15,223** | **34.9** |
| 1 person | 564,309 | 26.3 | 13,087 | 30.0 |
| 2+ persons | 70,135 | 3.3 | 2,136 | 4.9 |
| **Household with 1 family** | **1,489,817** | **69.5** | **27,991** | **64.1** |
| Married couple with family | 1,184,737 | 55.3 | 21,304 | 48.8 |
| no children | 520,806 | 24.3 | 9,147 | 20.9 |
| + depend children | 480,192 | 22.4 | 7,565 | 17.3 |
| + non-dependent children only | 183,739 | 8.6 | 4,592 | 10.5 |
| Cohabiting couple with family | 113,882 | 5.3 | 1,963 | 4.5 |
| no children | 71,783 | 3.3 | 1,296 | 3.0 |
| + depend children | 37,447 | 1.7 | 551 | 1.3 |
| + non-dependent children only | 4,652 | 0.2 | 116 | 0.3 |
| Lone parent family | 191,198 | 8.9 | 4,224 | 10.8 |
| + depend children | 112,246 | 5.2 | 2,284 | 5.2 |
| + non dependent only | 78,952 | 3.7 | 2,440 | 5.6 |
| **Households 2+ families** | **19,867** | **0.9** | **450** | **1.0** |
| TOTAL HOUSEHOLDS | 2,144,128 | | 43,664 | |

Source: Crown Copyright, Census 1991, Ethnic Group and Country of Birth Tables, table 18

**Table 3.2 Types of family, total and Irish-headed, 1991(10% sample)**

|  | Total families | | Irish-headed families | |
| --- | --- | --- | --- | --- |
|  | Number | % | Number | % |
| Married couple family | 1,208,606 | 79.0 | 21,689 | 76.2 |
| no children | 532,896 | 23.1 | 9,353 | 32.9 |
| + depend children | 487753 | 31.9 | 7632 | 26.8 |
| + non-dep children only | 187957 | 12.3 | 4,704 | 16.5 |
| Cohabiting family | 115,505 | 7.5 | 1,966 | 6.9 |
| no children | 72,708 | 4.8 | 1,300 | 4.6 |
| + dependent children | 38,051 | 2.5 | 548 | 1.9 |
| + non-depend children | 4,746 | 0.3 | 118 | 0.4 |
| Lone parent family | 206,040 | 13.5 | 4,811 | 16.9 |
| + dependent children | 124,272 | 8.1 | 2,290 | 8.0 |
| + non-depend children | 81,768 | 5.3 | 2,521 | 8.9 |
| TOTAL FAMILIES | 1,530,151 | | 28,460 | |

Source: Crown Copyright, Census 1991, Ethnic Group and Country of Birth Tables, table 19

**Table 3.3 Proportions never-married by age group and gender: total, Irish Republic-born and Northern Irish-born populations, 1991 (2% Individual SARS)**

|  | Women | | | Men | | |
|---|---|---|---|---|---|---|
|  | Total | IR born | NI born | Total | IR born | NI born |
| 16-19 | 97.5 | 88.5 | 97.6 | 99.3 | 100.0 | 98.9 |
| 20-24 | 73.3 | 88.0 | 88.5 | 88.9 | 93.0 | 93.4 |
| 25-29 | 46.7 | 60.4 | 54.1 | 53.9 | 66.4 | 63.0 |
| 30-34 | 18.1 | 30.0 | 22.7 | 28.2 | 45.5 | 33.2 |
| 35-39 | 9.7 | 14.7 | 13.3 | 16.2 | 19.5 | 17.9 |
| 40-44 | 6.4 | 9.0 | 10.5 | 11.5 | 17.4 | 9.7 |
| 45-49 | 5.1 | 7.2 | 5.1 | 9.1 | 11.9 | 8.0 |
| 50-54 | 5.1 | 6.9 | 4.5 | 8.2 | 14.1 | 7.1 |
| 55-59 | 5.4 | 9.6 | 5.1 | 7.8 | 14.0 | 6.5 |
| 60-64 | 6.5 | 9.7 | 10.6 | 8.3 | 14.6 | 11.9 |
| 65-69 | 6.9 | 11.2 | 8.5 | 7.9 | 12.3 | 6.3 |
| 70-74 | 7.8 | 13.3 | 9.6 | 7.1 | 10.0 | 4.9 |
| 75-79 | 8.9 | 11.5 | 8.0 | 6.6 | 11.8 | 10.3 |
| 80+ | 11.9 | 16.8 | 9.7 | 7.0 | 11.7 | 7.5 |

Source: Crown Copyright. Census 1991. ONS, Samples of Anonymised Records

**Table 3.4  Household size, total and Irish-headed households, 1991**

| | Numbers in household | | | | | | | |
|---|---|---|---|---|---|---|---|---|
| | 1 | 2 | 3 | 4 | 5 | 6 | 7+ | Av |
| **Total households** | | | | | | | | |
| 21,897,322 | 5,689,791 | 7,313,175 | 3,576,902 | 3,398,790 | 1,190,754 | 351,524 | 136,386 | 2.5 |
| % | 26.0 | 33.7 | 16.3 | 15.5 | 5.4 | 1.6 | 0.6 | |
| **IR-headed households** | | | | | | | | |
| 323,835 | 101,428 | 101,288 | 51,991 | 40,076 | 18,848 | 7,329 | 2,875 | 2.4 |
| % | 31.3 | 31.3 | 16.1 | 12.4 | 5.8 | 2.3 | 0.9 | |

Source:  Crown Copyright, Census 1991, Ethnic Group and Country of Birth Tables, Table H

**Table 4.1  Occupational groups of Irish-born in Britain by gender, 1991 (10% sample)**

| Standard Occupational Classification | Women | | | Men | | |
|---|---|---|---|---|---|---|
| | Number in employ | % Ir-bn in employ | % total | Number in employ | % Ir-bn in employ | % total |
| 1a  Corporate managers & administrators | 1,101 | 5.7 | 1.7 | 2,360 | 10.9 | 1.5 |
| 1b  Managers/proprietors in agric and services | 987 | 5.1 | 1.7 | 1,122 | 5.2 | 1.2 |
| 2a  Science & engineering professionals | 141 | 0.7 | 2.5 | 733 | 3.4 | 1.5 |
| 2b  Health professionals | 182 | 0.9 | 3.6 | 305 | 1.4 | 3.0 |
| 2c  Teaching professionals | 844 | 4.4 | 1.6 | 492 | 2.3 | 1.5 |
| 2d  Other professional occupations | 379 | 2.0 | 2.3 | 662 | 3.1 | 1.9 |
| 3a  Science, engineering and associate professionals | 211 | 1.1 | 2.0 | 549 | 2.5 | 1.3 |
| 3b  Health associate professionals | 2,374 | 12.3 | 4.3 | 212 | 1.0 | 3.0 |
| 3c  Other associate professionals | 686 | 3.5 | 1.9 | 744 | 3.4 | 1.4 |
| 4a  Clerical occupations | 2,351 | 12.2 | 1.3 | 1,115 | 5.1 | 1.3 |
| 4b  Secretarial occupations | 1,539 | 8.0 | 1.5 | 54 | 0.2 | 0.1 |
| 5a  Skilled construction trades | 15 | 0.1 | 1.9 | 1,540 | 7.1 | 2.6 |
| 5b  Skilled engineering trades | 37 | 0.2 | 1.4 | 1,165 | 5.4 | 1.2 |
| 5c  Other skilled trades | 338 | 1.7 | 1.0 | 1,967 | 9.1 | 1.4 |
| 6a  Protective service occupations | 96 | 0.5 | 1.6 | 840 | 3.9 | 1.9 |
| 6b  Personal service occupations | 2,896 | 15.0 | 2.3 | 782 | 2.5 | 2.2 |
| 7a  Buyers, brokers + sales reps | 139 | 0.7 | 1.3 | 382 | 1.8 | 1.2 |
| 7b  Other sales occupations | 1,083 | 5.6 | 1.1 | 205 | 0.9 | 0.8 |
| 8a  Industrial plant and machine operators, assemblers | 804 | 4.2 | 1.6 | 1,865 | 8.6 | 1.8 |
| 8b  Drivers and mobile machinery operators | 69 | 0.4 | 1.7 | 1,661 | 7.7 | 1.9 |
| 9a  Other occups in agric/ forestry/fisheries | 19 | 0.1 | 0.5 | 73 | 0.3 | 0.6 |
| 9b  Other elementary occupations | 2,827 | 14.6 | 2.9 | 2,432 | 11.2 | 2.8 |
| Not stated/inadequately stated | 199 | 1.0 | 2.3 | 281 | 1.3 | 2.0 |
| On a Government scheme | 120 | 0.6 | 0.9 | 166 | 0.8 | 0.8 |
| Total in employment | 19,347 | | 1.8 | 21,707 | | 1.6 |

Source: Crown Copyright, Census 1991, Ethnic Group and Country of Birth Tables, table 13.

**Table 4.2  Occupational groupings of Republic Irish-born, Northern Irish-born and total populations by gender, 1991 (2% Individual SARS)**

| | IR born | | | | NI born | | | | Total population | | | |
|---|---|---|---|---|---|---|---|---|---|---|---|---|
| | Women | | Men | | Women | | Men | | Women | | Men | |
| SOC | N | % | N | % | N | % | N | % | N | % | N | % |
| 1a | 140 | 3.8 | 344 | 8.1 | 94 | 5.7 | 191 | 10.1 | 14,019 | 4.8 | 34,952 | 10.0 |
| 1b | 217 | 5.8 | 239 | 5.6 | 90 | 5.5 | 135 | 7.2 | 16,505 | 5.6 | 27,543 | 7.9 |
| 2a | 23 | 0.6 | 92 | 2.2 | 14 | 0.9 | 78 | 4.1 | 1,393 | 0.5 | 12,032 | 3.5 |
| 2b | 18 | 0.5 | 45 | 1.1 | 26 | 1.6 | 42 | 2.2 | 1,302 | 0.4 | 2,568 | 0.7 |
| 2c | 115 | 3.1 | 65 | 1.5 | 100 | 6.1 | 56 | 3.0 | 14,044 | 4.8 | 8,323 | 2.4 |
| 2d | 61 | 1.6 | 69 | 1.6 | 47 | 2.9 | 77 | 4.1 | 4,195 | 1.4 | 8,029 | 2.3 |
| 3a | 50 | 1.3 | 114 | 2.7 | 31 | 1.9 | 75 | 4.0 | 4,571 | 1.6 | 14,390 | 4.1 |
| 3b | 443 | 11.9 | 33 | 0.8 | 152 | 9.3 | 20 | 1.1 | 14,041 | 4.8 | 1,791 | 0.5 |
| 3c | 88 | 2.4 | 75 | 1.8 | 62 | 3.8 | 54 | 2.9 | 7,979 | 2.7 | 9,919 | 2.9 |
| 4a | 392 | 10.5 | 223 | 5.3 | 207 | 12.6 | 100 | 5.3 | 48,754 | 16.6 | 22,687 | 6.5 |
| 4b | 316 | 8.5 | 19 | 0.4 | 13.8 | 8.4 | 14 | 0.7 | 32,360 | 11.0 | 2,179 | 0.6 |
| 5a | 5 | 0.1 | 380 | 9.0 | 2 | 0.1 | 96 | 5.1 | 277 | 0.1 | 16,614 | 4.8 |
| 5b | 8 | 0.2 | 349 | 8.2 | 5 | 0.3 | 148 | 7.8 | 1,089 | 0.4 | 35,334 | 10.2 |
| 5c | 70 | 1.9 | 334 | 7.9 | 27 | 1.6 | 101 | 5.4 | 10,518 | 3.6 | 28,886 | 8.3 |
| 6a | 24 | 0.6 | 121 | 2.9 | 9 | 0.5 | 131 | 6.9 | 1,717 | 0.6 | 11,699 | 3.4 |
| 6b | 567 | 15.2 | 134 | 3.2 | 208 | 12.7 | 65 | 3.4 | 37,717 | 12.8 | 10,546 | 3.0 |
| 7a | 23 | 0.6 | 57 | 1.3 | 12 | 0.7 | 32 | 1.7 | 2,685 | 0.9 | 8,125 | 2.3 |
| 7b | 218 | 5.9 | 41 | 1.0 | 136 | 8.3 | 30 | 1.6 | 30,381 | 10.3 | 8,019 | 2.3 |
| 8a | 142 | 3.8 | 199 | 4.7 | 71 | 4.3 | 70 | 3.7 | 15,234 | 5.2 | 19,775 | 5.7 |
| 8b | 26 | 0.7 | 552 | 13.0 | 10 | 0.6 | 173 | 9.2 | 2,497 | 0.8 | 31,289 | 9.0 |
| 9a | 4 | 0.1 | 17 | 0.4 | 3 | 0.2 | 14 | 0.7 | 1,380 | 0.5 | 3,523 | 1.0 |
| 9b | 723 | 19.4 | 685 | 16.2 | 195 | 11.9 | 184 | 9.8 | 31,874 | 10.8 | 29,627 | 8.5 |
| Total in employment | 3,724 | | 4,234 | | 1,639 | | 1,886 | | 294,432 | | 347,868 | |

See Table 4.1 for categories

Source:   Crown Copyright ONS, Samples of Anonymised Records.

**Table 4.3  Registrar General's Social Class by birthplace/ethnic group and gender, England, 1991 (2% Individual SARS)**

|  | Eng | Sco | Wa | NI | Ir Rep | Bl Car | Ind | Pak | Bl Afr |
|---|---|---|---|---|---|---|---|---|---|
| WOMEN |  |  |  |  |  |  |  |  |  |
| I | 3,328 | 148 | 107 | 55 | 68 | 30 | 149 | 16 | 24 |
| % | 1.5 | 3.1 | 3.1 | 3.8 | 1.9 | 1.0 | 4.2 | 2.6 | 2.9 |
| II | 55,209 | 1,614 | 1,295 | 508 | 1,082 | 880 | 717 | 122 | 255 |
| % | 24.6 | 34.1 | 37.9 | 35.5 | 31.0 | 29.3 | 20.0 | 20.1 | 30.5 |
| IIIN | 89,363 | 1,578 | 1,131 | 420 | 884 | 978 | 1,214 | 193 | 246 |
| % | 39.9 | 33.4 | 33.1 | 29.3 | 25.3 | 32.6 | 33.9 | 31.8 | 29.5 |
| IIIM | 16,987 | 260 | 185 | 69 | 233 | 202 | 225 | 39 | 44 |
| % | 7.6 | 5.5 | 5.4 | 4.8 | 6.7 | 6.7 | 6.3 | 6.4 | 5.3 |
| IV | 39,742 | 748 | 450 | 237 | 663 | 566 | 1,023 | 191 | 136 |
| % | 17.7 | 15.8 | 11.7 | 16.6 | 19.0 | 18.9 | 28.6 | 31.5 | 16.3 |
| V | 16,727 | 302 | 200 | 118 | 492 | 249 | 144 | 15 | 96 |
| % | 7.5 | 6.4 | 5.8 | 8.2 | 14.1 | 8.3 | 4.0 | 2.5 | 11.5 |
| Total | 224,084 | 4,731 | 3,419 | 1,432 | 3,490 | 3,002 | 3,581 | 606 | 835 |
| MEN |  |  |  |  |  |  |  |  |  |
| I | 16,585 | 571 | 486 | 162 | 193 | 62 | 505 | 106 | 119 |
| % | 6.3 | 9.2 | 11.9 | 9.9 | 4.8 | 2.2 | 10.7 | 5.7 | 13.3 |
| II | 71,128 | 1,967 | 1,508 | 449 | 815 | 384 | 1,245 | 324 | 204 |
| % | 27.2 | 31.7 | 37.1 | 27.5 | 20.3 | 13.7 | 26.4 | 17.4 | 22.7 |
| IIIN | 29,991 | 675 | 429 | 152 | 266 | 327 | 709 | 240 | 149 |
| % | 11.5 | 10.9 | 10.5 | 9.3 | 6.6 | 11.7 | 15.0 | 12.9 | 16.6 |
| IIIM | 84,551 | 1,488 | 817 | 443 | 1,462 | 1,048 | 1,099 | 565 | 147 |
| % | 32.4 | 2.0 | 20.1 | 27.1 | 36.4 | 37.4 | 23.3 | 30.3 | 16.4 |
| IV | 41,458 | 875 | 494 | 233 | 705 | 629 | 835 | 450 | 148 |
| % | 15.9 | 14.1 | 12.1 | 14.3 | 17.5 | 22.4 | 17.7 | 24.2 | 16.5 |
| V | 14,114 | 307 | 144 | 119 | 484 | 236 | 185 | 120 | 74 |
| % | 5.4 | 4.9 | 3.5 | 7.3 | 12.0 | 8.4 | 3.9 | 6.4 | 8.2 |
| Total | 261,314 | 6,208 | 4,068 | 1,635 | 4,022 | 2,803 | 4,711 | 1,863 | 897 |

Source: Crown Copyright ONS. Samples of Anonymised Records.

**Table 4.4 Social mobility 1971-81, total Irish-born and second-generation Irish populations (1% LS sample)**

A Total population

| | Class in 1971 | | | Class in 1981 | | |
| --- | --- | --- | --- | --- | --- | --- |
| | **PR** | **MA** | **PB** | **WC** | **BC** | **TOTAL** |
| **WC** | 2,654 | 4,549 | 1,338 | 24,072 | 8,253 | 40,902 |
| **BC** | 2,543 | 3,184 | 3,776 | 6,558 | 68,252 | 84,421 |
| | **TOTAL** | | **18,044** | | **107,135** | **125,323** |
| **PR** | 12,164 | 2,588 | 383 | 1,396 | 1,834 | 18,387 |
| **MA** | 1,072 | 7,953 | 966 | 1,736 | 1,760 | 13,506 |
| **PB** | 332 | 938 | 5,866 | 2,112 | 2,813 | 12,068 |
| | **TOTAL** | | **32,262** | | **11,651** | **43,961** |

B Irish Republic born

| | **PR** | **MA** | **PB** | **WC** | **BC** | **TOTAL** |
| --- | --- | --- | --- | --- | --- | --- |
| **WC** | 36 | 49 | 13 | 342 | 182 | 622 |
| **BC** | 31 | 47 | 64 | 161 | 1,475 | 1,788 |
| | **TOTAL** | | **240** | | **2,160** | **2,400** |
| **PR** | 250 | 23 | 6 | 27 | 33 | 339 |
| **MA** | 6 | 92 | 13 | 19 | 33 | 163 |
| **PB** | 6 | 13 | 82 | 12 | 75 | 188 |
| | **TOTAL** | | **491** | | **199** | **6,920** |

C Northern Irish-born

| | **PR** | **MA** | **PB** | **WC** | **BC** | **TOTAL** |
| --- | --- | --- | --- | --- | --- | --- |
| **WC** | 11 | 11 | 2 | 116 | 41 | 181 |
| **BC** | 12 | 14 | 20 | 42 | 401 | 489 |
| | **TOTAL** | | **70** | | **600** | **670** |
| **PR** | 93 | 15 | - | 8 | 13 | 129 |
| **MA** | 7 | 43 | 2 | 10 | 10 | 72 |
| **PB** | 2 | 2 | 24 | 7 | 17 | 52 |
| | **TOTAL** | | **188** | | **65** | **253** |

KEY:   WC: White collar; PR: Professional; PB: Petite Bourgeoisie; BC: Blue collar; MA: Managerial

Source: Crown Copyright, ONS Longitudinal Study

**Figure 4.5  Social mobility 1971-81: Transition rates (1% LS sample)**

| | Class in 1971 | | | Class in 1981 | | Upwardly mobile | Downwardly mobile |
|---|---|---|---|---|---|---|---|
| **A Total population** | | | | | | | |
| | **PR** | **MA** | **PB** | **WC** | **BC** | | |
| **WC** | 6.49 | 11.12 | 3.27 | 58.85 | 20.18 | | |
| **BC** | 3.01 | 3.77 | 4.47 | 7.77 | 80.85 | | |
| | TOTAL | | **14.40** | | **85.49** | **14.40** | **26.50** |
| **PR** | 66.16 | 14.08 | 2.08 | 7.59 | 9.97 | | |
| **MA** | 7.94 | 58.88 | 7.15 | 12.85 | 13.03 | | |
| **PB** | 2.75 | 7.77 | 48.61 | 17.50 | 23.31 | | |
| | TOTAL | | **73.39** | | **26.50** | | |
| **B Irish Republic born** | | | | | | | |
| **WC** | 5.79 | 7.88 | 2.09 | 54.98 | 29.26 | | |
| **BC** | 1.74 | 2.64 | 3.60 | 9.06 | 82.96 | | |
| | TOTAL | | **10.00** | | **90.00** | **10.00** | **28.84** |
| **PR** | 73.75 | 6.78 | 1.77 | 7.96 | 9.73 | | |
| **MA** | 3.68 | 56.44 | 7.98 | 11.66 | 20.25 | | |
| **PB** | 3.19 | 6.91 | 43.62 | 6.38 | 39.89 | | |
| | TOTAL | | **71.16** | | **28.84** | | |
| **C Northern Irish-born** | | | | | | | |
| **WC** | 6.08 | 6.08 | 1.10 | 64.09 | 22.65 | | |
| **BC** | 2.45 | 2.86 | 4.09 | 8.59 | 82.00 | | |
| | TOTAL | | **10.45** | | **89.55** | **10.45** | **25.69** |
| **PR** | 72.09 | 11.63 | - | 6.20 | 10.08 | | |
| **MA** | 9.72 | 59.72 | 2.78 | 13.89 | 13.89 | | |
| **PB** | 3.85 | 3.85 | 46.15 | 13.46 | 32.69 | | |
| | TOTAL | | **74.31** | | **25.69** | | |

Source: Crown Copyright. ONS Longitudinal Study

**Table 4.6: Measures of housing quality in London by ethnic birthplace group of head of household, 1991, %**

| | Irish born | White non-Irish | Ind | Bl Car | Bl Af | Pak | Bang | Bl other | Other |
|---|---|---|---|---|---|---|---|---|---|
| Overcrowded (1.5 + people per room) | 1.6 | 0.8 | 3.2 | 1.8 | 6.9 | 6.1 | 23.9 | 3.0 | 4.0 |
| Lack or share bath/shower and/or inside WC | 3.6 | 2.3 | 1.4 | 1.6 | 5.3 | 2.9 | 2.2 | 2.9 | 3.9 |
| No central heating | 22.0 | 19.8 | 7.6 | 14.8 | 14.8 | 13.5 | 12.1 | 17.9 | 12.8 |
| Not self-contained accommodation | 5.2 | 2.4 | 1.5 | 2.5 | 6.8 | 3.0 | 1.5 | 4.2 | 4.9 |
| No Car | 53.9 | 38.8 | 23.6 | 57.1 | 65.9 | 30.7 | 63.5 | 58.9 | 40.4 |

Source: Crown Copyright. Census 1991, Local Base Statistics (AGIY, 1995)

**Table 4.7: Housing/quality of life of life measures by borough, for all residents in households headed by four largest ethnic/birthplace groups, London boroughs, 1991**

| | %Lack/share use of bath /shower and/or inside WC | | | | %Lack Central heating | | | | % Not self-contained accommodation | | | | % No Car | | | |
|---|---|---|---|---|---|---|---|---|---|---|---|---|---|---|---|---|
| | Ir born | W non-Ir | Ind | B-C | Ir born | W non-Ir | Ind | B/C | Ir born | W non-Ir | Ind | B/C | Ir born | W non-Ir | Ind | B/C |
| City of L | 1.4 | 0.9 | - | - | 9.9 | 4.8 | 0.2 | - | - | 0.2 | - | - | 57.7 | 44.8 | 28.6 | 100.0 |
| Camden | 5.4 | 3.8 | 3.7 | 3.6 | 19.5 | 16.2 | 15.1 | 11.1 | 7.3 | 5.5 | 6.0 | 5.0 | 72.6 | 52.9 | 49.5 | 68.2 |
| Hackney | 4.7 | 3.4 | 2.5 | 1.9 | 25.8 | 23.5 | 0.1 | 16.0 | 6.1 | 3.9 | 4.2 | 2.6 | 69.8 | 59.1 | 45.0 | 71.4 |
| Hamm. | 5.2 | 3.5 | 1.8 | 2.1 | 35.9 | 25.5 | 18.6 | 23.3 | 7.9 | 4.8 | 3.8 | 3.7 | 69.6 | 48.0 | 45.0 | 69.9 |
| Haring. | 6.2 | 4.3 | 2.9 | 1.8 | 24.1 | 20.9 | 11.7 | 11.0 | 9.1 | 5.7 | 3.5 | 2.6 | 58.7 | 46.5 | 37.8 | 61.5 |
| sling. | 3.6 | 3.0 | 4.7 | 2.2 | 20.0 | 16.0 | 19.2 | 13.3 | 6.2 | 4.5 | 4.5 | 3.4 | 70.7 | 57.1 | 47.8 | 70.6 |
| Ken & C | 5.3 | 4.0 | 5.4 | 2.1 | 29.4 | 19.1 | 18.1 | 24.2 | 8.1 | 6.0 | 6.9 | 4.1 | 70.1 | 46.9 | 53.6 | 77.8 |
| Lambeth | 3.6 | 3.3 | 1.8 | 1.5 | 28.5 | 26.8 | 15.6 | 19.5 | 5.5 | 4.5 | 2.2 | 2.9 | 67.0 | 51.4 | 37.9 | 68.0 |
| Lewisham | 2.3 | 2.1 | 1.2 | 1.4 | 29.1 | 29.0 | 17.4 | 19.6 | 4.4 | 2.9 | 2.2 | 2.5 | 54.9 | 45.3 | 27.6 | 54.1 |
| Newham | 5.1 | 5.5 | 2.1 | 2.1 | 24.7 | 25.6 | 10.7 | 12.5 | 4.9 | 2.0 | 1.5 | 2.1 | 60.2 | 54.5 | 35.8 | 58.1 |
| Swark | 2.0 | 1.7 | 1.1 | 1.1 | 17.8 | 18.1 | 13.7 | 10.5 | 2.2 | 1.9 | 1.8 | 1.8 | 67.9 | 55.5 | 35.5 | 66.7 |
| THam. | 1.2 | 1.0 | 1.1 | 0.7 | 15.0 | 14.9 | 13.0 | 10.1 | 0.9 | 0.5 | 0.5 | 0.2 | 73.0 | 58.8 | 53.7 | 72.3 |
| Westmin. | 4.7 | 3.5 | 3.7 | 2.3 | 32.0 | 21.9 | 14.2 | 25.6 | 6.3 | 4.5 | 4.8 | 3.8 | 75.9 | 54.6 | 46.7 | 76.6 |
| B&Dag | 0.6 | 0.5 | 1.2 | 0.5 | 32.1 | 36.9 | 11.8 | 16.2 | 0.4 | 0.3 | 0.5 | 0.4 | 55.2 | 42.9 | 25.9 | 39.8 |
| Barnet | 3.1 | 1.8 | 1.2 | 2.0 | 15.0 | 12.1 | 4.3 | 9.3 | 4.0 | 2.0 | 1.5 | 3.2 | 41.7 | 30.2 | 18.3 | 41.9 |
| Bexley | 0.6 | 0.6 | 0.5 | 0.2 | 15.9 | 18.7 | 6.4 | 7.4 | 0.4 | 0.3 | 0.1 | - | 35.3 | 26.7 | 17.0 | 28.5 |
| Brent | 5.9 | 3.2 | 1.2 | 1.5 | 23.0 | 20.6 | 4.9 | 12.8 | 10.0 | 4.5 | 1.3 | 2.8 | 51.7 | 43.1 | 20.8 | 56.7 |
| Bromley | 1.8 | 1.2 | 1.0 | 1.5 | 15.0 | 12.8 | 5.7 | 11.6 | 2.3 | 0.9 | 1.2 | 1.5 | 35.7 | 25.3 | 14.2 | 38.7 |
| Croydon | 3.1 | 1.7 | 1.0 | 1.1 | 22.5 | 20.8 | 10.4 | 14.8 | 4.9 | 1.7 | 1.1 | 2.1 | 39.1 | 29.7 | 22.6 | 37.8 |
| Ealing | 3.7 | 2.5 | 1.3 | 1.7 | 18.2 | 18.9 | 6.2 | 10.1 | 5.4 | 3.1 | 1.1 | 2.3 | 46.1 | 36.7 | 23.8 | 47.5 |
| Enfield | 1.9 | 1.6 | 0.8 | 1.2 | 14.9 | 16.7 | 5.7 | 7.9 | 2.7 | 1.4 | 0.9 | 1.5 | 35.3 | 31.6 | 17.6 | 35.7 |
| Greenw. | 1.5 | 1.6 | 1.0 | 1.0 | 24.7 | 24.0 | 11.3 | 15.1 | 1.8 | 1.2 | 1.3 | 1.8 | 54.9 | 42.9 | 29.4 | 50.6 |
| Harrow | 1.7 | 0.9 | 0.7 | 0.9 | 12.5 | 13.3 | 2.4 | 6.5 | 2.8 | 1.0 | 0.7 | 1.3 | 33.3 | 28.2 | 13.7 | 27.9 |
| Haver. | 1.4 | 0.9 | 1.0 | 1.2 | 14.9 | 13.9 | 6.1 | 9.3 | 1.1 | 0.5 | 0.7 | 0.8 | 33.8 | 26.0 | 11.0 | 29.1 |
| Hilling. | 0.9 | 0.7 | 0.5 | 0.9 | 11.0 | 11.9 | 4.4 | 7.7 | 1.0 | 0.6 | 0.4 | 1.2 | 31.8 | 24.9 | 11.3 | 23.3 |
| hounslow | 2.6 | 2.2 | 0.9 | 1.3 | 20.1 | 20.9 | 5.0 | 12.9 | 3.5 | 2.1 | 0.9 | 2.2 | 41.6 | 33.7 | 17.1 | 39.9 |
| Kingston | 3.3 | 2.4 | 1.2 | 3.2 | 16.6 | 15.8 | 7.5 | 11.0 | 3.1 | 2.3 | 1.5 | 4.6 | 39.4 | 27.1 | 15.6 | 27.4 |
| Merion | 3.1 | 1.7 | 0.8 | 0.8 | 19.5 | 23.1 | 9.1 | 11.3 | 3.5 | 1.8 | 1.0 | 0.8 | 41.2 | 33.8 | 21.0 | 37.3 |
| Redbrid. | 3.1 | 2.0 | 1.0 | 1.4 | 19.2 | 19.2 | 4.7 | 9.4 | 4.9 | 1.8 | 0.9 | 2.7 | 37.9 | 30.9 | 15.1 | 31.2 |
| Richmond | 3.0 | 2.4 | 1.2 | 4.1 | 19.5 | 17.4 | 7.8 | 16.4 | 3.5 | 2.0 | 1.3 | 5.5 | 37.6 | 28.4 | 15.4 | 31.5 |
| Sutton | 2.2 | 1.4 | 1.3 | 0.8 | 15.4 | 15.6 | 6.9 | 11.0 | 1.7 | 1.1 | 0.5 | 1.4 | 33.7 | 26.5 | 12.2 | 23.6 |
| W.Forest | 3.3 | 3.9 | 2.2 | 1.5 | 26.4 | 30.6 | 12.4 | 14.5 | 4.4 | 2.0 | 1.6 | 2.0 | 48.3 | 42.0 | 31.0 | 48.1 |
| Average | 3.6 | 2.3 | 1.4 | 1.6 | 22.0 | 19.8 | 7.6 | 14.8 | 5.2 | 2.4 | 1.5 | 2.5 | 53.9 | 38.8 | 23.6 | 57.1 |

Source: Crown Copyright. Census 1991, Local Base Statistics (AGIY, 1995)

**Table 4.8  Higher level qualifications by ethnic/birthplace group and gender, Great Britain, 1991, percentages (10% sample)**

**WOMEN**

|  | Total | White | Ir-bn | Bl Car | Ind | Pak | Bl Afr |
|---|---|---|---|---|---|---|---|
| Total qualified | 10.9 | 11.5 | 16.4 | 12.0 | 10.6 | 4.0 | 22.1 |
| level a | 1.0 | 4.0 | 4.8 | 2.7 | 7.0 | 6.5 | 8.6 |
| level b | 11.1 | 38.0 | 28.8 | 20.0 | 56.4 | 61.8 | 34.0 |
| level c | 87.9 | 58.0 | 66.4 | 77.3 | 36.6 | 31.7 | 57.4 |

**MEN**

|  | Total | White | Ir-bn | Bl Car | Ind | Pak | Bl Afr |
|---|---|---|---|---|---|---|---|
| Total qualified | 15.5 | 15.4 | 13.2 | 6.0 | 19.4 | 9.8 | 30.9 |
| level a | 9.3 | 9.0 | 15.5 | 9.0 | 12.5 | 13.6 | 16.1 |
| level b | 52.6 | 52.5 | 56.1 | 38.8 | 63.0 | 60.6 | 45.2 |
| level c | 38.1 | 38.5 | 28.4 | 52.2 | 24.5 | 25.8 | 38.8 |

Source: Crown Copyright, Census 1991, Ethnic Group and Country of Birth Tables, table 17.

**Table 4.9  Higher level qualifications by age and gender, total and Irish-born populations, Great Britain, 1991(10% sample)**

|  | WOMEN | | MEN | |
|---|---|---|---|---|
|  | Total pop. | Irish-born | Total pop. | Irish-born |
| **18-24 % qualified** | **7.4** | **18.2** | **7.8** | **18.4** |
| level a | 1.4 | 2.9 | 2.4 | 4.6 |
| level b | 55.2 | 55.3 | 56.5 | 67.7 |
| level c | 43.4 | 41.8 | 41.1 | 27.6 |
| **25-9 % qualified** | **18.4** | **34.2** | **19.8** | **31.5** |
| level a | 3.9 | 6.7 | 7.2 | 11.4 |
| level b | 52.7 | 54.2 | 57.8 | 66.5 |
| level c | 43.3 | 39.1 | 35.0 | 22.1 |
| **30-44 % qualified** | **17.8** | **23.1** | **21.7** | **20.7** |
| level a | 5.5 | 6.6 | 11.3 | 18.7 |
| level b | 40.9 | 32.6 | 53.0 | 55.0 |
| level c | 53.6 | 60.7 | 35.7 | 26.3 |
| **45-59 % qualified** | **11.8** | **14.5** | **16.5** | **8.3** |
| level a | 3.9 | 3.6 | 10.5 | 16.3 |
| level b | 25.8 | 15.2 | 47.1 | 45.1 |
| level c | 70.3 | 81.2 | 42.4 | 38.6 |
| **60-4 % qualified** | **8.1** | **10.9** | **12.6** | **6.1** |
| level a | 2.6 | 2.9 | 7.5 | 15.1 |
| level b | 23.3 | 11.4 | 51.8 | 51.6 |
| level c | 74.1 | 85.6 | 40.7 | 33.3 |
| **65 + % qualified** | **4.7** | **9.3** | **8.9** | **6.8** |
| level a | 2.2 | 2.3 | 6.8 | 18.8 |
| level b | 22.5 | 12.6 | 55.5 | 54.9 |
| level c | 75.4 | 85.1 | 37.7 | 26.3 |

Source: Crown Copyright, Census 1991, Ethnic Group and Country of Birth Tables, Table 17.

**Table 4.10 Higher level qualifications, total and Irish-born populations by gender: change over time 1971-91, percentages (10% sample)**

| | WOMEN | | | | MEN | | | |
| | Total | | Irish-born | | Total | | Irish-born | |
| | 1971 | 1991 | 1971 | 1991 | 1971 | 1991 | 1971 | 1991 |
|---|---|---|---|---|---|---|---|---|
| Total qualified | 6.2 | 11.6 | 10.9 | 16.4 | 8.7 | 15.5 | 5.1 | 13.2 |
| level a | 0.9 | 4.1 | 1.0 | 4.8 | 4.8 | 9.3 | 10.2 | 15.5 |
| level b | 22.0 | 38.1 | 11.1 | 28.8 | 52.5 | 52.6 | 57.7 | 56.1 |
| level c | 77.1 | 57.8 | 87.9 | 66.4 | 42.7 | 38.1 | 32.2 | 28.4 |

Source: Crown Copyright, Census 1971, Qualified Manpower Tables, Table 3; Census 1991, Ethnic Group and Country of Birth tables, Table 17.

**Table 4. 11 Regional distribution of population with higher level qualifications, total and birthplace/ethnic groups, 1991, percentages (10% sample)**

| | Total | Ir-bn | Bl Car | Ind | Pak | Bl Afr |
|---|---|---|---|---|---|---|
| London | 17.51 | 14.47 | 8.97 | 16.20 | 12.90 | 25.09 |
| SE | 15.32 | 17.87 | 13.48 | 20.95 | 8.94 | 34.16 |
| SW | 13.84 | 18.17 | 36.13 | 22.13 | 13.03 | 36.13 |
| EA | 13.18 | 19.69 | 7.27 | 26.93 | 6.32 | 25.32 |
| EM | 11.64 | 12.38 | 10.36 | 9.28 | 6.72 | 26.03 |
| WM | 11.07 | 8.88 | 7.40 | 9.21 | 3.58 | 29.94 |
| YH | 11.42 | 14.63 | 7.18 | 13.98 | 3.15 | 30.19 |
| N | 10.79 | 18.02 | 10.59 | 27.34 | 8.91 | 38.30 |
| NW | 11.96 | 12.83 | 10.29 | 15.33 | 5.42 | 28.10 |
| Wa | 11.97 | 14.93 | 8.93 | 33.24 | 11.60 | 19.15 |
| Sc | 14.00 | 20.37 | 18.75 | 24.43 | 8.44 | 41.92 |
| TOTAL | 13.45 | 14.93 | 9.18 | 15.03 | 7.02 | 26.54 |

Source: GMB Report, 1993 Special Census tables.

**Table 4.12 Lower level qualifications: total population and ethnic/birthplace group and gender average 1989, 1990, 1991, UK, percentages**

| | WOMEN | | | | | MEN | | | | |
| | Total | White UK born | White Irish | Asian | Afro Car | Total | White UK born | White Irish | Asian | Afro Car |
|---|---|---|---|---|---|---|---|---|---|---|
| A level +equiv | 9.6 | 9.6 | 7.8 | 7.3 | 13.6 | 25.3 | 25.6 | 20.8 | 15.2 | 27.4 |
| O level | 16.7 | 16.8 | 7.2 | 15.6 | 18.1 | 11.2 | 11.2 | 5.0 | 13.7 | 13.1 |
| CSE | 3.7 | 3.8 | 0.9 | 3.5 | 8.3 | 3.0 | 3.1 | 0.7 | 2.6 | 5.1 |
| YTS | 0.5 | 5.0 | 8.2 | 9.8 | 5.3 | 3.6 | 3.5 | 7.0 | 7.1 | 3.9 |
| No quals | 24.9 | 24.3 | 29.9 | 44.6 | 27.9 | 16.9 | 16.4 | 25.0 | 15.4 | 22.6 |

Source: ONS Labour Force Survey

**Table 4.13 Unemployment rates\* by occupation group, ethnic/birthplace group and gender, 1991, percentages (10% sample)**

| Occupational group | Total | Ir-born | Bl Car | Ind | Pak | Bl Afr |
|---|---|---|---|---|---|---|
| **WOMEN** | | | | | | |
| 1 | 3.7 | 3.6 | 8.6 | 2.7 | 5.2 | 10.8 |
| 2 | 2.1 | 2.3 | 3.1 | 3.7 | 6.7 | 13.9 |
| 3 | 3.1 | 2.0 | 3.9 | 4.0 | 9.8 | 4.7 |
| 4 | 4.3 | 5.5 | 8.8 | 7.5 | 8.8 | 12.8 |
| 5 | 9.0 | 11.0 | 18.1 | 10.9 | - | 15.9 |
| 6 | 5.3 | 4.7 | 7.2 | 6.5 | 9.8 | 10.6 |
| 7 | 5.8 | 5.3 | 15.5 | 7.9 | 14.8 | 20.8 |
| 8 | 10.3 | 9.5 | 10.8 | 11.7 | 17.4 | 20.5 |
| 9 | 4.9 | 4.6 | 7.7 | 6.5 | 14.5 | 9.9 |
| **TOTAL** | **6.8** | **7.0** | **13.6** | **12.6** | **30.4** | **25.2** |
| **MEN** | | | | | | |
| 1 | 4.5 | 6.4 | 8.9 | 5.6 | 10.0 | 14.5 |
| 2 | 2.9 | 2.7 | 4.0 | 3.4 | 5.8 | 8.6 |
| 3 | 5.6 | 5.6 | 11.3 | 6.9 | 16.6 | 12.0 |
| 4 | 8.2 | 10.1 | 14.8 | 10.4 | 15.7 | 18.3 |
| 5 | 10.7 | 15.3 | 20.0 | 13.1 | 23.4 | 21.9 |
| 6 | 8.8 | 8.7 | 12.8 | 12.6 | 23.7 | 14.9 |
| 7 | 8.8 | 7.8 | 11.3 | 9.5 | 17.6 | 28.0 |
| 8 | 10.7 | 10.8 | 14.6 | 13.2 | 23.6 | 17.3 |
| 9 | 18.5 | 21.4 | 19.4 | 12.3 | 29.7 | 20.2 |
| **TOTAL** | **11.3** | **15.1** | **19.7** | **12.2** | **30.0** | **30.9** |

\* unemployed as % of economically active

Source: Crown Copyright. Census 1991, Ethnic Group and Country of Birth Tables, Table 13

**Table 5.1 Housing tenure by birthplace/ethnic group and gender, 1991, percentages (2% Individual SARS)**

| Tenure | Total | | RI-born | | NI-born | | Bl Car | | Indian | | Pakistani | | Bl African | |
|---|---|---|---|---|---|---|---|---|---|---|---|---|---|---|
| | F | M | F | M | F | M | F | M | F | M | F | M | F | M |
| Owner occupied | | | | | | | | | | | | | | |
| - outright | 20.3 | 18.2 | 22.7 | 18.7 | 17.0 | 13.8 | 8.7 | 9.5 | 17.7 | 16.7 | 23.1 | 20.8 | 3.6 | 4.8 |
| - buying | 48.3 | 52.5 | 37.6 | 39.7 | 44.4 | 46.6 | 43.0 | 44.6 | 67.9 | 68.4 | 58.6 | 60.5 | 27.2 | 25.6 |
| Private rental | 2.9 | 3.4 | 6.9 | 8.8 | 7.4 | 9.7 | 2.8 | 3.1 | 3.8 | 4.3 | 4.9 | 6.2 | 9.6 | 16.1 |
| - furnished | 3.0 | 2.7 | 3.1 | 3.5 | 2.7 | 2.8 | 1.9 | 2.2 | 1.2 | 1.4 | 1.7 | 1.7 | 2.3 | 2.8 |
| - unfurnished | 2.0 | 2.3 | 1.8 | 2.9 | 4.1 | 4.2 | 0.9 | 0.9 | 1.4 | 1.5 | 0.8 | 0.7 | 1.9 | 3.0 |
| Housing Assoc | 2.7 | 2.4 | 4.2 | 4.0 | 3.3 | 2.2 | 8.0 | 7.1 | 1.5 | 1.4 | 1.8 | 1.7 | 9.9 | 9.3 |
| Local Authority/New Town | 17.4 | 15.7 | 22.0 | 21.0 | 17.5 | 17.4 | 34.7 | 32.6 | 6.4 | 6.3 | 8.7 | 8.1 | 45.5 | 38.0 |
| Total | 559,249 | 526,383 | 6,078 | 5,283 | 2,540 | 2,260 | 4,983 | 4,557 | 8,338 | 8,405 | 4,470 | 4,835 | 1,935 | 1,903 |

Source: Crown Copyright. ONS, Samples of Anonymised Records

**Table 5.2 Household space type by birthplace/ethnic group and gender, 1991, percentages (2% Individual SARS)**

|  | Total | | RI-born | | NI-born | | Bl Car | | Indian | | Pakistani | | Bl Afr | |
|---|---|---|---|---|---|---|---|---|---|---|---|---|---|---|
|  | F | M | F | M | F | M | F | M | F | M | F | M | F | M |
| Detached | 22.1 | 22.9 | 13.7 | 12.1 | 19.4 | 18.7 | 3.8 | 3.2 | 14.2 | 14.2 | 5.2 | 6.6 | 5.7 | 5.0 |
| Semi-det | 31.7 | 32.5 | 25.1 | 25.5 | 27.5 | 26.7 | 17.2 | 18.0 | 28.7 | 28.8 | 18.9 | 18.8 | 9.8 | 10.8 |
| Terraced | 30.4 | 30.3 | 32.5 | 34.8 | 30.7 | 31.6 | 44.5 | 45.1 | 43.6 | 43.8 | 66.1 | 64.6 | 30.2 | 32.9 |
| Flat-resid | 11.4 | 9.7 | 19.0 | 16.6 | 14.7 | 14.4 | 25.5 | 24.7 | 6.3 | 5.7 | 5.2 | 5.4 | 39.1 | 36.0 |
| Flat-comm | 3.7 | 3.6 | 7.6 | 8.3 | 6.4 | 6.5 | 0.9 | 0.7 | 4.8 | 4.8 | 2.8 | 2.7 | 1.2 | 1.6 |
| Flat-converted | 2.5 | 2.3 | 5.7 | 5.3 | 4.6 | 4.3 | 6.8 | 6.3 | 1.8 | 1.8 | 1.2 | 1.3 | 9.8 | 8.6 |
| Total | 526,383 | 559,249 | 6,078 | 5,283 | 2,540 | 2,260 | 4,983 | 4,557 | 8,338 | 8,405 | 4,470 | 4,835 | 1,935 | 1,903 |

Source: Crown Copyright. ONS, Samples of Anonymised Records

**Table 5.3 Over-crowding in households by birthplace/ethnic group and gender, 1991, percentages (2% Individual SARS)**

|  | Total | | RI-born | | NI-born | | Bl Car | | Indian | | Pakistani | | Bl Afr | |
|---|---|---|---|---|---|---|---|---|---|---|---|---|---|---|
| Persons per room | F | M | F | M | F | M | F | M | F | M | F | M | F | M |
| 1-1.5 | 3.7 | 4.0 | 3.3 | 3.6 | 3.0 | 3.3 | 6.5 | 6.4 | 17.8 | 15.9 | 29.6 | 30.4 | 15.7 | 15.4 |
| Over 1.5 | 0.9 | 0.9 | 1.7 | 1.6 | 0.9 | 1.1 | 2.1 | 2.2 | 4.5 | 4.4 | 13.1 | 12.0 | 8.5 | 7.5 |

Source: Crown Copyright. ONS, Samples of Anonymised Records

**Table 5.4: Housing tenure in London by ethnic/birthplace group, ethnic/birthplace group of household head (%)**

|  | Irish born | White non-Ir | Indian | Black Carib | Black Af | Pak | Bang | Black Other | Other |
|---|---|---|---|---|---|---|---|---|---|
| **Owner Occupied** | | | | | | | | | |
| owned outright | 13.5 | 20.0 | 11.9 | 6.8 | 2.7 | 10.1 | 2.5 | 4.4 | 8.7 |
| buying | 30.5 | 39.2 | 66.9 | 37.4 | 21.4 | 56.9 | 23.8 | 29.0 | 42.1 |
| **Rented** | | | | | | | | | |
| privately | 16.8 | 12.1 | 7.3 | 5.4 | 16.5 | 11.2 | 6.0 | 11.6 | 21.8 |
| Housing Ass. | 8.0 | 5.1 | 2.6 | 10.5 | 11.7 | 3.5 | 8.3 | 13.6 | 5.9 |
| Local Authority | 28.9 | 21.9 | 9.7 | 39.0 | 46.1 | 16.9 | 57.6 | 40.0 | 19.1 |

Source: Crown Copyright. Census 1991, Local Base Statistics (AGIY, 1995)

**Table 7.1:       Women by ethnic origin and grade, Haringey Council, June 1986, %**

|  | Irish | UK&Eur | Afro-Car | Asian | Total |
|---|---|---|---|---|---|
| 1. £15,981 - 22,161 | 0 | 1 | 1 | - | 1 |
| 2. £13,292 - 15,600 | 0 | 3 | 2 | 5 | 3 |
| 3. £10,251 - 13,035 | 4 | 11 | 7 | 8 | 10 |
| 4 £4,245 - 9,954 | 23 | 35 | 34 | 48 | 34 |
| Manual & crafts | 72 | 49 | 57 | 39 | 53 |
| Number | 681 | 3,627 | 631 | 158 | 5,827 |

Key 1: PO4 & equiv; 2: PO1-PO3 & equiv; 3: scales 6-502 & equiv; 4: scales 1-5 & equiv
Source: Haringey Women's Employment Project, 1987

Figure 1.1    Total Irish born population in England and Wales, and Scotland, 1841 - 1991

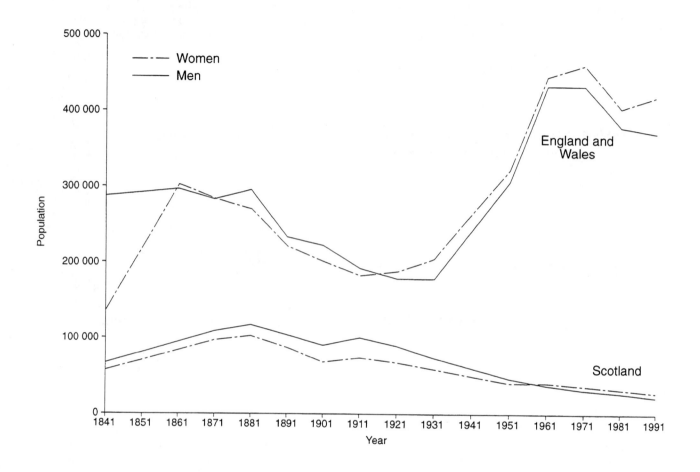

Source:    Census of G.B., 1841, Vol. II, Preface pp. 14-16; 1851 Pop Tables II, Vol. I, Tables XXXIX, XL; Census of England and Wales,
1921. Gen. Tables, Table 52; 1951, Gen. Tables, Table 39; 1961 Birthplace and Nationality Tables, Table I; Census of Scotland,
1951, Vol.III, Table 31; 1961, Vol. V, Table 1; Census 1971, G.B. Country of birth Tables, Table 3; Census 1981, Country of Birth
Tables, Table 1; Census 1991, Ethnic Group and Country of Birth Table 1.

Figure 1.2    Northern Ireland : proportions of population of Ireland
and of Irish migrants in Britain, 1951-1991

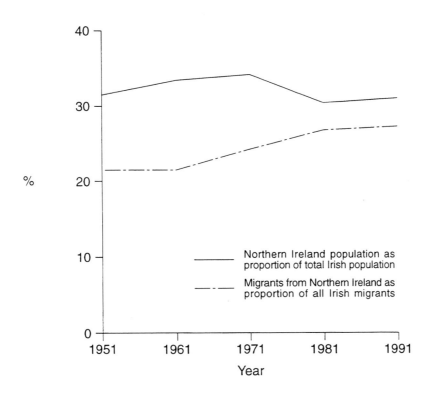

Source:    Census 1951-1991; Statistical Abstract of Ireland, 1992

Figure 1.3    Age-sex pyramid of population born in the United Kingdom to Irish-born parent/s and living in London, 1983

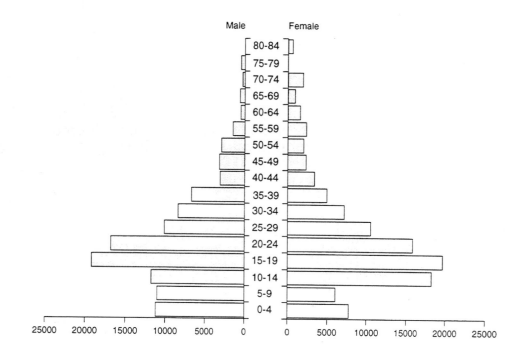

Source:   Labour Force Survey, 1983

Figure 2.1    Total Irish-born as a percentage of regional population, 1851-1991

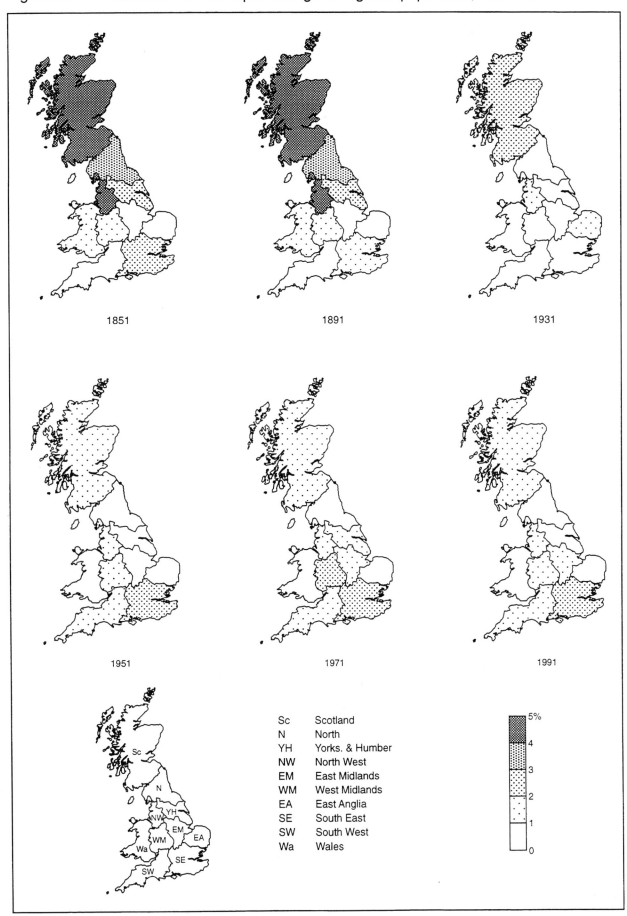

1851

1891

1931

1951

1971

1991

| Sc | Scotland |
|----|----------|
| N | North |
| YH | Yorks. & Humber |
| NW | North West |
| EM | East Midlands |
| WM | West Midlands |
| EA | East Anglia |
| SE | South East |
| SW | South West |
| Wa | Wales |

5%
4
3
2
1
0

Source:    See Figure 1.1

Figure 2.2    Cumulative proportions of population in Britain by region : Republic Irish -
born, Northern Irish-born and total 1971, 1981, 1991

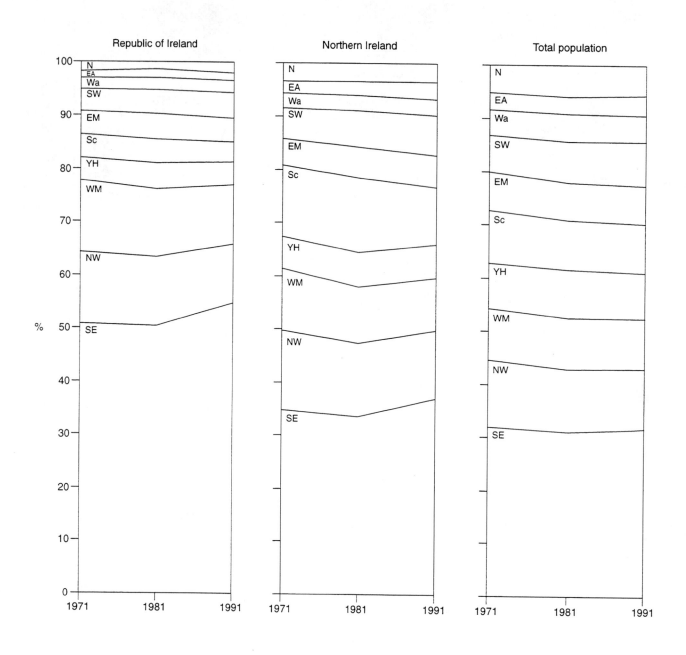

Source:    See Figure 1.1
Key:       See Figure 2.1

Figure 2.3    Regional population distribution of Irish-born and total
populations in Britain, 1991

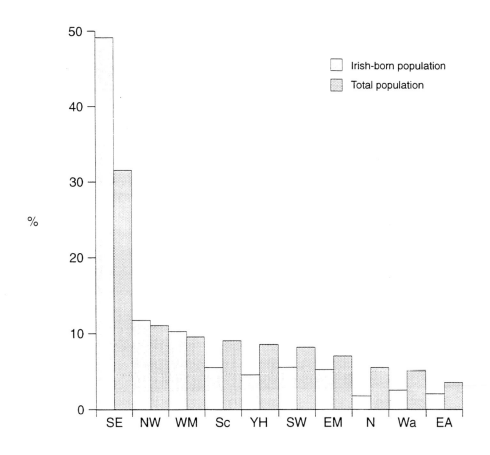

Source:    Census, 1991

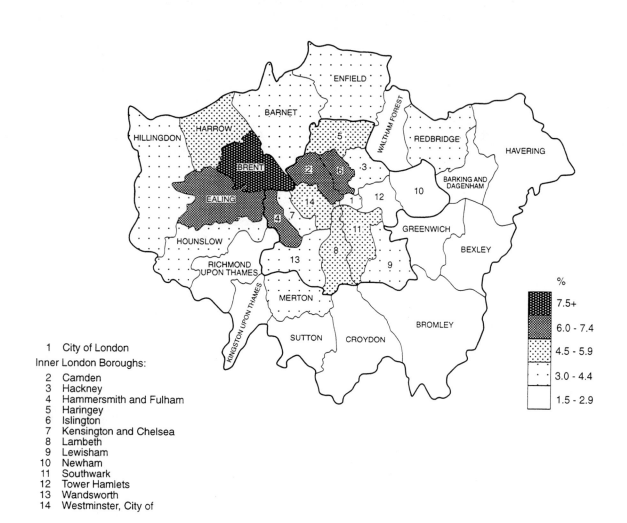

Figure 2.4    Irish-born as a percentage of total population,
              Greater London boroughs, 1991

%
7.5+
6.0 - 7.4
4.5 - 5.9
3.0 - 4.4
1.5 - 2.9

1    City of London
Inner London Boroughs:
   2    Camden
   3    Hackney
   4    Hammersmith and Fulham
   5    Haringey
   6    Islington
   7    Kensington and Chelsea
   8    Lambeth
   9    Lewisham
  10    Newham
  11    Southwark
  12    Tower Hamlets
  13    Wandsworth
  14    Westminster, City of

Source:   1991 Census, Local Base Statistics

Figure 2.5    Irish-born as a percentage of total population, Birmingham Wards, 1991

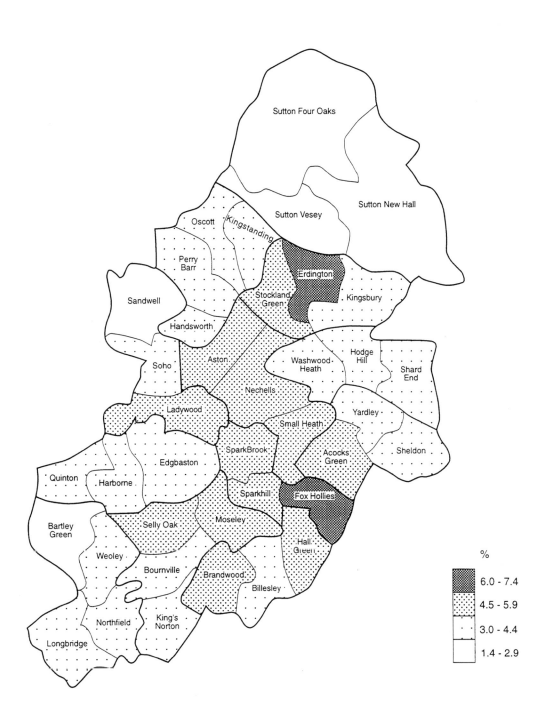

Source:   1991 Census, Local Base Statistics

Figure 2.6   Distribution of the Irish Republic-born population in England
and Wales, 1991

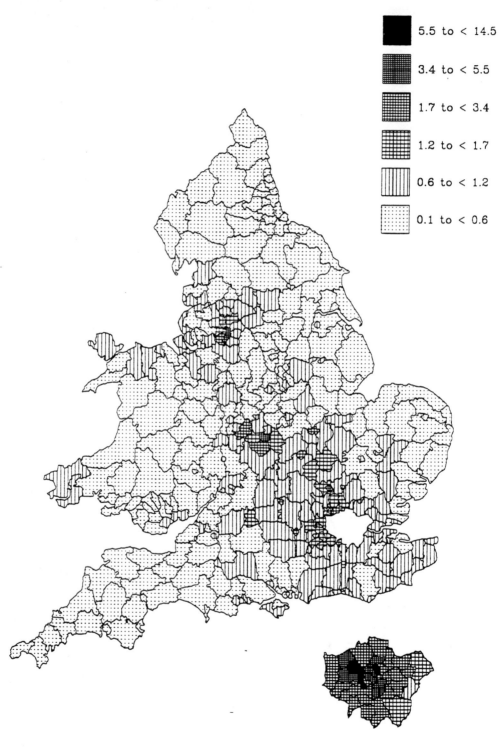

| | |
|---|---|
| ■ | 5.5 to < 14.5 |
| ▨ | 3.4 to < 5.5 |
| ▨ | 1.7 to < 3.4 |
| ▦ | 1.2 to < 1.7 |
| ▥ | 0.6 to < 1.2 |
| ▦ | 0.1 to < 0.6 |

*Source*: 1991 *Census of Population*

*Population and Housing Research Group*

*Crown Copyright*

Figure 2.7   Distribution of the Northern Irish-born population in England
and Wales, 1991

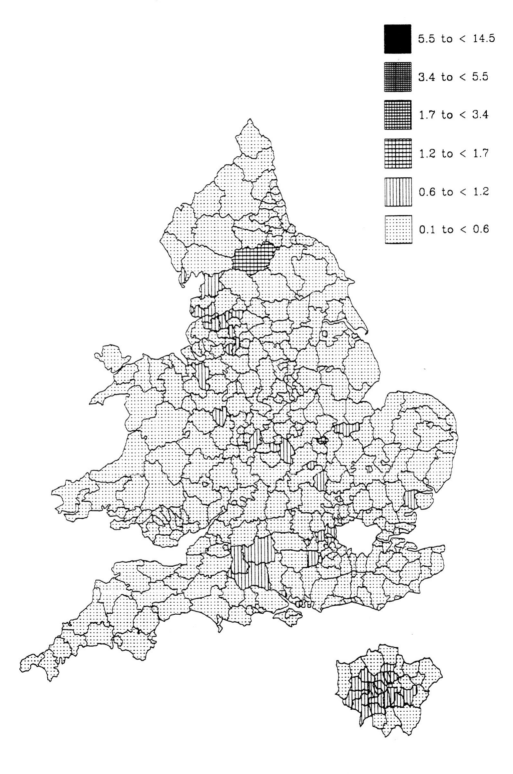

5.5 to < 14.5

3.4 to < 5.5

1.7 to < 3.4

1.2 to < 1.7

0.6 to < 1.2

0.1 to < 0.6

Source: 1991 *Census of Population*

*Population and Housing Research Group*

*Crown Copyright*

# Figure 2.8    Distribution of the Irish Republic-born population in Scotland, 1991

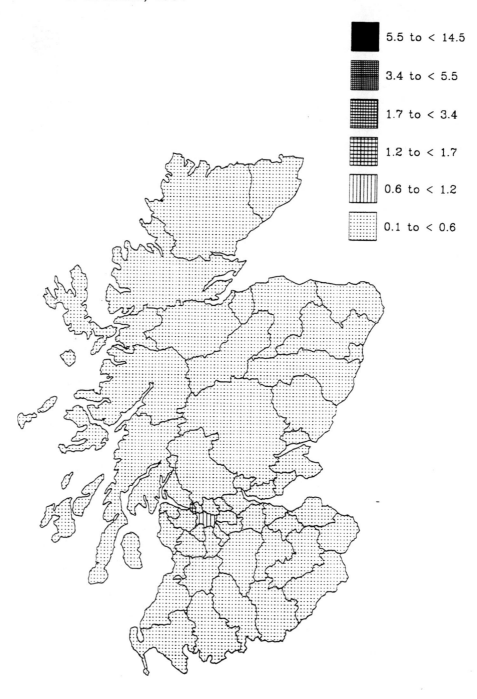

| | |
|---|---|
| ■ | 5.5 to < 14.5 |
| ▦ | 3.4 to < 5.5 |
| ▦ | 1.7 to < 3.4 |
| ▦ | 1.2 to < 1.7 |
| ▥ | 0.6 to < 1.2 |
| ▦ | 0.1 to < 0.6 |

Source: 1991 *Census Of Population*

Crown Copyright

*Population and Housing Research Group*

Figure 2.9    Distribution of the Northern Irish-born population
              in Scotland, 1991

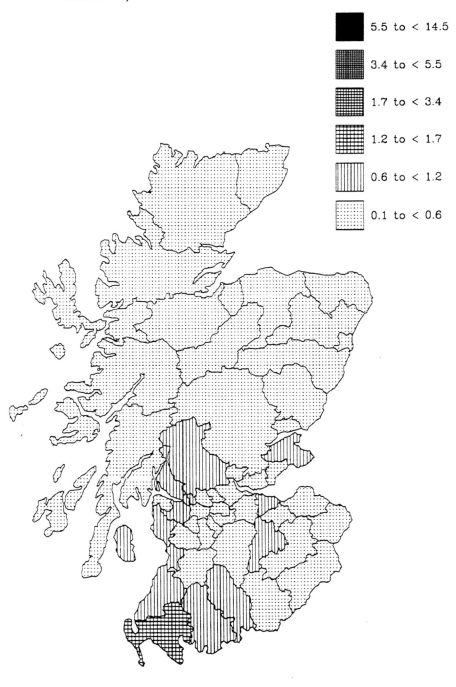

| | |
|---|---|
| ■ | 5.5 to < 14.5 |
| ▨ | 3.4 to < 5.5 |
| ▦ | 1.7 to < 3.4 |
| ▦ | 1.2 to < 1.7 |
| ▥ | 0.6 to < 1.2 |
| ▫ | 0.1 to < 0.6 |

*Source*: 1991 *Census Of Population*

*Population and Housing Research Group*

Figure 2.10   Region of settlement in Britain of one-year migrants :   Total
Irish-born and Irish Republic-born, 1971, 1981, 1991

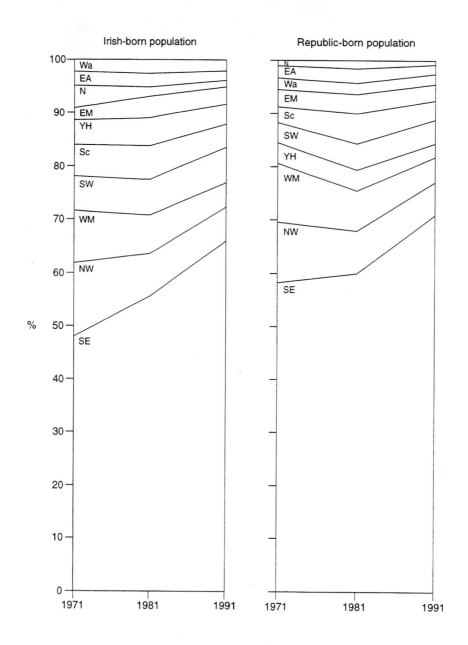

Source:   Census, 1971, 1981, 1991

Figure 3.1    Age-sex pyramid of (A) Republic Irish-born, (B) Northern Irish-born and
              (C) total population in London, 1991

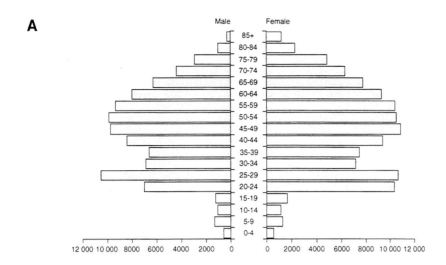

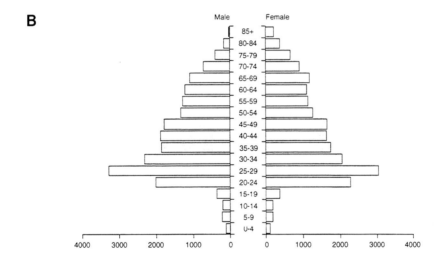

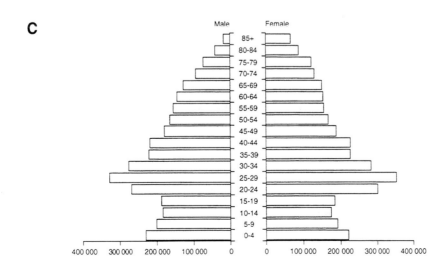

Source:   1991 Census Ethnic Group and Country of Birth Table 2

Figure 3.2　　Age distribution of Irish Republic-born by region in Britain, 1991

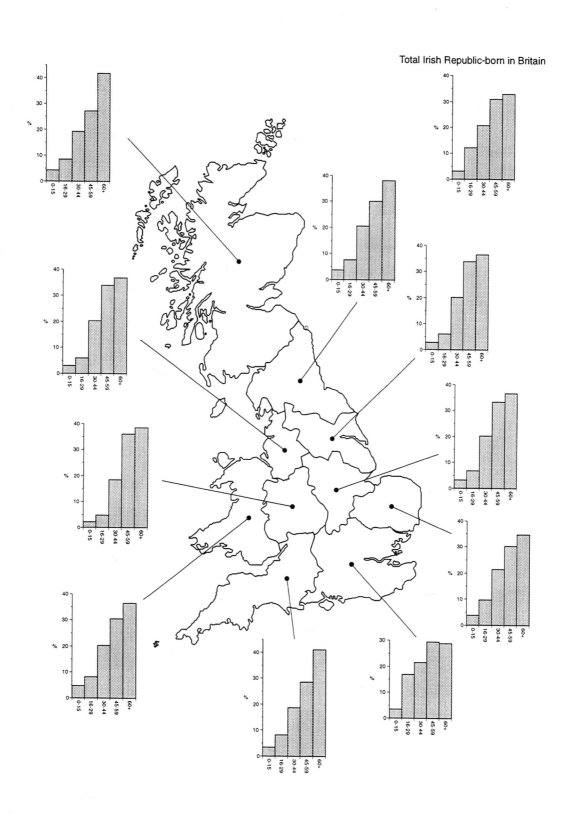

Total Irish Republic-born in Britain

Source:　Census, 1991

# Figure 3.3    Age distribution of Northern Irish-born by region in Britain, 1991

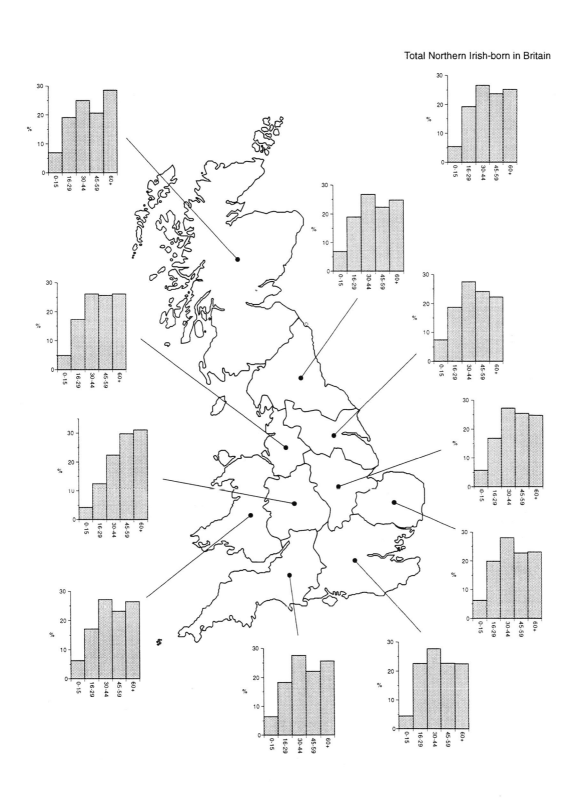

Total Northern Irish-born in Britain

Source:    Census, 1991

Figure 4.1    Occupational groupings of Irish-born and total populations by gender, 1991 (10% sample)

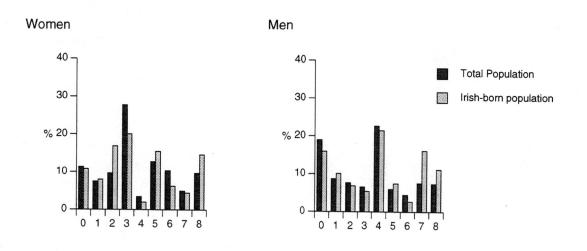

Occupational groups

| 1 | Managers and administrators | 4 | Clerical | 7 | Sales |
| 2 | Professionals | 5 | Skilled trades | 8 | Industrial |
| 3 | Associate professionals | 6 | Services: personal, protective | 9 | Other manual |

Source:    Census, 1991, Ethnic Group and Country of Birth Tables, Table 13

Figure 4.2    Industrial groupings of Irish-born and total populations by gender, 1991 (10%) sample)

Women

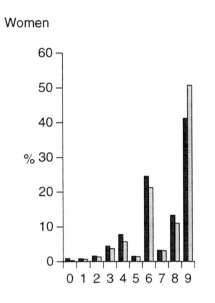

Men

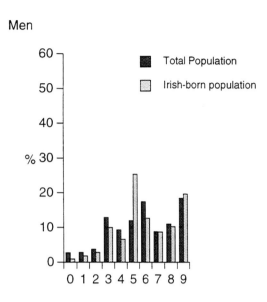

Occupational groups

| | | | | | |
|---|---|---|---|---|---|
| 0 | Agriculture, forestry, mining | 4 | Other manufacturing | 8 | Banking & finance services |
| 1 | Energy & water | 5 | Construction | 9 | Other services |
| 2 | Mining | 6 | Distribution & catering | | |
| 3 | Manufacturing metal etc | 7 | Transport | | |

Source:   Census, 1991, Ethnic Group and Country of Birth Tables, Table 14

Figure 4.3    Occupational groupings of Irish-born and total populations by gender and age, Britain, 1991

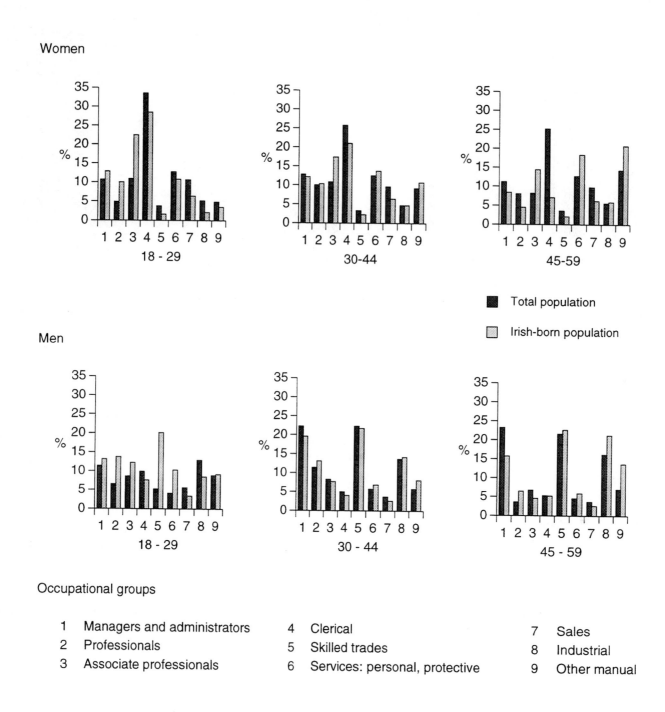

Women

Men

Total population

Irish-born population

Occupational groups

| 1 | Managers and administrators | 4 | Clerical | 7 | Sales |
| 2 | Professionals | 5 | Skilled trades | 8 | Industrial |
| 3 | Associate professionals | 6 | Services: personal, protective | 9 | Other manual |

Source:   1991 Census, 2% Individual Samples of Anonymised Records

Figure 6.1    Limiting long term illness by age: Republic Irish-born, Northern
             Irish-born and total population in Britain, 1991

Women

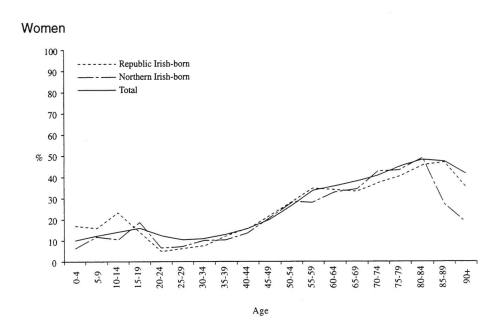

Men

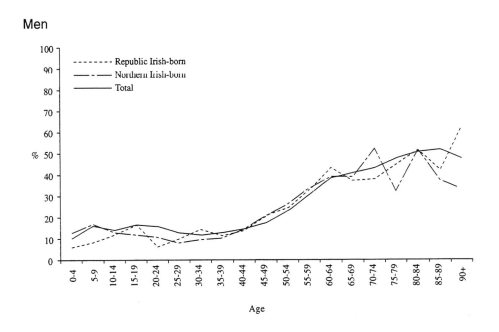

Source:   2% Individual SARS, OPCS, 1991

# Appendix B
# **Interview schedule and sample characteristics**

# Interview Schedule

**1**      Interviewee Number                 Interviewed by ...................

**2**      Male/Female

**3**      Area

## SECTION A: INTRODUCTORY DATA

**4**      Where are you from in Ireland? (city/county)

**5**      What year did you leave Ireland?

**6**      When you left Ireland, why did you choose to come to Britain?

**7a**     Since your arrival in Britain, have you always lived in Birmingham/London? Yes/No

       <u>If NO</u>

       **7b**      Where else have you lived? Place? Dates?

**8**      Do you own or rent this accommodation? Own? Rent: with work; local authority; housing association; private; other.

**9**      Are you: employee; self-employed; paid home-working; unemployed; working in the home; retired; student; sick; other (specify).

**10**     Were you born before or after 1945 (1.1.45)?  Before /After

**11**     How do you think Irish people are view in

|  | Positively | Negatively | Neither/Mixed | Don't Know |
|---|---|---|---|---|
| USA | | | | |
| Britain | | | | |
| The rest of Europe | | | | |
| Australia | | | | |
| Other countries | | | | |

## SUPPLEMENTARY QUESTIONS - for those who do not fit the quota

**12**     How do you think the Irish are treated in this country?

**13**     Have you personally experienced any difficulties because you are Irish?

## SECTION B: HOUSING

**14**     Who lives in this household with you?

       no-one; spouse/partner;

       number of children under 16;

       number of children over 16;

       parents/in law; other relatives;

       unrelated lodger/s (Number);

other (specify).

**15a**   Have you ever been homeless either on arrival in Britain or subsequently (eg had to stay with relatives, or stayed on a friend's floor)?  Yes /No

If YES

    **15b**   Why were you in that situation?

    **15c**   How did you then obtain accommodation?

**16a**   Have you ever tried to obtain housing from your local council? Yes/No

If YES

    **16b**   Were you successful? Yes/No

    **16c**   Did you experience any difficulties? (eg. in being taken on to the list or being allocated housing) Yes/No

**17a**   IF RELEVANT   Did you experience any difficulty in obtaining a flat, house or bedsit to rent? Yes/No

If YES

    **17b**   Please give details

**18a**   Have you ever tried to obtain a mortgage? Yes/No

If YES

    **18b**   Were you successful? Yes/No

    **18c**   Did you experience any difficulties? Yes/No

If YES

        **18d**   Please give details

**19a**   Have you experienced any difficulty obtaining any of the following type of accommodation?

|  | Yes | No | Not relevant |
|---|---|---|---|
| Hostels | | | |
| Bed and Breakfast | | | |
| Housing association | | | |

If YES

    **19b**   Please explain

**20a**   Do you know other Irish people who have experienced difficulties in gaining satisfactory accommodation? Yes/No

If YES

    **20b**   Please give details

## SECTION C: EMPLOYMENT

### C1   Qualifications

**21**   At what age did you leave school? Before 12; 12; 13; 14; 15; 16;17; 18+

**22**   What qualifications did you have when you left Ireland? None; Primary Certificate; Group Certificate; Intermediate Certificate; Leaving Certificate;

CSEs/O-Levels/GCSE's; A levels; Degree; Vocational; Nursing Qualification; other (specify)

**23a** Have you obtained any further qualifications since coming to Britain? Yes/No

If YES

    **23b** Please give details

## C2 Employment history

**24** Can you tell me what paid employment, if any, you have had since you came to Britain? (Put an asterisk next to current, or last main job). Job/Employer; Grade; Dates

**25a** Have you experienced any difficulties in getting employment at any point since you came to Britain? Yes/No

If YES

    **25b** Please give details

**26a** Have your Irish qualifications always been acceptable? Yes/No/Not relevant

If NO

    **26b** Please give details

**27a** Have you experienced any difficulties in getting promotion or training opportunities at any point? Yes/No/Not relevant

If YES

    **27b** Please give details

## C3 If currently in paid work (see Q.9), or else go to C4

**28** Is your present job: Full-time/Part-time

**29** What is your basic take-home weekly/monthly pay? (show card)

**30a** Do you feel that you are being employed at an appropriate level for your experience and qualifications? Yes/No

If NO

    **30b** Please explain

**31a** Are there other Irish people where you currently work? Yes/No

**31b** Describe the ethnic background of the people doing the same work as yourself

**32** How would you describe the atmosphere where you currently work?

## C4. All respondents who have had paid work at any time

**33a** Has there been a good atmosphere at all the places you have worked in the past? Yes/No

If NO

    **33b** Please explain

**34a** Have you ever heard anti-Irish comments or jokes at work? Yes/No

If YES

**34b**   Please describe what was said and in what circumstances

**34c**   Did you find these comments/jokes offensive or not? Yes/No/Sometimes

**34d**   Please explain your answer

**35a**   Have Irish issues, or your Irish background, been discussed at work? Yes/No

If YES

**35b** Please describe what was said, and in what circumstances.


## SECTION D: TREATMENT OF THE IRISH

**36a**   Have you ever been stopped at a port or airport when travelling between Britain and Ireland? Yes/No/Not relevant

If YES

**36b**   For how long were you stopped?

**36c**   Did anything else occur?

**37a**   Do you know of anyone else who has been stopped travelling between Britain and Ireland? Yes/No

If YES

**37b**   Please give details

**38a**   Have you seen or heard anything directed against the Irish in Britain which you objected to? Yes/No

If YES

**38b**   Please give details

**39a**   Have you ever decided not to join any community organisation because its Irish associations might draw unwelcome attention? Yes/No

If YES

**39b**   Why was this?

**40a**   Have you ever decided not to join political activity because its Irish associations might draw unwelcome attention? Yes/No

If YES

**40b**   Why was this?

**41a**   Have you ever decided not to join any cultural activity because you thought it might draw unwelcome attention? Yes/No

If YES

**41b**   Why was this?

**42a**   Have you ever felt the need to play down your Irish identity? Yes/No

If YES

**42b**   Why was this?

**43a**   When speaking on the phone or in shops or other public places, have you ever received any particular response to your Irish accent? Yes/No

If YES

P-120-
P-124
P128-9*
P130-133
P187-

**43b**     Please give details

**44a**     Have you ever received any particular response to your Irish name? Yes/No

<u>If YES</u>

**44b**     Please give details

**45a**     [BIRMINGHAM ONLY] Were you living in Birmingham in 1974 when the Birmingham bombings occurred? Yes/No

<u>If YES</u>

**45b**     What was your experience and reaction at the time?

**46**     During the past 25 years what has been your experience after various bombing incidents?

**47a**     Have you ever had any contact with the police or appeared in court? Yes/No

<u>If YES</u>

**47b**     What was your experience? Were comments made? Were you allowed bail?

**48a**     Has your Irishness ever been a factor in your relations with your neighbours, now or in the past? Yes/No

<u>If YES</u>

**48b**     Please describe the circumstances

**49a**     Are most of your friends: Irish; English/British; English and Irish; Other ethnic groups; a mixture?

**49b**     Why is this the case?

**50a**     IF RELEVANT   What schools have your children attended? Primary RC State; Primary State; Primary RC Private; Primary Private; Secondary RC State; Secondary State; Secondary RC Private; Secondary Private; Other

**50b**     Have your children ever told you about any anti-Irishness they or some other children have experienced? Yes/No

<u>If YES</u>

**50c**     Please give details


## SECTION E: OBTAINING SOCIAL SERVICES/ PROFESSIONAL ADVICE/ HEALTHCARE

**51**     What is your age group? (Show card: 16-19; 20-29; 30-39; 40-49; 50-59; 60-69; 70-79; 80+)

**52a**     Have you ever claimed Social Security benefit? Yes/No

<u>If YES</u>

**52b**     How were you treated by the DSS? Was your Irish background ever mentioned? Describe the attitude of the DSS staff

**53a**     Have you ever claimed any other benefits from Social Services (eg: housing benefit, disability allowance, invalidity allowance, attendants allowance)

<u>If YES</u>

**53b**    Which ones?

**53c**    Did you encounter any difficulties in obtaining the benefits you were entitled to? Yes/No

<u>If YES</u>

**53d**    Please give details

**54**    What form of identity did you have to provide in claiming benefit?

**55a**    Have you ever decided not to claim benefit or stopped claiming benefit because of the attitude of the benefit staff? Yes/No

<u>If YES</u>

**55b**    Please give details

**55c**    Have you ever turned to an Irish agency or other advice agency to help you obtain the benefits you are entitled to? Yes/No/Not applicable

<u>If YES</u>

**55d**    Please give details

<u>If NO</u>

**55e**    Why not?

**56a**    Have you ever turned to any other agency for help in claiming benefits? Yes/No/Not applicable

<u>If YES</u>

**56b**    Please give details

<u>If NO</u>

**56c**    Why not?

**57a**    Do you think it would be desirable if more Irish people were employed as staff dealing with benefit claims? Yes/No/Don't know

**57b**    Please explain your answer

**58a**    Would describe your experiences of the healthcare services here as: very good; quite good; mixed/neither; quite bad; very bad

**58b**    Please explain your answer

**59a**    Are you registered with a GP? Yes/No

<u>If NO</u>

**59b**    Why not?

<u>If YES</u>

**59c**    Have you ever had any comments made to you by a doctor, nurse or receptionist which connected your healthcare issue with your Irishness? Yes/No

<u>If YES</u>

**59d**    What were they and what was your reaction?

**59e**    In your view has this influenced any treatment you received?

## SECTION F: CONCLUSION

**60** What is your religion? Catholic/Protestant/Other

**61a** Do you consider yourself settled in Britain? Yes/No/Don't know

**61b** Please give reasons for your answer

**62a** Do you think the Irish should be recognised as an ethnic group in Britain? Yes/No/Don't know

**62b** Please give reasons for your answer

**63** Would you like to add any comments to your earlier answers?

**64** Do you know of other Irish people living in this area? (additional names/addresses if possible)

## Sample characteristics in Birmingham and London

| | Total Sample | | 1991 census (GB) | Birmingham sample | | census | London sample | | census |
|---|---|---|---|---|---|---|---|---|---|
| | N | % | % | N | % | % | N | % | % |
| **Sex** | | | | | | | | | |
| Women | 46 | 52.3 | 53.0 | 16 | 48.5 | 49.5 | 30 | 54.5 | 53.4 |
| Men | 42 | 47.7 | 47.0 | 17 | 51.5 | 50.5 | 25 | 45.5 | 46.6 |
| **Irish origins** | | | | | | | | | |
| Irish Rep. | 75 | 85.2 | 72.7 | 27 | 81.8 | 79.9 | 48 | 87.3 | 83.5 |
| N.Ireland | 13 | 14.8 | 27.3 | 6 | 18.2 | 20.1 | 7 | 12.7 | 16.5 |
| **Age groups** | | | | | | | | | |
| 20-39 | 31 | 35.2 | 27.7 | 3 | 9.1 | 15.5 | 28 | 50.9 | 35.6 |
| 40-59 | 28 | 31.8 | 39.9 | 16 | 48.5 | 45.2 | 12 | 21.8 | 37.7 |
| 60-79 | 28 | 31.8 | 29.0 | 13 | 39.4 | 36.8 | 15 | 27.3 | 24.1 |
| 80+ | 1 | 1.1 | 3.4 | 1 | 3.0 | 2.4 | 0 | 0 | 2.6 |
| **Housing tenure** | | | | | | | | | |
| Owner occupied | 42 | 47.7 | 55.4 | 20 | 60.6 | 52.3 | 22 | 40.0 | 44.0 |
| Rented: | | | | | | | | | |
| private | 8 | 9.0 | 10.9 | 3 | 9.1 | 7.0 | 5 | 9.1 | 16.8 |
| local authority | 27 | 30.7 | 26.6 | 10 | 30.3 | 33.0 | 17 | 30.9 | 28.9 |
| housing assoc | 4 | 4.5 | 5.1 | 0 | 0 | 6.0 | 6 | 10.9 | 8.0 |
| work | 5 | 5.7 | 2.4 | 0 | 0 | 0 | 3 | 3.4 | 0 |
| Other | 1 | 1.1 | 0 | 0 | 0 | 0 | 0 | 2 | 2.3 |
| **Economic activity** | | | | | | | | | |
| Employed | 33 | 37.5 | 45.2 | 13 | 39.4 | 38.2 | 20 | 36.4 | 48.7 |
| Self-employed | 10 | 11.4 | 6.9 | 3 | 9.1 | 4.0 | 7 | 12.7 | 7.4 |
| Unemployed | 11 | 12.5 | 6.8 | 6 | 18.2 | 9.9 | 5 | 9.1 | 8.4 |
| Student | 3 | 3.4 | 1.3 | 0 | 0 | 0.6 | 3 | 5.5 | 1.0 |
| Sick | 4 | 4.5 | 6.0 | 2 | 6.1 | 8.7 | 2 | 3.6 | 2.3 |
| Retired | 20 | 22.7 | 21.7 | 8 | 24.2 | 26.2 | 12 | 21.8 | 17.8 |
| Other | 7 | 8.0 | 11.6 | 1 | 3.0 | 10.9 | 6 | 10.9 | 10.3 |